CONTEMPORARY
MUSLIM
APOCALYPTIC
LITERATURE

Religion and Politics
Michael Barkun, *Series Editor*

DAVID COOK

CONTEMPORARY
MUSLIM
APOCALYPTIC
LITERATURE

Syracuse University Press

First Paperback Edition 2008
08   09   10   11   12   13   6   5   4   3   2   1

The paper used in this publication meets the minimum requirements
of American National Standard for Information Sciences—Permanence
of Paper for Printed Library Materials, ANSI Z39.48–1984.∞™

For a listing of books published and distributed by Syracuse University Press,
visit our Web site at SyracuseUniversityPress.syr.edu.

ISBN-13: 978-0-8156-3195-8
ISBN-10: 0-8156-3195-2

Library of Congress Cataloging-in-Publication Data
Cook, David, 1966–
Contemporary Muslim apocalyptic literature / David Cook.— 1st ed.
p. cm.—(Religion and politics)
Includes bibliographical references and index.
ISBN 0–8156–3058–1 (hardcover (cloth) : alk. paper)
1. Eschatology, Islamic. 2. Apocalyptic literature—History and
criticism. 3. Islam—21st century. I. Title. II. Series.
BP166.8.C65 2005
297.2'3—dc22
                                                2005011242

Manufactured in the United States of America

For Dr. Richard Landes,
who encouraged me in this study

David Cook is associate professor of religious studies at Rice University. He is the author of *Studies in Muslim Apocalyptic, Understanding Jihad,* and *Martyrdom in Islam* and has contributed articles to *The Encyclopedia of Millennialism* and *The Encyclopedia of Fundamentalism.*

CONTENTS

PREFACE

This book follows my previous volume, *Studies in Muslim Apocalyptic* (2003). I originally intended to provide a complete overview of Muslim apocalyptic literature at the year 2000; however, because of lack of funding the materials in this present work are confined to Sunni Muslim, Arabic-language apocalyptic literature. The Arabic language is the common currency for the Sunni Muslim world as a whole, and frequently ideas and motifs found in the corpus on which this book is based have wide currency throughout that world. I hope eventually to write on the apocalyptic literature found among Muslims in South Asia, Turkey, Africa, Indonesia and Malaysia.

I would like to thank my parents, Dr. W. Robert and Elaine Cook, for reading through this manuscript and making their enormously helpful suggestions and corrections. I am also grateful to Thomas Andrusko, Elisabeth Blanchard, Valerie Haeder, and Deborah Tor, who have each read through and corrected the manuscript at various stages; to Michael Barkun, editor of Syracuse University Press's Religion and Politics series, and to the other anonymous readers for their comments, corrections, and suggestions. I would like to thank Martin Gardner for inspiring me, and Richard Landes, director of the Center for Millennial Studies at Boston University, for encouraging me (and in certain cases, compelling me) in the study of Muslim apocalyptic literature and movements over the years. His comments and advice have been particularly useful, and this book is dedicated to him. I would also like to thank Carolyn Russ for her thorough job of editing.

The materials used were obtained with funds from various sources, notably the Center for Millennial Studies at Boston University, the Jon R. and Paula Mosle Fund, and the Rice University Junior Faculty Summer Research Fund (2002, 2003); my thanks to each. All mistakes are, of course, my own responsibility.

CONTEMPORARY
MUSLIM
APOCALYPTIC
LITERATURE

ONE

CLASSICAL MUSLIM APOCALYPTIC LITERATURE

Introduction to Classical Muslim Apocalyptic Literature

Mankind has always been fascinated by the future and has frequently sought to understand it by means of predictions, exegesis of holy texts, and interpretation of the various natural and cosmic signs available to everyone. Islam probably began as an apocalyptic movement, and it has continued to have a strong apocalyptic and messianic character throughout its history, a character that has manifested itself in literature as well as in periodic social explosions. It is important to understand precisely how apocalyptic and messianic beliefs are manifested in contemporary Islam.

One cannot understand contemporary Muslim society without a thorough grasp of the classical foundations from which it has been derived. This is as true for study of modern Muslim apocalyticism as for other aspects of Muslim soci-

1

ety. Therefore, despite the fact that this study is intended to stand alone, reference will be made to classical Muslim traditions.[1] Muslim apocalypticism is not only an important area of study in its own right; it is also part of the rapidly changing field of Qur'anic exegesis, as well as of modern political and religious thought. Muslims' beliefs about the end of the world ultimately reflect their views both of themselves and of the direction of their society's development—the challenges it faces and how to overcome those challenges.

It is not uncommon for researchers to regard the field of apocalyptic thought as entirely irrational and to dismiss its writers as unstable, or even as lunatics. This approach should be avoided, however, if only because of the number of people being characterized in this manner. When a substantial proportion of a population—even if not the majority—shares a particular worldview, value judgments that would dismiss their beliefs as lunatic are unhelpful, to say the least. This is not to say, however, that the scholars studying these beliefs, or even those of other, more moderate believers, are going to consider such a worldview entirely balanced (Collins 1979; D. Cook 2002c, 1–24; Hellholm 1989).

Many monotheistic faiths encompass strains of belief that the end of the world is approaching, but such strains are not usually deemed "respectable." The more specific these beliefs, the less respect they receive—especially since it is not uncommon for their adherents to deny or underplay them when the predicted "end" fails to occur. The general disdain for such beliefs is so great that a scholar publishing on this subject is a source of acute embarrassment to any established religious institution of higher learning with which he—or very rarely she—is associated. Even if the scholar is writing a refutation of the material, established institutions tend to be disdainful of the entire subject. Apocalyptists often receive negative reviews of their books and are sometimes forced either to recant or to disassociate themselves from any institutions to which they were attached. It is rare to find an established scholar who actually writes in support of the idea that the world is going to come to an end. Far from encouraging expositors of these attitudes, for example, the faculty of al-Azhar University—the most respected Muslim institution of higher learn-

---

1. See, among numerous studies, D. Cook 2002c; Madelung 1981; 1986a; 1986b; Bashear 1991; 1993; M. Cook 1992a; 1992b; D. Cook 1996; and 1997.

ing in the Sunni world—generally publish books rebutting popular apocalyptic writers, even when those writers received their education at al-Azhar.

If apocalypticism is (or can be) an embarrassment, what can be gained from studying it? Writers who believe sincerely in the imminent reality of the end of the world may say the most unguarded things and support the most extraordinary and outlandish ideas; this does not necessarily mean that there is *no* truth to be found in what they write, even if the truth they reveal is not the "truth" they sought to convey. The very nature of apocalypticism liberates its adherents from the codes and mores of this world: as they prepare for its end, writers may reveal hidden facets of their society and culture to deal with problems previously submerged and undetected. This is exciting and interesting, especially in the context of Muslim religious culture, which tends to excise innovations rather than embrace new ideas. The apocalyptist functions as something of a fulcrum in the process of cultural and religious transition. Often marginal characters, apocalyptists tend to inhabit a sort of no-man's-land, subject to the winds of whatever fads grasp the populace as they write—especially given their hunger for new ideas to support their views.

The apocalyptist constantly seeks new interpretations of ancient material to bolster his convictions, an approach diametrically opposite that of the conservative religious scholar. The latter is committed to preserving established tradition, tradition that can be lost but never added to, commented on but never reinterpreted or reformulated into a new creation. Conservative scholars take the long view of their tradition, seeing themselves at the end of a chain stretching back to the prophet Muhammad. Therefore they specialize in *not* reacting to events, involving themselves in damage control but not in radical change. Apocalyptists, on the other hand, are compelled to react to everything happening in the world around them.

The two most important concepts for the apocalyptist are time and meaning. Time is important because it is so unbelievably short and there is so much to do before the world ends. Meaning is to be found in everything as the apocalyptist seeks to divine God's will in the approach to the end of the world. His absolute conviction of the coming end gives the believer unparalleled energy and a sense of liberation. As old restraints fall away, the apocalyptist is finally free to speak out without fear of repercussions. In the repressive societies that exist in the vast majority of Muslim states, this release is tremendous, even overwhelming—often the first such liberation experienced by either the apocalyptist or the reader. The writer's sense of liberation can give him a confidence and assurance that in turn stimulates his readers, providing a breath of fresh air in a stifling society (cf. Matt. 7:28–29). The fact that this attitude is essentially a bluff is not important: merely the fact that the "truth" is spoken is sufficient to be exciting. The intellectual boldness of the apocalyptist stands in stark contrast to the caution and relativism of traditional scholars and religious dignitaries, who the apocalyptist sees as hidebound. Whereas established scholars look back to their intellectual predecessors, relying on footnotes, references, and tradition, apocalyptists are creators, looking ahead toward the inevitable end of the world and the meeting with God.

In light of this view, the apocalyptist becomes acutely sensitive to the world around him. In one sense, time slows—a paradox, since at the same time it is moving ever faster toward the end of the world—as though it were near the event horizon of a black hole, just previous to the final drop into oblivion. The apocalyptist looks for meaning everywhere, investing the most infinitesimal and random events with cosmic importance—at least those events and actions that he sees as relevant to his interpretation of the future. Frequently, proof of their significance falls by the wayside in the pell-mell rush to understand God's intentions for the immediate future. Inadvertently, this tendency can create humor for the reader of an apocalyptic work.

For the same reason, the apocalyptist is not a careful writer. He is not a scholar, searching to write a magnum opus that will ensure his lasting fame, but a messenger whose sole desire is to communicate to his audience the incredibly important discovery he has made: the world is going to end! Confined by the immediacy of time and his sense of urgency at this discovery, the apocalyptist sees no point in stylistic subtlety or lengthy proofs. He lacks the time to engage in lengthy debate with his opponents.

One can see time and again the hasty nature of the writing in the apocalyptic genre. Since my research has drawn on political and literary material as well as apocalyptic writings, I have been able to compare writing styles to some extent. Arabic apocalyptic writing is often rife with bad grammar and spelling mistakes. It is not unusual for writers of apocalyptic works to plagiarize whole sections either from their own earlier works or from the works of others. F. Da'ud (1999b), for example, plagiarized Ayyub (1987) without acknowledgment, while Harbi (1998) detailed the same concerning Amin Jamal al-Din. Arabic religious material is usually well edited; writers of Muslim religious literature are usually steeped in the classical Arabic tradition and try as best they can to uphold it. In this respect, apocalyptic writers are the exception. Often they do not even care to give their books titles in good Arabic style, and their citations of classical material are frequently incomplete, inaccurate, or even deliberately fraudulent, requiring vigilant checking. Such deficits arise not only from their sense of urgency but from their fatalistic view of their readers: those who are prepared to be convinced will be convinced; those who resist or oppose the apocalyptic view will see the truth soon enough, when the end of the world occurs before their eyes (Landes 1996). Given this certainty of the coming apocalypse, such writers apparently regard errors or misrepresentations as very minor affairs.

An understanding of the emotional state underlying apocalyptic writing, which is frequently both obscure and very intense, allows one to read and appreciate such texts. The materials surveyed here are graphically anti-Semitic and virulently anti-Western, very frequently exhibiting a blood lust and level of hatred stunning to the unprepared reader (Kenney 1994). Without making any excuses for the writers, one should understand the constraints under which they are operating: they believe they *must* get the message across to their audience. As long as they achieve this imperative—conveying their message to their Muslim audience—they regard the reactions of others as unimportant.

We should also speak here of definitions. Usually Muslim apocalyptic writers speak of "Islam" and "the West" (or sometimes "the Christian West" or the "Crusader West") as if these categories were self-evident and apparent. They clearly are not, yet it is difficult to define these problematic terms in line with at least some scholarly consensus. Such terms cannot be mentioned without reference to Samuel Huntington's controversial thesis, *The Clash of Civilizations,* in which the author presents a vision of the world divided into a number of civilizations (either seven or eight total) that will inevitably conflict as a result of fundamentally differing cultural and religious systems. Among these civilizations Huntington identifies the West and Islam, with the West being the only civilization not religiously defined. No matter how attractive this thesis might be at first glance, its value is nullified by the insurmountable problem of defining such terms as "the West," let alone "Islam." Muslim apocalyptic writers (and Muslim intellectuals in general) take issue with Huntington's thesis. Despite their opposition to Huntington's ideas, however, the apocalyptic writers use his terminology freely, and some of the same authors who attack Huntington present their vision of the world in terms strikingly similar to his (van Nieuwanhuijze 1995a; 1995b; Wallerstein 1999). These terms are attractive to Muslim apocalyptic writers because they allow them to divide the world into stark, easily identifiable categories and bolster a worldview in which the West and Islam are in total opposition. This opposition is not necessarily apparent, if only for the simple reason that "the West" is not a religiously based term. Moreover, the assumed definitions of these terms may vary from one writer to another, creating further levels of confusion and contradiction. Despite these problems, the scholar exploring such writing must use the terms used by the apocalyptic writers themselves, even while acknowledging their faulty nature.

This seems the point to make a note on the translations from apocalyptic literature in this book. All of them are mine, and although the process of transliteration has allowed me to silently correct such basic mistakes of spelling and grammar as might interfere with the reader's ability to apprehend the writers' meaning, I have sought to retain the full flavor of the original writing—not only its intensity and urgency but also the carelessless, obscurity, and bluntness arising from the writers' sense of mission. All of these qualities are indicators of the genre that I have sought to preserve. In my translations, all material in parentheses is from the original; any material supplied by me is in square brackets. All translations from the Qur'an are from Fakhry (1997), and all biblical translations are from the New International Version (Grand Rapids, Mich.: Zondervan, 1985).

With these ideas and reservations in mind, let us explore some of the sources of modern Muslim apocalyptic literature.

Prophetic Apocalyptic Traditions

According to the traditional Muslim view, classical Muslim apocalyptic traditions come in their entirety from the milieu of the prophet Muhammad (d. 632) and his closest companions. Non-Muslim scholars have rejected this view, but I have chosen to avoid a lengthy discussion of the issues involved in precisely dating the original material because the groups that probably produced the apocalyptic traditions during the first and second Muslim centuries are entirely anonymous. In their early manifestations, apocalyptic predictions took the literary form of the hadith (tradition) in which either Muhammad or one of his close companions makes a statement about what will happen at the end of the world. These statements varied in length from phrases of several words to single sentences to passages equivalent to several pages. The longer statements, known as "lengthy traditions," are assumed to be compilations of the shorter hadiths (see Juynboll 1983). They are the closest examples in Islam to what is known in Judaism and Christianity as the "literary apocalypse," of which Daniel 7–12 and the book of Revelation are the best-known examples. Because the Muslim traditions have no apparent context, except that provided artificially by the lengthy traditions (which are essentially attempts by scholars to place the material into usable chronological order), it is hardly surprising to find that there has been considerable disagreement as to the order in which events are to take place before the end of the world (see D. Cook 2002c, chapters 1–3). What follows is based on the scenario accepted by modern Muslim scholars, as well as certain elements of my own reconstruction (see al-Tuwayjiri 1994 for discussion).

Historical and literary texts of the period of classical Islam contain a large body of apocalyptic literature and speculation. This material enables us to speak of a "tradition," although it is not unified or codified in the manner of the Islamic legal tradition. From the condition in which we find the apocalyptic traditions today, one might speculate that this disorganization was a result of the marginal importance generally given the subject of an apocalypse; it commanded the attention of revolutionaries rather than theologians. Nonetheless, certain elements of the Islamic apocalyptic tradition have been important to Muslims at all times. The most prominent element is the simple belief that the world is due to end at some time—although the Qur'an specifically says that the knowledge of when that time will be is in the hands of God (see the present book, 84). It is likely that apocalyptic speculation during the first century of Islam (seventh century C.E.) largely concentrated on the date of the end and did not detail a complicated apocalyptic scenario other than those cataclysmic events described in the Qur'an. This can be deduced from the fact that many dateable traditions, most listing dates from the first and second centuries of Islam (seventh and eighth centuries C.E.), have survived; Bashear lists almost all of this material (1993).

Another key element of Islamic apocalyptic tradition concerns the return of Jesus to earth. (Although such a return is not mentioned specifically in the Qur'an, it is strongly implied by the wording of Qur'an 3:55.) Jesus' return is followed by descriptions of Gog and Magog and of the rising of the sun from the west, an event expected to immediately precede the end of the world. All of these events are commonly mentioned in the apocalyptic tradition literature and are specified in creedal statements.

Although these signs are generally agreed on, another field of apocalyptic material exists that has not become authoritative but remains at least peripheral to the tradition. Theologians have divided these apocalyptic signs into two groups: the Lesser and the Greater Signs of the Hour. The Lesser Signs are moral, cultural, political, religious, and natural events designed to warn humanity that the end is near and to bring people into a state of repentance. The vast majority of these signs are general and have been present in all known societies: moral decay, crime, natural disasters, and wars, for example. However, certain of them are specific political events, usually those connected with occurrences in the first and second centuries of Islam. The modern apocalyptists whose work forms the focus of this book contend that these Lesser Signs of the Hour have been fulfilled to a large degree; in fact, however, they could be applied with equal weight (and in many cases has been so applied) to almost any period of Islamic history after the first century. Apocalyptists point out the fulfillment of the Lesser Signs of the Hour as a mechanism for inciting apocalyptic enthusiasm at any given time.

The Greater Signs of the Hour are regarded as a map of the future. They detail a series of events of ever-increasing severity that will precede the end of the world, at which time the damned will be judged and the blessed will begin to taste the pleasures God has in store for them in heaven. This scenario will be a time of extremes, opening, in the classical accounts, with warfare between the Byzantines and the Muslims, an event in close accordance with the reality of the first three centuries of Islamic history. While the accounts of this warfare lack any real eschatological element—except for the achievement of the highly desirable and previously unattainable goal of conquering Constantinople, the capital of the Byzantine Empire—the battles are the precursors to the end of history. With the conquest of Constantinople, the Antichrist *(Dajjal)* appears on the scene, according to most accounts. His purpose is to tempt and seduce the Muslims and to torment and ultimately fight and kill those who resist his wiles. Accounts are very divided about him, but he is usually said to be a Jew who will appear from the east at the head of an army. The Antichrist will proceed throughout the world, tempting each person he encounters, and finally come to Jerusalem, the last refuge of those few Muslims who have refused to be seduced by him. At this critical point, as the last faithful Muslims in Jerusalem gradually dwindle in number, Jesus—one of the two generally accepted messianic figures in classical Islam—will come down from heaven to fulfill the rest of his earthly mission, which was cut short by God's lifting him up from the cross (Qur'an 3:55; see al-Kashmiri 1964; *Fatawa Islamiyya* 2002, 1:304–5; Addams 1944; Ibn Baz 1991, 166–71).

Jesus' arrival will usher in a messianic age; he will kill the Antichrist and afterward convert the Christians to Islam. Traditions about this messianic period are very confused: many hold that the alternative messianic figure (the Mahdi) will appear during the previous period of apocalyptic wars with the Byzantines and even that the Mahdi will be the one to emerge victorious. A sharp conflict exists between the Jesus and Mahdi traditions, signalling the intense discomfort of many Muslims with the Jesus scenario. Since Jesus is so revered by the Christians, it was apparently dangerous to leave him alone in control of the Muslim messianic future. Thus in many traditions he is made subordinate to the Mahdi, a purely Muslim messianic figure, to whom is assigned the more traditional roles of conquest and subjection of enemy countries.

Descriptions (including citations from Isaiah 11:6–9) of the Muslim messianic age that follows the defeat of the Antichrist contain elements of worldwide peace and prosperity; however, they also contain many violent events, such as the conquest and subjugation of non-Muslim territory—an idealized re-creation of the first Muslim conquests.

Other figures abound in the apocalyptic vision of the future, thanks to the numerous competing ideas and traditions that arose during classical times, to polemics between the government and opposition (mainly Shi'i) groups, and to the existence of a vast (and as yet uncharted) number of tribal and regional messianic figures; some of these were absorbed into the larger scheme of Mus-

lim apocalyptic literature, while others appear as demonic or ambiguous figures. Chief among these auxiliary figures is the Sufyani, who is at the same
time a Sunni hero in the region now forming Syria and a demonic figure in
Shiʿite sources for the classical Muslim apocalyptic scenario. Almost all of the
modern apocalyptic writers included in this book perceive the Sufyani as an
evil character, even though they themselves are Sunni; at best they are am-
bivalent about him.[2]

Beyond the cosmic battle between good and evil personalities, the
Greater Signs describe some universally detested groups that must appear at
the end. Principal among these are Gog and Magog (Yajuj and Majuj), groups
descended from Japheth (mentioned in Qur'an 18:94, 21:96) that, for no apparent reason, act as killing machines designed to destroy the entire world.
Ultimately they are defeated only by God, who miraculously causes them to
perish all in one night. (Apparently this was expected to create something of a
public health nuisance; some sources speak of Muslims begging God to remove the bodies because of the stench.)

While it is difficult to speak of a definite end to the world in Muslim apocalyptic tradition—because there are no traditions that make the leap from the
scenario described here and the actual Day of Resurrection—most accounts
agree that the end will occur in the immediate aftermath of the destruction of
Gog and Magog.

Classical Muslim apocalyptic literature accurately reflects the world and
the reality in which Muslims existed during the seventh to ninth centuries.
The peoples described, the political and social currents—even the technology—are accurate for that time; thus we are able to date the material with a
reasonable level of certainty. Western critical methodology is of course irrelevant to believing Muslims, who look to this material to guide them over the
yawning abysses and along the treacherous slopes of modern times. They want
to believe that these apocalyptic events will indeed happen as described by the
Prophet and his companions; they regard the traditions as a lens through
which to see the contemporary world. Seeking to understand conditions in

2. This is probably because Syrian apocalyptic writers were not free to promulgate their
views during the al-Asad dictatorship, allowing Egyptians and others to dominate the discourse.
By default the Sufyani figure has been moved to the evil column.

the modern world, they want verification that they are on the right path. Above all, they hope that everything will end as it should, since the present self-image of Muslims is frequently low. Citing a prophecy from the prophet Muhammad, one apocalyptic writer says: " 'You will be many on that day [in the apocalyptic future], but like scum.' [3] You were right, my lord, O Messenger of God, we are 220 million [Arabs] today, but we are scum, like the scum of the flash flood, without us having either value or weight" (A. 'Ali 1996, 101; cf. B. 'Abdallah 1994, 139; and M. 'Arif 1995, 50–52).

Another writer speaks in a similar vein:

> In this present time period despair has overcome some Muslims as a result of what they feel of the tyranny, the affliction, and the lack of justice—both specifically and in general. They have placed the issue of the expected Mahdi as their only hope. Some contemporaries have drawn upon their understanding of the traditions and have seen that his days are close, and some of them have even seen that the texts attest that we are on the verge of the appearance of the Antichrist and the descent of Jesus, son of Mary. The [fact that the] Jews rule most of the authorities of the world and the Christians and Majus [Zoroastrians] are helpless before them and are employed for their interests in their lording it over the Muslims has verified that for them. (Tawila 1999, 4; cf. B. 'Abdallah 1994, 139)

As it stands in the collections of classical traditions, this material cannot supply the believing Muslim with vitally needed hope. It is in need of an overhaul, a refurbishment, a reinterpretation in light of the realities of the modern world.

There is every reason to believe that the early Muslim community realized that there was a substantial difference between these traditions, which described a political reality of their times, and the other traditions, which are mostly legal in nature. The earliest compositions rarely attempt to "fulfill" the

---

3. The prophetic hadith quoted here is not one that is widely cited; see Ibn Hanbal (n.d., 5:278) and Ibn al-'Adim: "When your [i.e., Muslims'] evil actions multiply, God will remove the fear [of you] from the breasts of your enemies, and you will be like the scum of the flash flood in their eyes" (n.d., 1:98). Now we frequently find the hadith in literature on jihad. See, e.g., www .alribat.com, "The Battlefield: The Safest Place on Earth"; see also the present book, 182–83.

predictions or relate them to current events, if only for the simple reason that they were known to be current. The traditions, therefore, remained in their original form, transmitted with very little alteration both orally and through written transcription. As the traditions were gradually absorbed into the canonical collections (unlike most of the messianic traditions, which never were accepted), commentators began to treat them as material in need of interpretation and to look for explanations of the traditions and their ultimate fulfillment. The first such interpretations appeared in the genre of religious literature known as "the proofs of prophecy," composed by apologists and polemicists searching for proof of Muhammad's prophethood. These groups were later joined in interpretation by commentators on tradition; even in classical times apocalyptic scenarios from previous centuries were frequently reinterpreted in terms of a given contemporary situation; ancient names of peoples and places were given new meanings, and in general the story lines were brought up to date. Until very recently, however, reinterpretation did not continue after classical times; for the most part, the material stood on its own merits.

The exigencies of the present-day world have stimulated a new body of apocalyptic literature, however. Modern conditions are such that the traditional view of the hadith cannot be held to have much value. Muslims need new interpretations, applicable to the world of today. This book explores Muslims' attempts to update the meaning of the hadith and focuses on the Arabic-language apocalyptic literature current among Sunni Muslims. Contemporary Shi'ite apocalyptic literature is not examined in this book; it needs a separate treatment. Therefore, the word *Muslim,* as used in this book, refers to "Sunni Arabic-language Muslim," and the literature examined is the literature based in that culture. It is in this literature that the greatest changes have registered during the past thirty-odd years, especially since the Six Days' War of June 1967.

TWO

BUILDING A NEW VISION OF THE FUTURE IN THE WAKE OF THE SIX DAYS' WAR

Apocalyptic Writers and Their Schools of Thought

Apocalyptic writers do not stand alone in their reevaluation of Muslim tradition. The catastrophic defeat of Egypt, Jordan, and Syria in June 1967 brought about a revolution in Islam that has come to be known as the Islamic revival *(al-sahwa al-Islamiyya)*. This revival has led to the growth of political Islam, best represented by Islamic political parties in most Arab and Muslim states, and also to renewed prominence of Islam in society. In general, Islam was the primary beneficiary of growing popular disillusionment with secular and socialist regimes in the 1970s and 1980s, and during the 1990s political Islam—usually called radical Islam—challenged several of these regimes (notably those of Egypt, Algeria, and Saudi Arabia) using guerrilla tactics.

13

Radical Muslims also succeeded in establishing regimes in marginal Muslim countries such as Afghanistan and the Sudan.

Underlying the ferment of political Islam, however, has been an intellectual ferment. While radical Muslim intellectuals are sympathetic to the agenda of radical political Islam in certain cases, the two groups are by no means identical. Radical intellectuals have sought to develop new interpretations of Islam—often starting from traditions in Islam such as Wahhabism intended to denude Islam of any Sufi aspects (such as saint worship)—that would build a complete system separate from any European-derived political or social system. With the slogan "Islam is the solution," many of these intellectuals, such as Yusuf al-Qaradawi, have tried to build a system that is entirely Islamic and yet relevant to the modern world. (Whether they have succeeded is not the subject of this research, although they—along with Samuel Huntington, in his *Clash of Civilizations*—are probably naïve to believe that any system could be hermetically sealed.) The apocalyptic writers discussed in this book are part of this ongoing intellectual upheaval in the Muslim world.

Apocalyptic discourse was not initially under the intellectual control of apocalyptic writers. Until the middle of the twentieth century, Islam's apocalyptic heritage, like other elements of Islamic religious discourse, was for the most part dominated by the *'ulama'* (conservative religious leadership). The *'ulama'* are characterized by their rigid adherence to the texts received from previous centuries. They have tended to write pamphlets, or sometimes volumes, in the wake of a wave of apocalyptic interest or after a political setback that is deemed detrimental to the Arab or Muslim cause and that is drawing people to accept apocalyptic beliefs.[1] Examples of these writings abound, especially because the past several centuries have provided few successes for Arabs or Muslims to boast about. For example, many books by *'ulama'* came out in the wake of the 1948 Arab-Israeli war (often called al-Nakba, the disaster), after the Six Days' War of 1967, during the Gulf War interlude (1990–91), during the last years of the millenium, and in relation to the sec-

---

1. The following are recent examples of conservative and neoconservative writings: Ru'ud 1985; al-Tibi 1991; al-Shahawi 1992; Sa'd 1995; al-Ta'if 1995; al-Jabi 1996; al-Shami 1996; al-Tahtawi 1997; al-Ta'mi n.d.; 'Amr 1997. A number of these pamphlets were written as refutations of radical writings.

ond Intifada of September 2000 to approximately July 2003 (see, for example, Fa'iz 1983 and Haras 1993).

However, this type of writing makes no effort to relate the traditions to the events taking place around the reader. It is entirely up to the reader to make any necessary connection, although occasionally pamphlets written for popular consumption supply translations or explanations of difficult words in the classical texts. Writers of the conservative school are uniformly anti-apocalyptic. They are not writing to start a wave of expectations; they are writing to dampen and hopefully destroy that which is currently present in society. While they could perhaps serve their cause better by pointing out the differences between the classical texts and the modern realities, the books they write are usually simple reference books, presumably designed for religious leaders to use like a bucket of cold water on the excited masses. The new interpretations put forward by the apocalyptists have, for the most part, put the conservatives on the defensive.

This new school, which could profitably be called the radical school, has made a serious effort to create new apocalyptic scenarios based on classical Muslim material, more or less in the same manner that evangelical Christians use biblical material. The radical school has also assimilated into its scenario anti-Semitic conspiracy theories—which are very popular in many parts of the Middle East—as well as using Christian interpretations of the Bible or playing off of them. Although there may be some intellectual connections between apocalyptic writers of the radical school and Muslims who are politically radical (such as antigovernmental groups) or globally radical (such as Usama bin Ladin and al-Qa'ida), the intellectual apocalyptists do not necessarily overlap with these groups. However, themes and ideas common to all three are explored in this book, especially in chapter 8, which presents the apocalyptic scenarios of globalist radical Islam. It cannot be a coincidence that the rise of radical apocalyptic writers has been concurrent with the rise of radical Islam, but there is no evidence of actual interdependence, other than the fact that radical apocalyptic writers feed off the events and trends that radical Muslims have either generated or benefited from, and interpret them in terms of their apocalyptic framework.

While radical apocalyptic writers come from all sections of the Muslim world, most of the writers examined in this book come from Egypt. This is not surprising because Egypt is the intellectual capital of the Arabic-speaking world, and Cairo is one of its principal publishing centers. Much of the most recent discourse has been initiated by Sa'id Ayyub, an Egyptian writer, and his followers. Ayyub writes on religious and "clash of civilizations" issues, although he is not known to be associated with any religious institution. His first book on an apocalyptic theme, *al-Masih al-Dajjal* (1987), could be viewed as a religious book because it uses the Muslim apocalyptic heritage as its base; it is billed as "a political reading of the foundations of the great religions." Most of his other books stay within this general subject, except his book attacking Salman Rushdie.

Many other Egyptian writers have followed in Ayyub's footsteps. Probably the most popular of these is Muhammad 'Isa Da'ud, who calls himself "the Egyptian Sinbad, a great thinker." He has expanded the synthesis pioneered by Ayyub, using it to explain a number of so-called mysteries of the modern world, such as the Bermuda Triangle and the question of UFOs, and to relate these mysteries to the material in the classical Muslim traditions. His books are found all over the Arabic-speaking Muslim world, and anecdotal evidence culled from speaking with booksellers in Cairo, Beirut, Casablanca, and Amman suggests that he is a best-selling author. Other Egyptians—for example, Bashir Muhammad 'Abdallah, Khalid 'Abd al-Wahid, and Hisham Kamal 'Abd al-Hamid—have written specifically on such questions as the ultimate fate of the state of Israel and the future punishment of the United States, as well as on unresolved difficulties within the larger context of Muslim apocalyptic literature, such as the question of Gog and Magog.

But there are radical apocalyptic writers from other places as well. A number of Palestinians, such as Bassam Jirrar, who heads an organization called al-Nun li-Dirasat al-Qur'aniyya in Ramallah and is affiliated with Hamas, and Salih al-Din Abu 'Arafa, who came into prominence recently as a result of his prophecies concerning the end of the United States, have contributed to the apocalyptic scenario. Saudi Arabians, such as Safar al-Hawali, who is closely associated with globalist radical Islamic groups, have also written apocalyptic books. Syrians, Moroccans, and Jordanians are also cited in this study. There is a growing body of apocalyptic literature on the Internet, in either Arabic or English, most of it from the radical school and associated in a more obvious manner with globalist radical Islam. Thus, the radical interpretation of the

Muslim apocalyptic heritage has come to have a pan-Islamic (or at least a pan-Arabic Muslim) aspect.

Most of these authors subscribe to the idea of an international conspiracy against Islam and Muslims everywhere and to the idea that the best manner in which to counter such a conspiracy is to unite all Muslims into one state ruled by a caliph. This goal is closely parallel to that of globalist radical Muslims; the only difference is that globalist radical Muslims appear to believe that this should be achieved by fighting. Many of the radical apocalyptic school have written about wars that lend themselves to an apocalyptic interpretation, such as those in Bosnia and Kashmir or the Gulf War, and have tried to develop them into full-scale, end-time, apocalyptic wars. Yet other writers have concentrated on the moral and religious decay of Muslim society and how this is to be seen in light of the radical synthesis.

There has been a great deal of polemic between the conservatives and the radicals. At first the conservative school tried to overcome the radicals by reviewing their books negatively and occasionally by writing pamphlets against them, pointing out the weak connection of their writings to the classical Islamic sources and what the conservatives held to be illegitimate interpretations of the material. However, they quickly discovered that nobody was listening to them because of their conservative and boring writing style, and in any case they did not have an alternative vision to offer. In addition to this, they did not polemicize with their opponents by name (for example, Murad 1997)—unlike the radicals, who regularly insult their opponents in every way possible—and were in general too dignified to sling the mud necessary to win the battle. As a result, the conservatives' writings have nearly disappeared from the marketplace, although occasionally one of their big names (Muhammad 'Abd al-Qadir 'Ata' or Shaykh Ahmad Mustafa Tahtawi, for example) will produce a new volume. Their criticisms of the radical approach did, however, produce one variation that proved to be fruitful. While the conservatives criticized the assimilation of the anti-Semitic conspiracy theory on the same evidential level as the hadith, they apparently accepted it in the end, probably because it was too central to be fought and no one disbelieved it enough to even try. However, along with this innovation the radicals also introduced a huge wave of biblical exegesis, which was too much for the conservatives, who are well aware that this is abrogated material from the despised faiths of Judaism and Christianity.

The school I refer to as the neoconservative school was founded as a result of criticism of the assimilation of the biblical material, and numbers among its adherents writers such as Amin Jamal al-Din, 'Abd al-Wahhab Tawila, and Mustafa Murad. They took the radical synthesis and sought to rid it of the biblical material, and rebuilt the scenario using Muslim sources as much as possible. They continued to assume the truth of the anti-Semitic conspiracy theory, although spending a good deal less time on it, and concentrated on the material from the prophet Muhammad's struggle with the Jews (appearing extensively in the Qur'an and historical narratives). In rebuilding, the neoconservatives have been at least partially successful because of their training by classical scholars, the conservatives; they have considerable mastery of the hadith material and have used it far more effectively than did their predecessors. Essentially they have abandoned a boring writing style, brought the Islamic sources back into the discourse, and assumed the rest of the radical approach that they could not prove from their own material.[2]

Assimilation of the Anti-Semitic Conspiracy Theory

The first and most powerful stimulus in the new interpretation of classical apocalyptic materials has been the assimilation of classic European anti-Semitic conspiracy theory. A good general statement of it is the following:

> The people [i.e., Muslims] have never discovered who the evil and dangerous [one] is who manipulates this world and pushes it without mercy toward hell, who it is that moves the chess pawns on his wide board, and who has an interest in everything that happens on the face of the earth. There were enlightened opinions and thoughts, and true voices proceeding from some of the intelligentsia in civilized areas, raised in protest and warning at the beginning of the [twentieth] century, saying that there is a hidden hand, half of which is human and half of which is satanic, making a concerted effort to de-

2. The neoconservatives are also concerned with restoring the belief in the apocalyptic nature of the times to respectability, something that their conservative predecessors would not have wanted. See, for example, Jamal al-Din (1997, 11).

stroy this world, and that there is an evil enemy preparing disasters for humanity. There have been many names describing this hidden enemy: Masons,[3] the Hidden Hand, the secret world government, pieces on the chessboard—meaning the world—the game of Israel.[4] This enemy has remained surrounded by walls of fear, holiness, and secrecy, and none are able to pass through the secret barrier to this enemy and reveal his reality to the people, despite the fact that there have been those who have penetrated those organizations and have written about them. But the writings perpetuate and augment the secrecy even more, and lately voices have drowned out the intelligentsia and hidden the light of truth; the voices of lies and deception have risen and the deceived are those who believe themselves to be writers and thinkers. The world has become a beggar, listening to the melody of Satan playing in every place. "There is no conspiracy against the world, there is no conspiracy against the Muslims, there is no conspiracy against the Arabs, there is no conspiracy against morals, there is no conspiracy against religion—the idea of a conspiracy is the most dangerous idea against humanity, and we must fight it." Yes, by my Lord, this is what Gog and Magog have done to the minds of people.[5] This enemy has become arrogant [see Qur'an 17:4],[6] to the point where it can conceal its real name from the people of the earth. (F. Salim 1998b, 9–10)

Fundamentally, as the anti-Semitic conspiracy theory has been absorbed into Arab Muslim apocalyptic belief, it takes one of the following forms.

The first one is a historical introduction lifted out of anti-Semitic European and American writers. In general, these writers perceived the Jews as being part of a Communist world conspiracy and sought to discern a Jewish hidden hand behind the numerous revolutions, the social turmoil, and antireligious agitation of the first half of the twentieth century. It is not unusual for pictures on the covers of apocalyptic books in Arabic to have the characteris-

---

3. On the Masons, see Shalabi (1992); and Sharbasi (1977).

4. This is probably a reference to William Guy Carr's book *Pawns in the Game* (1950), which is one of the most influential of all foreign apocalyptic books for the Arab Muslim writer.

5. According to Fahd Salim, the writer of this extract, the Jews are Gog and Magog.

6. All Qur'anic translations are from Fakhry (1997).

tics of anti-Semitic portrayals of Jews. Jews are perceived as the eternal enemy of Christianity, subverting it at every level and controlling its history for their nefarious purposes, and driving ultimately toward the rule of the Jewish Antichrist. While it might seem that this element of the conspiracy would not have much relevance for the Muslim Arab because it largely concerns the experiences of another religious group (Christianity), one finds that this historical element is not suppressed. Perhaps it shows a certain schadenfreude and triumphalism that the Jews—who through the state of Israel have resisted repeated Arab attempts to defeat them on the battlefield—have subverted the all-powerful West as well, and much more thoroughly even than they have done to the Arabs. Arab Muslim writers add to this conspiracy scenario all the history of the Jews with the prophet Muhammad and various other unsavory episodes from their own history books.[7] The original European authors did not include this material; they focused exclusively upon their own continent's history and religious prejudices. However, the Muslim material is not given the same prominence as the Christian material, and it is obvious that there is simply not that much upon which to draw.

The depth of this historical material has to be read to be believed. Functionally, so these writers would have us believe, all of history has been controlled by a group of Jews who, because they knew more than anybody else and had unlimited amounts of money and unassailable positions of power, together with satanic authority and the monomaniacal purpose of subverting all of humanity and driving it into hell, have directed all past historical events.[8] While it is sometimes hard for the apocalyptists to pin down exactly when this conspiracy became operative, it clearly was organized at the latest shortly after

---

7. See al-Maydani (1974, 41–217); Ferooz (1979); Zallum (1962); Hamidullah (1982); Bayumi (1995b, 47; the Jews destroyed the caliphate). See also Veliankode: "This situation [of disunity] was fully utilized by Christian and Jewish lobbies [during the Crusades] to recapture the masjid [al-Aqsa] from the Muslim hands . . . The Zionist synagogue and Christian Colonialist lobbies successfully endeavored to weaken the Islamic solidarity" (1995, 57); and "Once Zionists planned to overpower the Muslims during Crusader War. Allah sent down his grace and great help to Salah-ud-Din al-Ayyubi and defeated the Zionist lobby's plot and freed the Bait-ul-Maqdis Mosque" (1995, 248).

8. According to Abu Zayd (1999, 36–37), Jews worship Satan in the form of the Antichrist, and all Satanists are Jews as well; see also M. Mustafa (1998, 52–54).

Jesus' time, since the apostle Paul was one of its most effective agents (Shihabi 1997, 13–14). It was he who successfully perverted Jesus' teachings and corrupted the New Testament (Ayyub 1987, 28, 295; al-Bar 1998). Many of these Arab Muslim apocalyptists are fully convinced that this Jewish conspiracy led directly to the prophet Muhammad's confrontation with the Jews of Medina (recorded in part in the Qur'an).

The second level of the conspiracy theory is represented by the state of Israel. It is fair to say the vast majority of modern Arab Muslim apocalyptic writers are obsessed with Israel. Israel is offensive to them on many grounds: because of Arab nationalism, because of Muslim supercessionism toward the Jewish faith, and because of the feeling that no country that has become Muslim should ever go back to being non-Muslim (also operative with regard to Spain; al-Buti 1997, 241). Israel has control over Muslim holy places and has a reasonable claim to the sites upon which many of them are built (such as the Dome of the Rock), the control of which is not an issue subject to compromise for most Muslims. In particular, Israel is a symbol of the hated and envied West, a cultural intruder, a country that has succeeded in building a democratic and progressive society when the Muslims overwhelmingly have not (if they are from the Left and have sympathy for such goals). For the devout Muslim, Israel represents something of a Trojan horse, culturally speaking, because its society is so clearly incompatible with the Muslim value system. It also represents an attraction for both them and their children, which is much closer to home than the hated and envied America and the European countries.

> In summary, the Jewish presence in occupied Palestine constitutes a great danger to the culture of the Islamic community, and this danger is typified by the Jewish cultural invasion that is infiltrating the countries of the area in accordance with a written plan, whose originators took advantage of the experience of the Western cultural invasion of the Islamic community, and use different methods and media for the purposes of this invasion: universities, educational and scientific curricula for schools, fine literature, arts, different informational media, such as the newspaper, radio, and television, research centers and cultural centers, and other things as well. Thus the Islamic community is threatened in its culture, and thus it is threatened in its identity and personality, which distinguish it from other communities and protect its exis-

tence and independence. The meaning of this is a sentence of dissolution into the [other world] communities and then disappearance and conclusion. (Shabir 1992, 42; cf. Zarzur, Rabi', and al-Ansari 1996, 71–74, 78–80)

In addition to all of the above, the apocalyptically conscious Muslim knows that Israel is in control over many of the most important areas in which the apocalyptic future is to take place. For Jerusalem is none other than the apocalyptic capital of Islam (Jirrar 1995, 48–49; M. 'Arif 1996, 126). It is the location from which the Mahdi will rule, and it is where the Muslims will take refuge from the Jews, led by the Antichrist, when he attacks the lands of Islam. It is the site to which Jesus will return, and he will defeat the Antichrist near the present-day Ben-Gurion Airport. Many other equally important events are to occur there. Thus the end of the world literally cannot take place until Israel is removed and a Muslim state is put in its place.

For this reason there is a striking emotional similarity between Jewish and Muslim messianic expectations. Both Jews and Muslims feel that they are incredibly and frustratingly close to the realization of their goals. For many religious Jews, it is incomprehensible that the Third Temple cannot be built upon the Temple Mount, the area of the Dome of the Rock, because control over it was won during the 1967 war. Israel reigns over the Temple Mount but does not rule over it. It has the authority to do what it wishes, but dares not use it in a manner that could make that control effective. This is a source of incredible frustration for many religious Jews, even more so than if this holy spot were far outside their jurisdiction. They feel as though it is almost, but not quite, within their grasp (Gorenberg 2000, 138–56). Muslims feel this frustration as well, since they control the actual Haram al-Sharif, if just barely, and for this reason they focus intensely upon the site. Muslims are also aware of Jewish claims to the site, they know that Israel has the power to enforce these claims, and they do not completely understand why this dreaded event has not happened.

The Jews claim, starting from an understanding of their civilizational hatred, that Jerusalem is their heritage and belongs to them alone, and that it is Jewish by birth, origin, and history, while the truth is that religiously, essentially, and geographically Jerusalem was Arabic previous to Islam, previous to Christianity, and previous to Judaism, and that Islam has more rights to it because it is [the] correct [faith] and any other is false. (M. 'Arif 1996, 132)[9]

Other writers focus on the emotions felt by this generation of Muslims in the face of their helplessness: "If the Jews reach the al-Aqsa Mosque and put into action their plots, in the midst of a generation of Muslims reaching a quarter of the inhabitants of the earth, may God help us for the shame *('ar)* that would not be wiped away by time nor washed away by water" (A. Mustafa 1990, 284).

In a way, the very tenuousness of each side's control of this sensitive site contributes significantly to apocalyptic expectations.

The third level of the anti-Semitic conspiracy theory stems from the frustration Muslims feel about their inability to deal with Israel and their inability to convince the larger world of the justice of their concerns.[10] Such feelings have prompted the creation of a larger and existentially evil Zionist world government. Based on *The Protocols of the Elders of Zion,* which virtually all modern Muslim apocalyptists from both the radical and neoconservative schools cite as an authoritative text, this level of the conspiracy theory depicts the world as totally dominated by the Jews—both as a people and as an evil, demonic presence somehow transcending the Jews as a people—and ultimately controlled by the Antichrist. According to the theory at this level, the An-

9. According to the reworking of history common in parts of the Arab world, the inhabitants of the area currently controlled by Israel and the Palestinian National Authority have always been Arabs (and sometimes even Arab Muslims), from the time when this territory was conquered by Joshua (see Josh. 6–11) and sometimes even before that, back to the period of the El Amarna Letters (approx. 1500–1200 B.C.E.). See chapter 5 of this book.

10. There is also the inability to understand the freedom of choice and the marketplace of ability created by a free society, which promotes the view that since the Jews are prominent in Western society (and regarded as even more so by the exaggerations created by discovery of "hidden Jews"), there must be some conspiracy to explain this fact. Coming from a hierarchical society where ability is not necessarily rewarded and where it is more important to have a protective group supporting an individual than to get a good education and to work hard, the conspiracy accusation at this level is understandable. See H. 'Abd al-Hamid (1996, 5–6).

tichrist's power is now so great as to be unquantifiable. This power cannot be overestimated, and vast numbers of people have been tainted by it or are puppets directly controlled by it.

> I speak to Muslims especially and to the entire world [additionally]: that this is the dark and definitive Zionist page [of history], shedding blood, killing its sons, propagating corruption in every area of the world, the sweeping plague of drugs and immorality—both what is open and what is concealed. They [the Jews] have tyrannized and fornicated until there has not remained any holiness in the laws of God upon the earth that they have not profaned. (M. 'Arif 1996, 14; cf. 'Amaluhu 1992, 115–16)

In many cases this conspiracy is divorced from actually belonging to the Jews per se, although many Jews are supposedly tainted by it, but for the most degraded writers it involves racial affiliation. Muslims often insist that they are not racists (Lewis 1986, 81–139, 192–235), and in a sense even most of these offensive apocalyptic writers are not. If one could coin a word, one would be forced to call them religionists. That is, they define their superiority to the rest of the world in terms of religious affiliation rather than race. Many of them in any case take the classic Muslim position that Jews are not a race but a religion:

> Judaism is not a divine faith, and most especially not the faith of the prophet Moses, but is a very old mixture of superstitions that Jewish devils and their evil ones have woven together since ancient times to form a way for the most loathsome attack history has ever known [i.e., Zionism]. (Zaytun 1996, 7)

> Judaism is the very creed of Satan, and it has dwelt in the evil soul from ancient times, even a long time previously to Moses. . . . In short, Judaism does not have any connection to Moses, and it constitutes infidelity and enmity toward Moses. His mission was to liberate [people] from it [Judaism] completely, as was the mission of Jesus and all of the prophets. (Zaytun 1996, 12–13; cf. 'Amaluhu 1992, 167–68; and Ya'qub 1988)

Clearly, Muslim apocalyptic writers have not closed themselves off from anti-Semitic racist obscenities, and more than occasionally they cite the type of pornographic anti-Semitic material that has made *Der Stürmer* and other Nazi literature infamous.[11] Not all apocalyptists are guilty of this—it is true—but few make any effort to differentiate.

This sort of anti-Semitism has an entirely different meaning and power over the reader. It contends that the Jewish conspiracy is vast and all-encompassing, ruthless and entirely evil. Therefore, no mercy can be extended to Jews in any way, shape, or form, and that part of humanity tainted with the conspiracy has no redeeming qualities whatsoever. One writer, for example, compares other ruthless peoples, such as the Romans and the Aryans, with the Zionists and asserts that while these other conquering peoples were restrained by a sense of fellow humanity toward those supposedly inferior peoples temporarily subjected to them, Zionists lack even this lowest common denominator of human feeling:

> At a glance at *The Protocols of the Elders of Zion*, which is the primary document upon which Zionism built the bricks of the Zionist entity's foundations, both conceptually and in practice, astonishment and bewilderment takes one vis-à-vis those Zionists, since they anchor the principles of the Zionist idea in this book, and the foundations of the appearance of their entity in the future [from when it was written], from an age previously. You are amazed at how these [Zionists] began to plan corrupting the entire world, all of its nations and peoples, and how they used knowledge, progress, nudity, vilification of morals and values, and how they made all of these into implements for their goals that they attained, using all monstrous lies and deception, breaking of treaties, and biting the hand that is extended to help them, and destruction of countries, killing of the sons of nations that work for their benefit. In short, they have surrounded themselves with all of the implements that make them into a terrifying and frightening race to all who deal with them. Whenever anyone deviates from their path, then you see them tempted—even the *'ulama'* [Muslim religious leadership]—with money, and if they refuse, then with women, and if they refuse, then with prominent positions and the publication of their sciences and their inventions. If they refuse to deal with them [the Zionists], in the end they are killed, and thus they

---

11. For example, M. Da'ud, who details the disgusting and incestuous means by which Jews supposedly turn their children into prostitutes (1999, 289–327); M. 'Arif (1996, 96–97); al-Musayri (1998, 165–89).

[the Zionists] have succeeded in subverting the programmed sciences in accordance with their opinions, and interpreted according to their desires to service their lower goals in the corruption of the world. In *The Protocols* there is a picture of people more animal-like than animals, trying to make the world into a red hell. ('Amaluhu 1992, 160–61)

It is difficult to recognize any aspect of the actual Jewish people when reading selections of this nature.

There are no noncombatants in the war with world Zionism; according to many of these apocalyptic fantasies, all Jews must be killed for the evil to be extirpated, as in this quotation from a chapter entitled "The Jews: A Spreading Plague":

The present reality of the world (just like a slide under a microscope)[12] . . . proves that the Jewish bacteria is in the process of being diffused and its spread throughout the body of the planet is consistent with those savage diseases that destroy in a devastating manner. There is no cure except by the leadership and lordship of Islam, that great faith that completes the felicity of humanity. As for Zionistic Jewry, they are a bog of evil qualities and plagues—for this reason their great hatred is against Islam and Muslims. . . . Among the pictures of Jewish shamelessness and criminality against Islam and the Muslims during our own lives are the propagation of those shameless, brazen, low crimes for which even one of them deserves the punishment of death and annihilation from off the face of the planet entirely. (M. 'Arif 1996, 97)[13]

According to such writers, Islam is the only refuge from the evil of the Jews—but not just any brand of Islam. One must embrace *true* Islam—what-

12. These parentheses and the material they contain appeared in the original text.
13. Among the things that offend 'Arif are the use in the English language of the word "Mecca" to indicate the center of something, as in "a Mecca of vice." He also accuses the Jews of putting out a group of pornographic pictures in which a woman was pictured performing lewd actions with a copy of the Qur'an, and he claims that Jews put the name of Allah under shoes so that people can walk on it (M. 'Arif 1996, 154). See also Ayyub (1987, 9–10); Murad (1997, 3); and M. Mustafa (1998, 88–89).

ever that is—because so many Muslims have themselves been tainted by the Jews' evil and must be either saved from it or killed. One should note at this juncture that apocalyptic writers do not hesitate to accuse large numbers of Muslims of being non-Muslims, although they don't explain how one differentiates between true Muslims and false Muslims.

Muslim apocalyptic writers consider Israel and—even more so—the United States as the natural homes of the Antichrist because the United States is the source of the Jews' power and the seat of the Antichrist's authority (see chapter 7).

> As to the rule of the Jews or Banu Isra'il [Israelites] of the world, it is dependent upon their rule of America, and the perfection of their grip upon it, politically, economically, media-wise, morally, militarily, and educationally as well. The Christian American people have become a colony subservient to the Jews, despite their minority status. Afterward this minority has drowned the dominant majority in lusts and perversions and the pleasures of licit and illicit life, so that their consciousness has disappeared—I mean the American people—and they have become like a herd of animals led to the slaughter by inciting them through means of stalks of grass, [while they are] hoping thereby to stop up their hunger.
>
> The most debased and degraded of all of the peoples of the world to the Jewish Satan is the American people, and they toil and slave to fill the warehouses of the Jews with gold. Their lives are for the sake of the Jews, and they make war and die for the sake of fulfilling the strategic interests of the Jews throughout the entire world in general, and to protect Israel and its expansion in particular. They will live and die for the Jews. If a people is willing to live and die for another people or another group, then they are slaves to that group in every sense of the word. The most amazing thing about this whole matter is that this people [the Americans], which is in a state of societal slavery, extols freedom and lifts its slogans up, and is a universal example of it.
>
> There is no educated person in the entire world who will deny the truth of the Jewish rule of the United States, which has lately become the most powerful nation on the earth economically, militarily, and politically, and its rulers, leaders, and writers have proclaimed the era of the rule of America in the world under the name of the "new world order," so that the rule of the

Jews is a done deal and certain, not through Israel but through America. (B. 'Abdallah 1994, 98–99, 113; H. 'Abd al-Hamid 1997a, 44–54, 63–64)

From paranoid anti-Semites in the West, Muslims have also absorbed a great fear and loathing of the United Nations, seeing it as the tool through which the Antichrist and his Jewish minions exercise their control over the new world order.

Then part of his [the Antichrist's] plan to rule the world is to proclaim him-self as the king over it and to realize what they call "peace" by means of the international law through the Security Council of the UN, and the Interna-tional Monetary Fund. All of this will not happen despite the Jews, the Antichrist, their helpers, and their slaves from the infidel Masonic collabora-tionist governments, and their ignorant masses. (B. 'Abdallah 1994, 159; cf. Abu Zayd 1999, 23–39; and Sunnaqrat 1983, 46)

Others say about the UN:

From the time of the foundation of the UN until today it has been a tool in the service of world Zionism, and never has any resolution been issued by it in condemnation of Israel, with the exception of several nonbinding resolu-tions whose purpose was to throw sand in the eyes. (H. 'Abd al-Hamid 1997a, 61)[14]

The rule of the Jewish Zionists has extended until it has included the General Assembly of the UN and, secretly, the Security Council, under its new veil called the United States of America, under the new name of the "new world order." (M. Mustafa 1998, 17)

And what about the Muslim countries and the other countries of the world?

14. Because certain Muslim groups regard the United Nations as a Zionist tool, there have been calls for Arabs to leave it all together; see Abu Sahiliyya (1992).

The Islamic world remains [to be discussed], and here the Zionist control over this world is through the Masons. (B. 'Abdallah 1994, 101)

The Zionists control by imposing famine and scientific and technical backwardness upon the Islamic world. The most important thing is that most of the people of the world—the Crusader [Christian] world, the Islamic world, and the Buddhist and Hindu worlds—have all become subservient to the evil powers exemplified in institutions and great powers like mountains.[15] And these evil powers, which are like mountains—the Jews sit upon their peaks in the form of the Hidden Government. During the first period of corruption by the Banu Isra'il, God destroyed them as a result of the first promise [threat] at the hand of Nebuchadnezzar the Babylonian.[16] Now the Jews and all of humanity are living through the second corruption of Banu Isra'il and the second promise [threat] in response to this second corruption; its time is drawing near. (B. 'Abdallah 1994, 102)

Since the type of conspiracy detailed above is so overwhelming, what chance does a Muslim have to fight it? Is not the description of it such that many would wish to join the conspiracy rather than resist it? Furthermore, it is unclear what meaning the word "conspiracy" would have when such a substantial percentage of the world's population belongs to it and such a large part of human history was and continues to be controlled by it. One should rather call it a movement or by some more grandiose name. Although the apocalyptic Muslim is very conscious of the constant betrayal and treachery on his own side, he does not seem to be worried by these issues. On the contrary, he feels a sense of his own power, as if he is the only one to see the world as it really is. He is speaking to the entire world a word of truth concerning a reality that everyone else is either blind to or is willfully and malevolently ignoring. The Egyptian writer Muhammad 'Isa Da'ud, for example, says: "I speak to the entire world that the hidden hand, which prepares conspiracies and revolutions and causes the spilling of blood and disgusting events, continues to

---

15. B. 'Abdallah (1994, 127–29) describes many of these institutions as he discusses the identity of enemies against whom Muslims should wage their jihad.

16. The destruction of the First Temple in 586 B.C.E. by the Babylonians.

prepare to get at whatever it wants, whatever the price. This is a man like Satan [the Antichrist] in his hatred of humanity" (M. Da'ud 1992b, 42; cf. Ayyub 1987, 120–29).

Therefore, the sense of destiny and arrogance of these writers is part of their self-perception, which in itself is part of their liberation from the servitude imposed on them by the Antichrist's new world order. Do they personally feel persecuted? Why, if the conspiracy is so powerful and all encompassing, does it not remove these writers who try to expose it? Ironically, this theme of suppression of the truth behind the conspiracy, which is so widely developed in Western paranoid fantasies (where the society is free), does not seem to bother the Muslim apocalyptists living in more repressive societies. Very few of them speak of a sense that they personally are being watched or are in any personal danger.[17]

The conspiracy can still be fought, and that is the struggle for which the apocalyptist is calling:

It is incumbent upon the Muslims to raise the flag of jihad in the face of the Jews, to exalt the word of God on the earth, and not to leave the reins of their rule and their leadership to those who were satisfied when Zion sheathed its poisoned knife in the breasts of the Muslims, or that their impure feet would pollute the land of the mosque of al-Aqsa, the first of the two directions of prayer, and the third [holy site] after the two Harams [Mecca and Medina], and the destination of the Night Journey of the beloved Muhammad, the birthplace of Jesus, the habitation of Abraham, and the gathering place of the Muslims under the leadership of the Imam of the end of time, the Mahdi, and the place of prayer of Jesus, and the place of his marriage, his progeny, and his death. (M. 'Arif 1996, 180)

There is a great fear and (apparently to overcome the fear) an incredible arrogance on the part of the apocalyptic writer. For it is supremely arrogant on

17. The sole exception to the apocalyptists' freedom from a sense of being personally watched and threatened is Muhammad Mustafa, who says that he worries whether the Mossad will kill him for his previous book, *Nihayat Isra'il*, in which he uses gematria to calculate the length of Israel's duration (1998, 11). However, this theme of personal danger is more developed in the Muslim material on the Internet.

his part to believe that a conspiracy that has been (supposedly) dominating humanity for between two and three millennia will be single-handedly exposed and brought down by solitary efforts. The apocalyptic writer's rejection of accepted Muslim tradition and his inability to be self-critical augment this arrogance. The fear stems at least partially from the perceived lack of knowledge. Apocalyptists sense that their enemies know everything and so feel that they alone understand this reality. Since these enemies are in control of the world situation, they are capable of understanding the apocalyptist, and strangely enough actually give him sincere advice that usually has to be decoded from their writings. For this reason we find apocalyptic writers combing the Israeli press, and many books authored by Israeli or Jewish political or religious figures are then translated into Arabic in order to divine the otherwise inexplicable Zionist plots. It is somewhat ironic to find David Ben-Gurion, Shimon Peres, Benjamin Netanyahu, and even religious Israeli figures such as Rav Ovadia Yosef and Rav Zvi Yehuda Kook appearing in Muslim apocalyptic volumes and actually appearing to tell the Muslim masses what to do; this is doubly ironic in light of the fact that so many times the self-same writers say that everything the Jewish (controlled) media publishes is a lie (see, for example, M. 'Arif 1996, 152; and A. 'Ali 1996, 138–43).

It is perhaps also this type of fear and loneliness that prompted Muhammad 'Izzat 'Arif to dedicate one of his books, *Hal al-Dajjal yahkum al-'alam al-an?* (Is the Antichrist presently ruling the world?), to the Antichrist himself.[18] It is as though they alone (the writer and the Antichrist) in the world know the truth, possessing hidden secret knowledge, and so they can speak above the heads of the ignorant masses. The masses do not all understand what is really going on, but these two share in this gnostic insight that is denied everybody else. In a certain way, therefore, *The Protocols* is a gnostic text for the anti-Semite, one that reveals knowledge only a few can comprehend or are willing to face and to use. The apocalyptist is part of that high priesthood of knowledge.

Therefore, the third level of the anti-Semitic conspiracy theory is the most dangerous. It is by its very nature both paranoid and irrational because no ar-

---

18. A similarly odd dedication appears in a book by al-Sharbati (1994), who dedicates his book to Pontius Pilate for asking the rhetorical question: "What is truth?" [John 18:38].

gument or proof to the contrary has any bearing on it. Once a person has reached this level of belief in the conspiracy, anything that happens in the outside world will inevitably confirm it. Therefore, one must always be conscious of the fact that there is a world of lies and deceits awaiting the unsuspecting person. To the apocalyptists, as demonstrated by the following series of short quotations from several sources, everything originating in the outside world comes from the Antichrist and his Jewish followers:

> Know, O Muslim, that all of what is shown, broadcast, or distributed from the media in every place, in every time, and under any guise, from the beginning to the end, comes from the Jews and is in service to the Jews.[19]

> If the nations that claim to be Islamic, if they were Islamic in truth and ruled according to the law of God *(shari'a)* and forbade what God forbids, they would not receive or accept this flood of moral disintegration and proclamation of the forbidden. This is the conspiracy, whose roots are Zionist, assailing the minds of the people like an octopus.[20]

> I charge the ministers of communications in every Arab and Islamic country with the sin of realizing this dangerous plan for the continuation of the obliteration of the Islamic identity, and the transformation of the human innate character[21] and the propagation of corruption of the Jahiliyya[22] in every place.[23]

19. See the discussion of al-Tibi concerning the "tribulation of the television" (1990, 254ff); and further M. Mustafa (1998, 15–16).

20. Oddly, the octopus is the most common image used to describe the Jewish world conspiracy.

21. One should remember that Muslims believe that the true innate character of humanity is Islam and that people are transformed into idolaters, Jews, or Christians (or other groups) by their environment.

22. The Jahiliyya is the pre-Islamic time of idolatry. Modern radicals frequently say that we are living through another such time; see M. Qutb (1991, 30–52).

23. See M. 'Arif (1996, 152) and also his discussion of the results of the purported Jewish control of the media (1996, nn. 154–55); 1997, 118–19); Abu Zayd (1999, 73–105), especially 102–6, where Abu Zayd asserts that the Internet is the Jews' new tool for mind control; M. Mustafa (1998, 16–17); and 'Abd al-Hakim (1998a, 55–56).

The paranoid anti-Semite has placed himself in a closed circle from which neither logic, facts,[24] nor reality, can extricate him. He is literally in a prison of his
own creation.

Muslim apocalyptists are aware that they are accused of being paranoid,
and occasionally they do try to defend themselves from this charge.[25] However, paranoia is a major theme throughout all of the texts, both those of a
conservative and those of a radical bent.

The use of *The Protocols of the Elders of Zion* is a predominant feature of the
contemporary Arabic-language Muslim apocalyptic scenario.[26] It is the lens
through which the apocalyptic writers view the world and interpret everyday
events occurring in the political, religious, economic, and cultural arenas. One
can see how and why they have focused on the concept of freedom as being the
enemy, because for them it is the *true* enemy, denying them their power over

24. M. 'Arif (1996, 71–72); al-Musayri (1998, 14–15); and Abu Zayd (1999, 19–22) know
all about the correct historical facts of the origins of *The Protocols*; in fact, al-Musayri admits that
it is a forgery (1998, 20). Yet 'Arif shows no hesitation in dismissing the historical facts as lies put
out by the Jews, and al-Musayri maintains that even if they are a forgery, the Jewish conspiracy
they purportedly expose does exist, and other documents prove the general thesis (1998,
278–80).

25. See, for example, F. Salim 1998c, 24; 1998a, 9. Note M. Mustafa's writing (1998,
7–12) about the destruction of the United States. In it, he expounds on his respect for the United
States and his gratitude to the people who allowed him to tour through it and extended hospital-
ity to him, and states that in consequence he is reluctant to write about its destruction. However,
he continues, he is required to because "of what we have seen and heard about what has happened
in Bosnia, Kashmir, India, Afghanistan, Pakistan, Iraq, Indonesia, Somalia, and other places,
which proves that there has been a large-scale attack on the part of the Jewish Zionists against
Islam and the Muslims" (18–19). A. 'Ali (1996, 161–66) attacks those who point out the danger
of conspiracy theories (as did the newspaper *al-Sharq al-Awsat* in a special issue dated August 14,
1994).

26. *The Protocols of the Elders of Zion* are cited by Nawfal (1973); Tantawi (1987, passim,
e.g., 9–11, 25–29); al-Waqfi (1990, 108–21); Ayyub (1987, 114); M. 'Arif (1996, 73–82; 1997,
24–25, 54–55, 104–5); M. Da'ud (1992b, 100–104; 1999, 233–44); 'Amaluhu (1992, 117–23,
159–76); M. Mahmud (1997, 29–42; 1993, 111–26); al-Musayri (1998, 14–21 and passim); M.
Qutb (1991, 65ff); A. Mahmud (1995, 163–66 and passim); H. 'Abd al-Hamid (1997a, 59, 170;
1996, 199–204, 210–19); Abu Zayd (1999, 5–22); al-Shihabi (1997, 68–69, 74–75); and Musa
(1998, 222).

their audience. Many, like 'Arif in the following passage, describe it as a Jewish plot to cause chaos, which is the basic theme of *The Protocols*:

> Secular groups go along with a plan built upon the slogans of freedom and democracy. When they [the secular groups] reach their goals, these slogans themselves will have accomplished the desire of the sons of Zion by the propagation of chaos and societal aimlessness and destructive agitation for the people. This is what we are feeling during the present, which is based upon something other than fearing God. The pillars of the Jewish rule are built upon the axis of the propagation of corruption, the spread of drugs and alcohol, prostitution and depravity, corruption, [taking of] interest, and gambling, and the rule of the people through relativistic laws that increase the tyranny and lead to conflict between the people. All of that shows without a shadow of a doubt that policy in most of our Arab Islamic countries is Masonic serving the Jews, and that Islam and the Arabs have absolutely no part in it. (M. 'Arif 1996, 157; cf. Mahmud 1993, 145–46; and M. Mustafa 1998, 46–51)

The examples 'Arif provides here of "democratic" leaders—Kamal Ataturk and Gamal 'Abd al-Nasser—are usually described in the West as populist dictators (F. Salim 1998a, 19–20). Nonetheless, he can say—and apparently be believed by his audience—that generally Arabs and Muslims have tried democracy and freedom and found them to be a sham. Now it is time to stop deluding themselves and get rid of these governments that have been imposed upon them by the Jews and their Masonic followers and return to the freedom of the *shari'a*.

> There can be no doubt that the Jews are behind the rejection of the *shari'a* of God and the preference of relativistic laws, because it [the *shari'a*] is more just, more compassionate, and more right. This is what proves the deviation of the ruling politicians, who rule according to something that God has not revealed and disgrace their identities through the fact that they are named by Muslim names. (M. 'Arif 1996, 160)

While many other elements of the conspiracy theory are covered in this book, these are the primary features with regard to the Jews.

Use of Evangelical Protestant Exegesis of the Bible

While perhaps it is understandable that Arab Muslims, confronted with the powerful reality of the state of Israel, would embrace the anti-Semitic conspiracy theory, it is initially unclear why the radicals have chosen to use massive amounts of biblical material to flesh out their scenario. From classical times there have been very strong prohibitions against using the Bible. That some have chosen this unexpected step indicates a sense of the desperation Muslims feel when confronted by the modern world. This method has not been accepted without criticism, but overwhelmingly it continues to be used, and lately even certain neoconservatives have begun to use some biblical material in their works. The first step in assimilating biblical material was indeed to use the anti-Semitic conspiracy theory, whose European creators—conscious of the slight but crucial difference between their own racist creed and that of Christian-based anti-Semitism—enhanced the credibility of their publications by citing large amounts of biblical material, some of it clearly concocted. In many cases they did this by basing their writings on apocalyptic beliefs expressed in the New Testament, which forms the basis for the most pronounced Christian anti-Semitism.

However, there were other reasons for the radicals' attraction to biblical material. Muslim apocalyptists from the radical school avidly seek new sources to support their scenarios. Although their scholarship is not nearly as careful or as thorough as that of the neoconservatives, it is apparent they have been disappointed with the material they find in the classical hadith literature. Having absorbed the anti-Semitic conspiracy idea, they then read classical Muslim apocalyptic literature and are disappointed to find that it does not concern itself very much with Jews. They are obliged to fall back primarily on a single hadith known as the "tradition of the rocks and the trees": "The Hour [of Judgment] will not arrive until the Muslims fight the Jews, and the Muslims will slaughter them, until the Jew will hide behind the rocks and the trees. The rocks and the trees will say: 'O Muslim, O Servant of God ('Abdallah)—there is a Jew behind me, come and kill him!' " (Ibn Hammad 1993, 348, 350; see also, for example, A. Mustafa 1990, 285).[27]

Unfortunately for the radical school, however, this hadith stands virtually alone as an example of anti-Jewish animus in the classical apocalyptic sources. While the Antichrist is Jewish in Muslim apocalyptic beliefs—and many of his followers are said to be Jewish, as well—the vast majority of classical Muslim apocalyptic literature is concerned with the powerful enemies facing Islam during the seventh to ninth centuries, the period in which it was written— namely the Byzantines and the Turks. It was not concerned with Israel or United States, neither of which existed yet and both of which were well beyond the range of the classical Muslim imagination that produced the original apocalyptic literature.

So the apocalyptist is forced to search for new material. Although going to the Bible probably would not be a first choice (others have sought materials varying from ancient gnostic texts to UFO literature and everything in between), it has served apocalyptists well.[28] Ayyub pioneered this technique using the book of Revelation as his basis. It goes without saying that this exegesis necessitates some changes in the biblical text. These changes are usually explained in terms of the classical Muslim doctrine of *tahrif* (alteration), according to which Christians or Jews are said to have deliberately altered their holy texts in various ways. In many cases the apostle Paul or his close associates are singled out, since Jesus himself is a Muslim prophet and cannot be legitimately attacked (H. 'Abd al-Hamid 1997a, 212).[29] Previous to their presentations many of these apocalyptists have had to explain themselves to their audiences and to justify the use of biblical texts: although the legal material

27. This is perhaps the single most widely quoted tradition in modern Muslim apocalyptic literature. For an English translation see "Hamas Covenant," *Journal of Palestine Studies* (1993) 22:122–34 at 123. One should note that although Jews are the most prominent subjects of this tradition, there are a number of classical versions in which Jews are not mentioned: see Ibn al-Munadi (1998, 247); al-Majlisi (1983, 52:388); and Ibn Abi Shayba (n.d., 15:167 no. 19402). However, only the versions mentioning the Jews are cited in modern Muslim apocalyptic literature.

28. See A. 'Ali's work (1996, 123–37) for a large selection of Nostradamus prophecies related to the future victory of Islam. There are also forgeries, such as the Gospel of Barnabas cited by Veliankode (1998, 371–73); on this, see Jomier (1959–61) and Slomp (1978; 1997).

29. This connection was made in classical times as well; see van Koningsveld (1996); Stern (1968); and al-Zu'bi (1997).

and the predictions of the prophet Muhammad's coming—which were supposedly in the Bible originally—were changed by the Jews and the Christians, the material prophesying the end of the world was not (B. 'Abdallah 1994, *lam-nun,* introd.); H. 'Abd al-Hamid 1997a, 5–6). Some early writers, such as Ayyub, did not bother with this justification process and paid for their carelessness by enduring endless criticism from the conservative scholars. They were less careful about the feelings of the Christians and how Christians would receive the unique exegesis that the apocalyptists have applied to the Bible, although Ayyub (1987, 11, 79) does touch on this subject. Now, even neoconservatives feel free to indulge occasionally in the use of biblical material, at least when they have a point that cannot be proven through the Muslim sources.

Since Sa'id Ayyub pioneered this synthesis, we will examine here some of his methodology, exegesis, and conclusions, and afterward look at several other apocalyptists. If his exegesis seems a little unpolished, remember that he is doing something that had not been done by Muslims for almost one thousand years. Ayyub begins with the book of Revelation and tries to find the description of the Mahdi in it. He mentions the name of the "leader who will rush into the battles at the end of time, his name is 'faithful and true' [Rev. 19:11]," which for him recalls the names of the prophet Muhammad (which is also the name of the Mahdi), and he notes that the reference in the description "with justice he judges and makes war" (Rev. 19:11) is comparable to the prophetic material about the Mahdi (Ayyub 1987, 76).[30] His major effort is saved for the vision of the new Jerusalem in Revelation 21 with this idea:

"And he carried me away in the Spirit to a mountain great and high, and showed me the Holy City, Jerusalem" [Rev. 21:10]. I say: Since the mountain is great and high and the "faithful and true" one is Muhammad bin 'Abdallah [the Prophet], who would go to this mountain previous to the revelation and be in solitude from the people, alone in his worship of his Lord inside the cave of Mount Hira[31] . . . "a new earth [for him, reading 'a new

30. All biblical translations are from the New International Version.

31. In other words, Ayyub is reading these verses as a prediction of the first revelations of the prophet Muhammad.

land'] . . . and there was no longer any sea" [Rev. 21:1]. I say: There is no sea in Mecca, and the land is naturally hard and rocky, and Bahira the monk, who was watching for the new prophet, understood that nature of the ground and did not go to Bethlehem or to the Dead Sea, because he read, "The house of the wicked will be destroyed but the tent of the upright will flourish" [Prov. 14:11], and the word of the Messiah [Jesus], "Therefore I tell you that the kingdom of God will be taken away from you and given to a people who will produce its fruit" [Matt. 21:43]. Therefore the man searched among the tents of the upright, who would have given to them the leadership of humanity, and read that the tents were those of "Edom and Moab," meaning the Ishmaelites and the Hagarenes, and then tried to get far away from where there was a sea, until he came to Mecca, just as the book of Revelation says. (Ayyub 1987, 79–80)[32]

"The city was laid out like a square, as long as it was wide" [Rev. 21:16]. They said in commentary that it was a square city *(madina muka"aba)*. . . . I have no commentary!![33]. . . . "Whoever is thirsty, let him come and whoever wishes let him take the free gift of the water of life" [Rev. 22:17]. . . . Since there is no ocean or river, then this water must come from a well, and this well has a long history. . . . 'Umar b. al-Khattab said that when he would drink of it [the water of the well of Zamzam], "I drink of it for the thirst on the Day of Resurrection."[34] "The new Jerusalem coming down out of heaven from God" [Rev. 21:2]. I say: It is certain that this was the first house [i.e., the Ka'ba] placed for people, since Adam was part of humanity. (Ayyub 1987, 83–85)[35]

32. Mecca is really only a half day's journey from the Red Sea.

33. By this Ayyub means that there is no need to point out what his interpretation is; because the words in Arabic are similar, the connection to the Ka'ba in Mecca is obvious. For a similar attempt at etymological usage, see al-Sharbati (1994, 66–71), who tries to prove that the name "Israel" has within it the element of the *isra'* (the Prophet's night journey to Jerusalem; see Qur'an 17:1–2) and therefore does not legitimately belong to Israel at all. The elipses in this passage were in the original.

34. 'Umar b. al-Khattab, the second Muslim caliph, reigned 634–44.

35. Most of the disrupted sentences are written this way in the text, as is usual with Ayyub, who tends to write in incomplete sentences.

With this line of commentary, Ayyub is trying for straight supercessionism and seeks to apply all of the above descriptions to elements of the holy places well known to Muslims. His exegesis will work only for someone who is not familiar with the original text, however, and not reading the Bible in Arabic substantially destroys much of the value of his identifications as well. In further commentary, he says the new songs described in Revelation 19:1–7 are those of the *shahada* (the Muslim confession of faith); the saints in the verses will speak in Arabic, which is the language of paradise (Ayyub 1987, 86–88); the impure who will not be allowed into the new Jerusalem (Rev. 21:27) are actually the Jews and the Christians themselves (Ayyub 1987, 88); and that the twelve angels guarding the gates of the new Jerusalem (Rev. 21:12) are the twelve righteous caliphs (Ayyub 1987, 90; also al-Hawali 2001, 35–46; compare Rubin 1997). Further polemicizing with Christians, he says:

> We say to those who said that Islam is the faith of the Antichrist, look to the length of the rule of this capital [the new Jerusalem]. "There will be no more night. They will not need the light of a lamp or the light of the sun, for the Lord God will give them light. And they will reign forever and ever" [Rev. 22:5]. The people of the new capital will be Muslims and they will reign forever, since the Antichrist and his followers and all the liars will be killed. The meaning of this is that the victorious side at the end of time will be the camp of Islam and Islam alone. (Ayyub 1987, 92)

Eventually Ayyub reaches the descriptions of the Mahdi (which are essentially those of the rider on the white horse in Revelation 19:11–13). Many other examples of his biblical exegesis could be adduced here, but this suffices to convey the general method.

Biblical exegesis did not end with Ayyub. Many others have followed in his footsteps and used this method. Among the most interesting is Bashir Muhammad 'Abdallah. He does not start out on a very literal note. To discuss the periods of the "corruption" of the Banu Isra'il upon the earth,[36] he

---

36. See chapter 5 of this book. According to the exegesis of this passage, there are two periods of corruption allowed by God for the people of Israel during human history. The first period was judged either by the destruction of the First or the Second Temple, and the second is occur-

chooses to start with a verse from Isaiah that he asserts relates to the occupation of the Palestinian lands by Israel: "Nevertheless, there will be no more gloom for those who were in distress. In the past he humbled the land of Zebulun and the land of Naphtali, but in the future he will honor Galilee of the Gentiles, by way of the sea, along the Jordan" (Isa. 9:1).

'Abdallah continues with: "I will wait for the Lord, who is hiding his face from the house of Jacob. I will put my trust in him. Here am I and the children" (Isa. 8:17–18). This is said by him to relate to the children of the first Intifada (1987–93), who hid their faces behind kaffiyas and threw stones at the Israeli troops in the West Bank (B. 'Abdallah 1994, 111–12, 170). To clinch the proof of the two corruptions of Israel, he cites Ezekiel 21:19: "Son of man, mark out two roads for the sword of the king of Babylon to take, both starting from the same country. Make a signpost where the road branches off to the city." According to 'Abdallah, this prophecy, which describes Nebuchadnezzar's attack upon the city of Jerusalem (586 B.C.E.), is a clear indication of the two corruptions of the Jewish people mentioned in the Qur'an (B. 'Abdallah 1994, 112–13).

However, 'Abdallah soon goes into considerable detail in his exegesis. Temporarily going back to Isaiah 9:1, he adds this about the future downfall of Israel:

> As to the "future" [v. 1] in this text, this is the promise of the second time in the Qur'an [17:4–8] when the new Babylonian with his army will enter into the community of Islam in Palestine. In other words, [this means] the Muslims of Palestine and his entrance upon them [which] will be a "humiliation" [v. 1] because he is from the community of Islam and his army is Muslim, although his entrance upon them will not be in punishment for their sinfulness, but his entrance will be upon the Zionist enemy as a redeemer for them, and as an aid to them from God in their jihad, which they began under the

ring during the present time as a result of the establishment of the state of Israel and will shortly be judged by God. This is a dominant idea among most radical apocalyptic writers (other than Ayyub, who wrote just before it became prominent). See also al-Fazazi (1983) and al-Tamimi (1998) for similar attempts to find a Qur'anic sequence mandating the destruction of Israel.

leadership of Hamas with stones, because aid is from God.[37] That is the meaning of "He will honor Galilee of the Gentiles, by way of the sea, along the Jordan." The last part is the promise of the end time, in other words the expected entrance of the Babylonian that will occur in fulfillment of God's threat to Banu Isra'il during the second corruption connected with their great arrogance in the land. "The way of the sea" because according to what is established from other texts in the books [of the Bible]—there is no point in noting them here—that the Assyrian, the Babylonian, al-Sakhri, al-Sufyani—all of these are names of the Iraqi leader who will lead his armies, entering upon Banu Isra'il and the mosque [of al-Aqsa] a second time. (B. 'Abdallah 1994, 174)[38]

Moving to the heart of his discussion—which for 'Abdallah consists of trying to find biblical evidence of the coming Earthquake of the Hour (mentioned in Qur'an 22:1, 99:1)—we find him reading Daniel 7, a text that has inspired many apocalyptic writers during the past millennia. 'Abdallah accepts that there are two possible lines of interpretation of this prophetic dream. One possible interpretation is what the angel tells Daniel (7:23–27). This simplistic answer, however, is rejected in favor of an interpretation in the light of future historical events. Because the vision begins with Daniel saying, "In my vision at night . . ." (7:2), 'Abdallah comes to the conclusion that

its events will begin during an era of darkness reigning over all the earth, after which humanity will be blessed with justice, peace, and truth for the length of the strong Islamic caliphate that subjected all of the infidel idolatrous states and peoples, and imposed the *jizya* [the tax imposed upon non-

37. 'Abdallah has a somewhat exaggerated opinion of the position of Hamas during the period of the first Intifada (1987–93), regularly crediting it for actions that were really the responsibility of the PLO.

38. 'Abdallah is developing a thesis according to which all of the above minor messianic titles will be attached to Saddam Husayn. See the present book, 89n.

Muslims] upon them. All of Europe and China used to pay the *jizya* to the Muslims, and India was a Muslim state. (B. 'Abdallah 1994, 146)[39]

Now that 'Abdallah has set up a chronological framework, he proceeds to the identification of the four beasts: the lion, the bear, the leopard, and the terrible, frightening fourth beast. The British empire is the lion, the Communist empire of Russia is the bear, and the leopard is the United States. The fourth beast with ten horns is the terrifying one that puzzled Daniel so much (7:19). 'Abdallah identifies this beast with the beast of Revelation 13:1—an identification well known from evangelical Protestant exegesis of these passages—but then bestows on it a further identity of his own, contending that it is the European Community and that it is ruled by the small horn (7:8), which is Israel. (According to him the three defeated horns of 7:8 are the Axis Powers of World War II.)

During the ensuing messianic age, 'Abdallah cites Daniel once again to say: "Then the sovereignty, power, and greatness of the kingdoms under the whole heavens will be handed over to the saints, the people of the Most High. His kingdom will be an everlasting kingdom and all rulers will worship and obey him" (Dan. 7:27). 'Abdallah says in comment:

The "saints" are the Muslims,[40] the believers and fighters in the path of God, since they are described in the present-day Antichrist media as fundamentalists, terrorists, and extremists.[41] His words "the sovereignty will be handed over [to the saints]" refers to the continuing victory they will have in the establishment of the Islamic caliphate at the hands of the Ancient of Days (the Mahdi) first of all, and then their victory over Crusader [Christian] Europe

39. It is an exaggeration to say that all of Europe and China paid this tax, although for certain periods of time certain areas did.

40. This was first brought out by Ayyub (1987, 247).

41. For a refutation of the idea that there are fundamentalists or extremists in Islam, see al-Nujayri (1998). B. 'Abdallah says: "The slaughter that will happen among those they call fundamentalists and describe as 'terrorists' will be nothing other than the plan of the Zionists and the Antichrist, who both know that Muslims who hold fast to the laws of their faith are their true enemies and that they will be the basis for the armies of the Mahdi" (1994, 138).

second of all, and then their final victory under the leadership of the true messiah, Jesus, the son of Mary, over the Antichrist and his armies of Masonic and hypocritical followers thirdly, and after that the purification of the earth from Gog and Magog.

Daniel then continues speaking of the present and continuous struggle taking place between the human kingdom under the leadership of the secret world government, headed by the Antichrist, and the Muslims, the believers, and the fighters in the path of God in every place in the world, in groups and as individuals: "As I watched, this horn (which is Israel on the outside and the secret world government on the inside)[42] was waging war against the saints and defeating them" [Dan. 7:21], in other words slaughtering them and annihilating them by making slaughters for them in Palestine, Afghanistan, India, Kashmir, Bosnia and Herzegovina, Azerbaijan, and Tajikistan, and in every place where they hold onto the confession that "there is no God but Allah and Muhammad is the Messenger of God."

The angel then interprets the tribulation falling upon the believers and the martyrs, and clarifies that it is from the leaders and the secret world government, meaning the Zionists mounted upon the Crusaders [i.e., Western Christians] and deceiving them as the jinn deceive [people] using human bodies, and the angel says about this hidden government, the Antichrist: "He will speak against the Most High and oppress his saints and try to change the set times and the laws. The saints will be handed over to him for a time, times and half a time" [Dan. 7:25]. (B. 'Abdallah 1994, 165)

From this point, 'Abdallah proceeds naturally into the calculations appearing in Daniel 8:14, which are examined in chapter 5 of this book. He also explores the possibilities of the book of Revelation. Starting with the vision of the woman in Revelation 12 (see the present book, 198–200), he says, dealing with the beginning of Revelation 13:

The meaning is that the Antichrist concentrates and relies now primarily upon the United States of America, and when God destroys its power with the Earthquake [of the Hour], then that will force him to hasten his plans for

42. The addition to the biblical verse is 'Abdallah's.

appearance and to alter his plans somewhat, so that he will rely primarily upon the polytheistic and idolatrous powers in the world, and those are the seven great nations: America, Russia, England, France, Germany, Japan, and China. The first stage of the implementation of his rule over the world is the completion of the institutions of that rule, and this was inaugurated by the proclamation of the new world order in 1990. [He quotes Rev. 13:1–10.] The sight of this vision has been fulfilled since the proclamation of the new world order and international law after August 1990, when the Security Council proposed in accordance with it a world government for every land. It will be ratified and implemented, and the opponents to it will be destroyed. The foundation was laid for this new reality led by America in the war that it waged together with more than thirty other states against Iraq, in obedience to the Zionists, headed by the Antichrist (the beast). This is the beginning of the first appearance of the beast. (B. 'Abdallah 1994, 185)

He goes on to explain how the seven heads of the beast (Rev. 13:1) represent the seven nations listed above and that either the Security Council or the United States is the embodiment of the beast—remembering that according to the vision the beast is said to be all-powerful—"Who is like the beast? Who can make war against him?" (Rev. 13:4)—as it causes slaughters and famines. On the other hand, he interprets the dragon (Rev. 12), which is usually interpreted by Christian exegetes as the devil, as the Zionist conspiracy (B. 'Abdallah 1994, 186–89).

Contemporary history of Jerusalem is to be found in his interpretation of Ezekiel 22:

Almost the entire chapter deals with two slaughters that precede the day of vengeance against the cursed Jews, with the entrance of the Sufyani [Saddam Husayn] and his army of mighty men [into Jerusalem]. [He then quotes Ezek. 22:1–7[43] and 9–16.] The interpretation of it is that Jerusalem is a city of blood, and there will be two slaughters in the Haram [the Temple Mount] because the Haram is in the center of Jerusalem, and his word, "O city that

---

43. He does not cite, among Jerusalem's crimes listed in the biblical passage, verse 8, where the people are condemned for not keeping the Sabbath.

brings on herself doom by shedding blood in her midst" [Ezek. 22:3], also "because of the blood you have shed" [Ezek. 22:4]. This shows that God will be very angry and will hasten the day of the end of Jerusalem with the servants who are mighty men because of the innocent blood shed by the Banu Isra'il [Jews] in the Haram of the mosque of al-Aqsa. (B. 'Abdallah 1994, 362–63; also Hashim n.d., 60–64)

'Abdallah then goes on to say that this slaughter, which occurred in 1990 during a confrontation between Palestinians and the Israeli police, is the immediate reason why God must judge Israel and finish the country off entirely. It has been polluted, according to 'Abdallah, by being the capital of Israel and must be purified by the blood of its Jewish inhabitants flowing through the streets. Fundamentally, 'Abdallah reads the Bible as a Palestinian document instead of as a Jewish one. The selections above give the reader a good example of his style of commentary.

Other Egyptian apocalyptic writers have followed in 'Abdallah's footsteps and expanded upon his line of interpretation. 'Abd al-Hamid also looks to Daniel for interpretations concerning the downfall of the United States. His books are basically spin-offs of those of 'Abdallah, Da'ud, and Salim, but some new ideas do appear. He starts by saying that he agrees with much of what 'Abdallah says but that he has new thoughts about the interpretation of the vision in Daniel. In the interpretation of the vision of the four beasts, Great Britain is still the lion, and the USSR is still the bear. However, the leopard is Germany and the Axis powers of World War II, and the final terrifying beast is NATO. The "little horn" of Daniel 7:8 is

none other than America, since America has appeared on the world scene as a great power after World War II . . . and the little horn is a hint at world Zionism, which manages America and rules through it, and it is also a hint at the Antichrist, just as the Christians interpret it, because world Zionism manages it [the world] and moves it from behind the veil of the Antichrist, as we have noted previously. There is a perfect correlation between the little horn and Zionist America because this Zionist state has waged many wars against the Muslims (the saints), and the Zionists have humiliated the Muslims with the aid of America that persecutes them, imposes an economic and military siege [upon them], and forbids them from weaponry and supplies.

Further correlating what the prophet Daniel says about this little horn is that it wages war upon the saints (the Muslims), and overcomes them, until the Ancient of Days comes (the expected Mahdi) and unifies them, empowers them, and redeems them from the present tyranny happening to them from the little horn and the fearful beast (NATO). America is the mother of corruption in the world and the originator of most of the corrupt, tyrannical, civil, social, economic, and political laws existing in the world today. Most of these are in opposition to the law of God and his commandments, like the laws and slogans allowing fornication and perversion that were proclaimed at the UN Conference on Population Control, and the Conference on Women, both of which were held under the auspices of the UN, which is ordered according to the orders of world Zionism and America. (H. 'Abd al-Hamid 1997a, 84–86)[44]

'Abd al-Hamid then has to prove that the "saints" of the selection are actually the Muslims, which he attempts to do by asking how the figure of the Son of Man could be coming down to help Christians (the other possibility for being the saints), since the saints are clearly being oppressed, and in reality it is Christians who are doing all of the oppressing in the world as we see it today. "The 'saints,' " he continues, "are the Muslims, because they are the community with which Jews and Christians, together with all of the other idolatrous nations, fight, and they are the community that the Antichrist will fight, together with the great powers allied with him at his appearance" (H. 'Abd al'Hamid 1997a, 88).[45]

Fahd Salim, another Egyptian apocalyptic writer, applies his exegesis to

44. See Barth (1997) on Islam and the U.N. Conference on Population Control.

45. H. 'Abd al-Hamid (1997a, 89–93) cites further proofs that the "saints" are Muslims: that they are described singing praises in Revelation 15:1–4 (which according to him only Muslims do); the saints are sealed on their foreheads (Rev. 7:3), which again only is common with Muslims who have the sign of prayer on their foreheads (someone who prays extensively will develop a permanent bruise, called *athar al-sujud*, on his forehead, a mark of honor among Muslims); the bowing elders in Revelation 11:16 cannot be Christians or Jews because the latter two groups do not prostrate themselves in prayer; and so on.

the prophecies about Gog and Magog in Ezekiel 38. He theorizes that the
Jews in Israel are themselves Gog and Magog:

In reality Israel is Gog because in the book of Ezekiel, in addition to what we
have already mentioned, God sometimes speaks to the rebellious house of Israel: "Son of man, I am sending you to the Israelites. . . . Go now to the
house of Israel and speak my words to them" [Ezek. 2:3, 3:4], and sometimes to Gog: "The word of the Lord came to me: 'Son of man, set your face
against Gog of the land of Magog. . . . Prophesy against him and say: This is
what the Sovereign Lord says: I am against you, O Gog' " [Ezek. 38:1–3].[46]
We find that God sometimes is made holy in this book among Israel, and
sometimes among Gog, which proves that Israel equals Gog and Magog
equals Israel. Only once in the book does the book say: "Then the nations
will know that I the Lord make Israel holy" [Ezek. 37:28], and the words directed to Gog, "so that the nations may know me when I show myself holy
through you before their eyes [Gog]." [Ezek. 38:16][47]

It is well known that Gog is the ten lost tribes [of Israel], and in reality,
as we have already shown, they were exiled to the north by the order of God:
"By the life of the Lord I will bring Banu Isra'il back from the land of the
north, and from all of the lands to which you were exiled, and I will return
you to the land that I gave to your fathers" [prob. Ezek. 11:17 or 37:21].
These groups will come to the land while the Palestinians are in it—which
will lead to their expulsion from it, and this is what happened. "Then I will
take all of the groups of the north and bring them to this land and upon all of
its inhabitants" [prob. Ezek. 39:2].[48] It is clear that these groups will rise in
airplanes to land in Palestine. "I will lift Banu Isra'il up from the land of the
north . . . and return them." This is the same Gog, and with it are many peoples, Magog. "Therefore, son of man, prophesy and say to Gog: This is what
the Sovereign Lord says: In that day, when my people Israel are living in
safety, will you not take notice of it? You will come from your place in the far

46. Ezekiel is also called to prophesy against the mountains (6:2, 36:1), false prophets
(13:2), the South (20:46), Tyre (26:2), Egypt (29:2), the shepherds of Israel (34:2), and Edom
(35:2).

47. The word "Gog" here is Salim's addition.

48. A close reading of Ezekiel does not reveal an exact match to either one of the two verses
cited. This could be because of inconsistencies in translation or additions by the writer.

north, you and many nations with you, all of them riding on horses, a great horde, a mighty army. You will advance against my people Israel like a cloud that covers the land" [Ezek. 38:14–16]. His words "a great horde" means Gog[49] and "a mighty army" means Magog. This is the people that Ezekiel raised up, and stood before him, a very great army [Ezek. 37:10], and this is all the rebellious house of Israel. His words "come . . . like a cloud that covers the land" is a vision of the planes filled with those Jews, and they are like a cloud covering the land of Palestine from all angles, "and they slink away from every quarter" [Qur'an 21:96]. (F. Salim 1998b, 190–91)

Most of this commentary needs no explanation; its supercessionist aim is clear, as is the reinterpretation of the words "Israel" and "Gog and Magog" away from their accepted (and sometimes from their plain) meanings.

More recently, as a result of the second Intifada (beginning in September 2000), the radical Saudi preacher Safar al-Hawali has explored the exegesis of the book of Daniel. It is clear that al-Hawali is making a major effort to redirect the focus of biblical prophecy texts away from the evangelical Protestant philo-Israel interpretation and claim them for radical Islam (al-Hawali 2001, 5–11, translated section entitled "Islamic Vision of Prophecy." See also Hilal 2000, 95–96). Safar al-Hawali makes the following identifications from the books of Daniel and Revelation, which are a synthesis of Ayyub's identifications and those of 'Abdallah:

The new Jerusalem [Rev. 21:2]	Mecca
The trustworthy, truthful one [Rev. 19:11], the head of creation, the Paraclete [John 15:26]	Muhammad
The Son of Man who will come in the latter days	Muhammad[50]
The Messiah	Christ Jesus, son of Mary

49. There is probably a misprint here, since "Magog" is written.

50. Al-Hawali argues that this must be Muhammad and not Christ since Christ is the son of a woman and it is he who announced the coming of the great Messenger after him who is the Son

The Antichrist	The false messiah
The beast	Zionism in its Jewish and Christian fundamentalist forms
The false prophet	Paul, the popes, and everyone who claims to be Christ or claims that Christ dwells within him or sends revelation to him
Gog [and Magog]	Yajuj and Majuj of the Qur'an [Qur'an 18:94, 21:96].
The little horn [Dan. 8:9]	The abomination of desolation. [Dan. 12:11] The state of Israel
The new Babylon	Modern Western culture; particularly American culture
The new Roman Empire	The United States of America

Source: al-Hawali 2001, 45–46, translated section entitled "Indisputable Evidence"

It is clear that these identifications have a good deal of internal coherence (from a Muslim point of view) and represent a strikingly new reading of these classical apocalyptic texts in the light of contemporary events.

The Lesser Signs of the Hour: Moral Attitudes, Natural Disasters, Cosmic Phenomena, and Political Events

Of the signs that the end is drawing close, the most apparent to the majority of Muslims are the so-called Lesser Signs of the Hour *('alamat al-sa'a al-sughra)*. These signs provide the basis for the picture the apocalyptist is painting of the future and consist of events that almost everyone can agree are actually happening. In reality they have always been true, and were true even during the time of the prophet Muhammad, as well as during every generation of Islam since then, as is clear from reading the historical literature of

---

of Man. The nature of Christ's birth disqualifies, argues al-Hawali, as well as Christians' own doctrine concerning him, since they hold that he is the Son of God.

Islam. This fact can additionally be demonstrated because in every generation, apocalyptists have stated that these Lesser Signs were true of their particular time period. Therefore, they enable the apocalyptist to win quick
points from otherwise skeptical members of the audience who are genuinely
concerned about the moral and ethical decay of the world around them.
These signs are the hook that draws the audience into the larger framework of
apocalyptic beliefs. The Lesser Signs of the Hour are also very general; it
would be almost impossible to prove they are not happening somewhere,
since they are by their very nature always occurring (or at least with enough
explanation they are).

One of the most comprehensive lists of signs is given by Amin Muhammad Jamal al-Din (who should be placed within the neoconservative school
since he is a graduate of al-Azhar). He has made a major effort to prove that
the present times are the end times. In order to demonstrate the truth of this
assertion, he issued a pamphlet on the Lesser Signs. For him there are seventy-
nine signs that must be fulfilled; an additional smaller number (four) are too
indistinct to tell whether they have been fulfilled or not. His starting point is:
"Before we will start our long journey with the Lesser Signs of the Hour, we
will affirm that the Lesser Signs have all been fulfilled, and we are eagerly
awaiting the sign that is the link between the Lesser Signs and the Greater
Signs, and that is the appearance of the Mahdi" (Jamal al-Din 1997, 12).

Jamal al-Din begins with those signs that were already fulfilled in classical
times: the appearance of the Prophet, the conquest of Jerusalem, plagues, and
the fire in the Hijaz (which according to him was probably the volcanic explosion in 654/1256).[51] Others that do not refer to historical events are far more
difficult for him to identify. Among them: being ruled by fools (or simple-
tons), the erection of tall buildings,[52] and the allowing of fornication, cosmet-

51. Although the conquest of Jerusalem was, of course, fulfilled by the Muslims in 636, he
notes that there is need for Jerusalem to be reconquered from the Zionist Crusaders, and that this
problem is one that concerns all Muslims (Jamal al-Din 1997, 19).

52. There is a strong leveling strain here. Jamal al-Din is disgusted, for example, by the
buildings at the Haram around the Ka'ba in Mecca, and he states that this is a fulfillment of the
sign (1997, 29); see also al-Tibi (1990, 229–34).

ics, silk, wine, and musical instruments (cf. B. 'Abdallah 1994, 305–10; M. Da'ud 1992b, 117–20; 1999, 431–53). While it is a little difficult for him to say that these latter items have actually been formally "allowed" (in the sense that the *shari'a* has been changed to allow for them), it is clear that throughout Muslim history these things have appeared. Many events are related to the moral decay of the West and its evil influence upon the Muslim world, and then used to "prove" the truth of the prophecies. 'Abdallah 'Ali, another apocalyptic writer, illustrates how disparate events are related: "Thus in the West the newspapers have described that a workingwoman hired the womb of her mother, who is living with her, so that she could have a child. During the same time as this is happening in the West, in the East the barefoot, naked sheepherders [Saudi Arabians] have caused buildings to be erected high" (A. 'Ali 1996, 95).

Since these two events are connected in the apocalyptic tradition describing the moral decline of the end of the world, this is viewed as confirmation of the larger picture as well. Natural events are noted: earthquakes, such as that which struck Iran in May 1997 (Jamal al-Din 1997, 98), the difficulty of seeing the moon (which is important for the delineation of the Muslim lunar calendar), and the appearance of comets and plagues. Other signs are indicative of the deterioration of the faith: that "true" Islam would be considered strange and Muslims would be persecuted and that there would be a general loss of faith. People will pay more attention to the economic situation than to their faith, and prices will rise, and there will be famines.

Instruments of modernity are frequently condemned. Jamal al-Din notes that the famous hadith specialist Nur al-Din al-Albani felt that the sign concerning the appearance of "houses for demons" was fulfilled by the invention of automobiles, but Jamal al-Din disagrees with this interpretation. He believes it concerns actual houses that wealthy parents build for their children to live in when they grow up but leave empty for many long years, allowing demons to dwell in them (Jamal al-Din 1997, 81–82; however, see B. 'Abdallah 1994, 9). Cars are also said to be a sign because they make it possible for women to drive; this allows men to see them in a state of immodesty that encourages fornication (Jamal al-Din 1997, 82–83). Another sign connected with women is women joining their husbands in economic ventures.[53] Jamal al-Din says:

> The woman has gone out to work with the men, facing them, contending with them, talking with them, and disputing with them. She looks at them and they look at her, and she is not embarrassed in front of them, and they are not embarrassed in front of her. The woman, by her going to work, has ripped every veil and has taken every calumny and sin. The issue is, as the Messenger of God said, "I went into heaven and saw that most of its people were poor people, and I went into hell and I saw that most of its people were women."[54] The sad thing is that the woman by her disobedience of this [that is, by going out to work] drags with her everyone who has guardianship or authority over her—husband, or father or brother who manages her affairs, or even lord, judge, and ruler (sultan). (Jamal al-Din 1997, 59, also 75; see also M. Da'ud 1999, 422–30; and Qutb 1991, 93–102)

Further moral or societal signs are described: the lack of mutual greetings between strangers, and extensive lying, corruption, and not caring about the shedding of blood. One of the signs is that at the end there will be many police (*shurat,* which probably meant in classical times the oppressive security forces of the government) (Jamal al-Din 1997, 69).[55] Jamal al-Din does not concentrate on the oppressive nature of many of the Muslim governments for the fulfillment of this sign; instead, he says that this indicates the rampant crime of the end times, otherwise, there would be no need for the police. It is clear that

53. Although an outside observer might say that classical Islam did not know about the participation of women in economic life, the fact is that from the literature of the 'Abbasid period, as well as from the documents of the Cairo Geniza, we know that women frequently ran businesses during the time when these apocalyptic predictions were first written (although during certain periods they had to do this using men as fronts).

54. Al-Shinawi wrote a misogynist booklet (1996) that takes its title from the last part of this tradition.

55. Jamal al-Din says about the sign of the police causing people to suffer that "this is apparent in our own time" (1997, 74).

with this comment he has missed a golden opportunity to attack the dictatorships in the Arab and Muslim worlds. The political situation is also described:

> The nations have assailed us since the caliphate fell at the hands of the sinner
> [Mustafa Kamal] Ataturk, and the Islamic community has dissolved into mi-
> nuscule states fighting each other and struggling because of passions, division,
> and dissension that have tossed it about on the waves caused by hidden sinful
> hands executing satanic plots. Their slogan is "Destroy Islam and annihilate
> its people!"[56] The Islamic community has become fragmented minuscule
> states, the Crusader states parceling them out as limited shares among them-
> selves. Our situation is like that of a weak prey pulled back and forth by the
> fangs of starving wild animals, who do not know limits other than the satiation
> of their enormous appetites by filling their empty stomachs with parts of this
> wounded, helpless prey. (Jamal al-Din 1997, 52; also Musa 1998, 143)

Although different words are used by other authors, the above list of
moral portents is an accurate summary of the picture of modern Islam in the
opinion of the apocalyptic writers. In most cases it is easy to see that the given
proof is highly subjective, and in many cases the reader apparently should simply agree that the sign has been fulfilled, as Jamal al-Din gives no further comment on it. While this lack of commentary is amazing, the amount of
comment that he does give is so substantially and qualitatively better than that
of the conservatives that it is clear where he stands.

'Abdallah, for his part, links his signs to those in Revelation 16, and he
speaks more of an apocalyptic language used in the West.

1. The spread of fornication and adultery

2. The pollution of the seas by oil spills and other contaminants

3. The pollution of the environment, especially the rivers

4. The depletion of the ozone layer, which has caused people to be
burned by the sun's rays

5. The appearance and spread of AIDS

---

56. This was actually the title of a book issued in Egypt by 'Alam, *Qadat al-gharb yaqulun:
Dammiru al-Islam, ubidu ahlahu* (1977).

6. The drying up of the Euphrates River (B. 'Abdallah 1994, 310–28; also al-Shihabi 1997, 55–66; and A. 'Ali 1996, 172–76)

The final sign in this list, concerning the Euphrates River, has been a major concern to many Arab countries; ever since Turkey built a series of dams in the upper reaches of the Tigris and Euphrates Rivers, Arabs have been uncomfortably reminded that their water resources are at the mercy of a foreign power—and Turkey's close relations with Israel does not reassure them. Most concerned are Syrians and Iraqis, but Egyptians have been reminded by this that the sources of the Nile River are far beyond their nation's political control.

Other writers have surveyed the Lesser Signs as well and obtained different results. Jamal al-Din is interesting because as a neoconservative, he at least makes an effort to relate the material to the present-day circumstances. Others make less of an effort and come to different conclusions than he did. Jamal al-Din's opponent Mustafa Murad goes much further, listing 142 Lesser Signs (Murad 1997, 33–37). It is difficult to tell what Murad hopes to accomplish by this list, other than trying to prove Jamal al-Din wrong. But then he lists nineteen additional signs that demonstrably have not happened, and this additional list almost certainly is given to prove his thesis that the end of the world is still distant. Among the signs: there would be no pleasure in the taking of spoils (since wealth would be so common); Islam would have reached every household in the world; each man would have fifty women; animals would talk; a shoe would tell its master about the infidelities of his wife; and there would be open immorality in the streets (ibid., 33–37). Al-Shaykh, a conservative, lists the signs and comes to the conclusion that there are sixty-one of them (1993, 27–63). Veliankode (1995, 47–273) lists sixty-three signs, but he does not comment on them and apparently assumes that the reader will know that they have or have not been fulfilled. Even Bashir Muhammad 'Abdallah, a more sophisticated writer, merely lists the majority of the Lesser Signs, although he does describe the fulfillment of some (1994, 8–15).[57] The neoconservative writer Tawila also gives very few comments, al-

---

57. B. 'Abdallah works harder to arrange the greater signs of the end, which are very disorganized in classical texts; see 'Abdallah 1994, 15–45. See also on the signs F. Salim (1998a, 29–31); al-Rahbawi (1987, 3–15); Mabruk (1986, 21–51, with 49–51 listing those signs not yet

though he organizes the signs neatly and more logically than others of his school do; there are, according to him, a total of seventeen signs, but he groups a number of similar signs (1999, 19–52).

Regarding the immediate signs of the end, the writers are at variance. Muhammad 'Isa Da'ud in his early books lists his own preferred signs. They are, among others, the appearance of Halley's Comet in 1985, the drought in Syria-Palestine (1986), the beginning of the Intifada in the West Bank and Gaza (1987), the Iran-Iraq War (1981–88), the invasion of Kuwait (1990–91), and the gathering of the Jews in Israel (from Russia in 1989–92).[58] The invasion of Kuwait is said to be the first of the major signs of the coming apocalyptic wars (apparently he wrote before the Gulf War of 1991 was actually fought; M. Da'ud 1992b, 143–56). In order to understand the political signs, it is important to understand the context provided by various traditions. For example, to understand comments about the appearance of the Mahdi and the Antichrist, there is what I refer to as the "a'maq tradition" (the *a'maq* were the valleys of northern Syria where most of the battles between the early Muslims and the Byzantines were fought). It is used as a hinge tradition between events of the here and now and the apocalyptic future, just as it was used in classical times. This tradition reads:

> The Byzantines will make a secure treaty with you [the Muslims], and you will raid together an enemy who is behind them, and you will defeat them, pillage them, and force them to make peace.[59] Then you will return until you settle down in a field with hills *(marj dhi tulul),* and a Christian will raise the cross and say: "The cross is victorious!" and a Muslim will be enraged and

---

fulfilled); al-Sha'rawi (1990, 68–70); Tahtawi (1997, 18–21); al-Shami (1996, 9–14); Shakir (1993, 7–15); al-Jabi (1996, 22–70); Al Mubarak (1991, 49–84); M. 'Arif (1997, 63–76); M. Da'ud (1992, 143–56); Bayumi (1995b); and Musa (1998, 86–142). H. 'Abd al-Hamid (1997a, 78) says that 95 percent of the Lesser Signs have been fulfilled, and he lists them on 158–68; see also 1996, 169–79; and 1998, 24–32). For material in English, see M. 'Arif (1995, 18–28, 46–70) and Veliankode (1998).

58. The conservative faculty of al-Azhar at the time resisted a proclamation that the Intifada was in any way connected with the end of the world: *Majallat al-Azhar* 61 (1989), 897–900.

59. The Byzantines are, ironically (from an Eastern Christian point of view), interpreted as Western Christians.

will crush him. Then the Byzantines will betray you and gather for the final apocalyptic battle.[60]

As Jamal al-Din notes, this tradition is the hinge tradition upon which his apocalyptic vision (and that of many others) is built. Whenever it appears in a text, it is an indication that the action is about to move away from the historically verifiable events and into the apocalyptic future. The origins of the tradition are obscure, but even in classical times it functioned as the hinge tradition par excellence between identifiable historical warfare between the Byzantines and the Muslims, and the final apocalyptic battles of the end of the world. Jamal al-Din interprets the a'maq tradition in terms of the Gulf War (1990–91) and states that for the present the West and the Muslims are in a state of secure treaty after having joined together to destroy Iraq. However, the Christian West will shortly betray the secure treaty with the Muslims, and the former will gather for the apocalyptic war (Armageddon) in a "field with hills" (the valley of Armageddon) (Jamal al-Din 1997, 123–27).[61] The a'maq tradition has been recently reinterpreted by radical Muslims (see the present book, 176–79).

'Abdallah, too, sees the Gulf War as the first battle of the series of wars culminating in the battle of Armageddon; in fact, he makes a major effort to reinterpret a wide range of the Muslim classical apocalyptic heritage to fit this scenario (B. 'Abdallah 1994, 247–56). Taking the classical tradition, "There will be a man from the Umayyads in Egypt who will rule, then be overcome in his government and it will be taken from him and he will flee to the Byzantines, and bring the Byzantines to the people of Islam and this will be the first of the apocalyptic wars," 'Abdallah begins his scenario. Discounting all of the obvious geographical and contextual difficulties, he states that this prophecy

60. See Ayyub 1987, 173–74; Jamal al-Din 1997, 123; B. 'Abdallah 1994, 247–62; F. Salim 1998a, 32–33; 'Abd al-Hakim 1998b, 196–97; 1998a, 76–79; and Tawila 1999, 73–76.

61. The apocalyptic atmosphere of the Gulf War was felt by everyone; even the conservative *Majallat al-Azhar* ran two pieces on the subject: Farag Allah 'Abd al-Bari's article, "al-Yawm al-akhir fi al-Yahudiyya, al-Nasraniyya wa-l-Islam," *Majallat al-Azhar* 63 (1991), 894–99, 1232–37, 1350–57; and in the French language section, Rokaya Qabr's article, "Les signes de l'Heure d'après le Coran et la Sunna," *Majallat al-Azhar* 63 (1991), 1308–16, 1449–56. See also the conservative writer Hashim (n.d.); and al-Hawali (1992).

was fulfilled by the emir of Kuwait, who fled to the West and brought the Western allies to the soil of Islam:

> Because it has never happened in the history of Islam that an Arab Umayyad ruler asked the Byzantines for aid,[62] and brought them to the people of Islam to fight between them the first of the apocalyptic wars, which will be followed after their occurrence in a short time by the apocalyptic wars and the signs, as the beads of a necklace when its string is cut. For this reason we say the Kuwait war, or the apocalyptic war of Kuwait, was the first apocalyptic war in the chain of apocalyptic wars between the Byzantines and the Muslims that continues [to this day]. The war in Bosnia and Herzegovina against the Byzantines in general, under the leadership of the Security Council and the United States, and behind them the Antichrist, and [more] specifically against the Serbians, is the second apocalyptic war.[63] The war of Azerbaijan against the Byzantines in general, and against the Armenians specifically, is the third; then the war in Tajikistan against the Byzantines in general, and against the Russians specifically, and the war of the Somalians against the Byzantines in general and the United States specifically [are the fourth and fifth apocalyptic wars respectively].
>
> All of these wars were incited by the secret Jewish world government under the leadership of the Antichrist, with the aim of uprooting Islamic societies or even Islamic blocs of peoples in Europe so that they would not have an independent state, so that their governments could return to the *shari'a* someday. Since the Kuwaiti war between the Byzantines and the Muslims was the first apocalyptic war, it was one of the signs. (B. 'Abdallah 1994, 259; cf. F. Salim 1998a, 101–2; and Ayyub 1987, 314–15)

The rest of the signs will become apparent in the immediate future. In more recent apocalyptic books, the creation of the Palestinian ministate, the

---

62. This is not true. A number of early caliphs (Mu'awiya, 'Abd al-Malik) in fact did take this step, and it is very likely that the tradition reflects these realities, which at the time were not as shocking as they are today.

63. He is, of course, using the name "Byzantines" as a euphemism for the Christian West.

presence of American forces on the holy Saudi Arabian soil, and the siege of Iraq by the United States are the final signs.[64]

For the apocalyptic writers, however, all the biblical exegesis and the lists of the signs merely set the stage for the principal issue of the contemporary world: the Zionist conspiracy.

64. See, for example, F. Salim 1998a, 102–5; Veliankode 1998, 249–50; Jamal al-Din 2001, 91–105; and www.asifa l3sim.org/_private/Taslsoul.htm, which lists a total of thirty-five signs from the Gulf War until the end of the world. See also the discussion in Farouki's essay (1995).

THREE

INTERPRETATIONS OF THE PRESENT

Domination by World Zionism

The anti-Semitic conspiracy theory is intensely real for the apocalyptic writers discussed in this book. In order to understand their conceptual framework, effort is made in this section to present the world as they see it. According to Ayyub, there is an overall conspiracy and several subconspiracies, as well as numerous layers of conspirators.

> There is a duality to the conspiracy. There is a general purely Jewish conspiracy, which comprises the entire world for [the purpose of] control over it. Then there is a larger conspiracy under the aegis of the general conspiracy, which is the Jewish-Christian conspiracy to subjugate the Arab world and the Muslim world and to enslave it. "Neither the Jews nor the Christians will be pleased with you until you follow their religion" [Qur'an 2:120]. (F. Salim 1998c, 15–16)

59

To those who claim that the Jews are God's chosen people who guide humanity in the right, we say that this is a sick and irrational idea. First of all, the Jews have lost the way themselves, and second of all, because they take no pleasure in people's goodness. They do not proclaim Judaism anyway—they only assist the Christians in their missionary efforts. (Ayyub 1987, 34–35; Tawila [1999, 273] plagiarizes Ayyub without acknowledgment)

Jews do not proclaim their own faith or allow others to enter into it because that would lead to impurity of the blood from which they derive their superiority over the rest of the world. Instead, they help the Christians in missionary efforts, and this is because the Christians are the carriers of the stones of the temple and the carriers of the hopes of the Jews, as we will clarify. (Ayyub 1987, 35n. 29; see also 184–85)

The history of the conspiracy is an issue to which a great deal of time and effort is devoted in the apocalyptic literature. These apocalyptic writers closely follow European and American anti-Semitic authors (Count Cherep-Spiridovich, William Guy Carr, *The Protocols of the Elders of Zion*, etc.) in their attempts to connect all of history with the Jewish conspiracy.[1] However, Christian anti-Semites usually do not seek to find the roots of this conspiracy within the Jewish Bible, preferring to propose a negative change in the Jewish people as a result of their collective rejection of Jesus after the time of the Bible and to date the beginnings of the conspiracy from that time. This reluctance has not been felt by Muslim apocalyptists, for whom the Bible is a forged and abrogated document (or at the very least a suspect document) and an example of the mendacious nature of both Jews and Christians (Ayyub 1987, 139; M. 'Arif 1996, 35–61).

1. Cherep-Spiridovich actually "quotes" the Qur'an to say: "Whoever is a friend of a Jew, belongs to them, becomes one of them. GOD cannot tolerate this mean people. The Jews have wandered away from divine religion (given by Moses). They are usurpers. You must not relent in your work which must show up Jewish deceit" (1926, 126). This appears to be a very loose paraphrase of Qur'an 5:51, but Cherep-Spiridovich does not mention that the Qur'anic verse cautions against both Christians and Jews as friends.

[From the preface of *Isra'il: Ila ayyina?*] This book contains—from the roots—a study of a poisoned satanic tree that burns with the hot fires of its breath every human, animal, or plant, even every inanimate object, upon the earth to which it is able to come near. This tree is the tree of Judaism. This tree has taken numerous colors, and its bark has changed with the centuries and has been called by many different names during different times. It began—according to the Jewish tradition—[first] Hebrew, then Israelite, then later turned Jewish-Israeli. [In the same way] this tree did not stay—as historical events will attest—in any one country, since its first sprout appeared in the Arabian Peninsula, then it stayed for a time in Mesopotamia (Iraq of today), then was taken to Syria and Palestine, and then to Egypt.

From Egypt the Jewish tree returned to stay in the land of Palestine for a time, and there its wood became strong, and its evil became out of control. But the Truth [God] did not wish to leave this satanic tree to cause harm to the land and to the faithful servants, and so he gave them over to the power of the Assyrians to uproot the larger group by the roots, by their finishing off the northern kingdom of Israel in the year 720 B.C.E., and in 586 B.C.E. the Babylonians uprooted the other roots of this evil tree, which was exemplified by the kingdom of Judah.

But the wisdom of the Truth willed that this cursed tree not come to an end from [influencing] humanity's life entirely, but the Truth granted it existence until the Hour [of Judgment] will arrive, just as he granted [it to] the devil and his evil angels. So its people have grown strong and have replanted seedlings of it [the tree], spreading widely over the entire world, to tempt the people, to propagate corruption as a wind surrounding the corners of the world, until its foreordained and predestined end in the Preserved Tablet *(al-lawh al-mahfuz)* will arrive, and it will become fuel in hell.[2] The present-day state of Israel constitutes the most arrogant and the most dangerous existence—in history—of the Jewish tree, because this tree has been planted in our land by the hands of injustice and error and continues to live under their protection. (Faraj 1993, 15)

Therefore, the apocalyptic writers do not hesitate to point out the dishonorable stories told about so many of the prophets in the Bible. Depending on

---

2. The Preserved Tablet is located in heaven, and on it are written all of the events that have occurred or will occur during the duration of the world.

their attitude toward these prophets, either the reaction is one of glee that the Jews themselves would tell such stories about their own origins, or one of disgust that such material would be published about God's honorable prophets.[3] Either way, the Jews are held up to ridicule.

Some Muslims are able to find conspiracies much earlier than Christian Europeans were able to:

> The Torah admits that the Hebrews—or Banu Isra'il [Israelites]—did not leave any type of hatred or blood lust that they did not practice against the Egyptians. Their Torah says, when the Hyksos occupied Egypt during a period between 1370 and 1580 B.C.E., for a period of 250 years, Banu Isra'il made a covenant with those foreign and invading Hyksos against Egypt and the people of Eygpt.[4] This also happened when they made a covenant with the Persians during the reign of King Cyrus against the Canaanites of the people of Palestine. Dr. Ahmad Shalbi, professor of Islamic history and civilization, says in his book about Judaism, "Previous to the exodus of Banu Isra'il from Egypt there occurred a number of disputes between them and the pharaoh of Egypt because of their attempts to stir up the lower classes of the people of Egypt against the regime of the pharaohs." (J. 'Arif 1999, 8)

After reminding us that the treatment of the Israelite slaves in Egypt was exemplary and that Egyptians have never been known for cruelty, he then mentions the circumstances of the Exodus (Exod. 12:31–42) during the course of which the Israelites took a large quantity of gold, silver, and other items as a "loan." These are described in the text as a loan but oftentimes are understood by commentators as just repayment for the years of slave labor in Egypt. 'Arif says that he was reminded of this text when he heard about the claims of Israeli Jews to their property left in Arab countries when they were forced to

---

3. In this criticism two versions of history are at war. The Judeo-Christian version emphasizes the humanity and fallibility of the prophets and heroes of the faith, while the Muslim version is an idealization of history in which each prophet is infallible. Any exploration of their personal histories is by definition an insult to their honor, according to this latter opinion. See Donner (1998, 75–85); and further M. Da'ud (1999, 301–17); M. Mustafa (1998, 92–93).

4. There is obviously a mistake as to the dates of the Hyksos occupation. Probably read 1830–1570 B.C.E.

flee to Israel during the late 1940s and early 1950s, and the claims of Holocaust survivors to their property in Swiss bank accounts.

> I cannot say anything other than that an action with this point of view, as long as the Israeli government persists on expressing itself as the legitimate heir of the Jews in the world, then it is incumbent upon this government to take responsibility for the crimes that Jews have committed in the lands in which they lived, and to pay the Egyptian government the price of the gold the Israelites stole from the Egyptians thirty-five hundred years ago. I cannot say anything but record that an Egyptian citizen, Dr. Nabil Ahmad Hilmi, a professor of international law and vice-dean of the law college at al-Zaqaziq University, took the initiative when he brought legal action before the Swiss courts against the government of Israel, demanding the return of the gold the Banu Isra'il stole from the Egyptians during their exodus from Egypt. (J. 'Arif 1999, 11)

Obviously the vice dean, Hilmi, put a good deal of time and effort into this matter, since he is able to supply the exact figures of the stolen gold and other items, which the original text does not:

> Banu Isra'il, who were treated courteously by Egypt, took advantage of the goodness of the Egyptians and their good intentions, and pulled off the greatest robbery in history by the "loan" of the gold, silver, goods, clothes, and cooking implements from the Egyptians. . . . He said that he estimates the weight of the stolen gold at approximately three hundred tons, and since the value of a ton of gold doubles once every twenty years—and the weight of this gold would include interest of approximately 5 percent[5] . . . since the weight of the stolen gold was approximately three hundred tons . . . the weight of the gold would be compounded to become approximately three

---

5. It is curious that a Muslim would include interest (forbidden in Qur'an 2:275, and especially 3:130: "O believers, do not devour usury, doubled and redoubled, and fear Allah that you may prosper"), although the word he uses is *fa'ida* and not *riba* (interest).

hundred thirty-eight million tons every one thousand years . . . and during
5,758 years,[6] in accordance with the chronology of the Jews . . . it would become approximately 2.1765 billion tons of gold. (J. 'Arif 1999, 11–12)[7]

Although there is a good deal of humor value in a selection of this nature,
one can also sense a certain futility in the spectacle of distinguished intellectuals wasting their time with such nonsense as a result of frustration, envy, and a
general attitude of "history done us wrong."

Ayyub and others spend a great deal of time with the "Jewish conspiracies" of the Middle Ages and the sixteenth to nineteenth centuries. Apocalyptists who write in this vein (Ayyub, Salim, 'Arif, Da'ud, 'Abdallah, and others)
have a deterministic view of European history as being controlled by the Jews,
who were in the know, while everyone else (mainly the Christians) blundered
around in the dark or were manipulated by them. For example, both Ayyub
and Salim (along with many other writers) understand the importance of the
discovery of the New World for Europe's development in the 1500s and
1600s. However, they do not look to economic motivations for these discoveries nor perceive the curiosity of explorers. Instead, Salim describes how the
Jews already knew about the existence of the Americas and arranged the entire
episode of their expulsion from Spain in 1492 because they had bilked that
country of its wealth and were ready to move on (F. Salim 1998c, 31–32).
The other great ventures of European colonial expansion easily fall into place
once this level of knowledge, manipulation, and malevolence is attributed to
the Jews.

Moreover, according to these writers, all of the major Reformers (Luther
and Calvin, for example) were Jews, and they designed their new belief systems specifically with the idea that Jews would be the true rulers once the
Protestant sect was forced to flee to the United States.[8] A century previous to

6. An obvious error; read 3,758 years.

7. For the entire (and ongoing) lawsuit, see "Egyptian Jurists to Sue 'the Jews' for Com-
pensation for Trillions of Tons of Gold Allegedly Stolen During the Exodus from Egypt," Special
Dispatch no. 556 (Aug. 22, 2003), memri.org.

8. For a humorously anachronistic "scholarly" rendition of this idea, see Lahmar, "Al-
Buritaniyya awwal ta'ifa masihiyya takhtariquha al-Sihyawniyya" (The Puritans: The First Christ-

Theodor Herzl, usually considered to be the father of political Zionism, George Washington (who was a Mason) already foresaw the coming of the state of Israel and made provision for it within the U.S. Constitution (F. Da'ud 1999, 14–15). Others apparently were on the opposing side, since Benjamin Franklin is cited as speaking about what would happen when the Jews took control of the United States (H. 'Abd al-Hamid 1997a, 7–8; M. 'Arif 1996, 98–99; al-Shihabi 1997, 46 [cited in English]; Qutb 1991, 108–9; Suwayd 1989, 196–97), as these writers contend did happen after their numbers became large in the wake of the great immigrations of the end of the nineteenth and beginning of the twentieth centuries. Since that time Jews have absolutely controlled the United States, just as the Rothschilds and other Jewish banking families controlled Europe, manipulating the rise and fall of governments and the beginning and ending wars (precipitating both World Wars I and II) for their own nefarious ends.

Little of this reworking of history can be credited to the Muslim apocalyptists, whose primary contribution was to extend the conspiracy back deep into biblical times (M. 'Arif 1996, 32–45; Ayyub 1987, 37–68; F. Salim 1998c, 135, 193, 196), expand it to include the Qur'anic material of which the Western anti-Semitic writers were ignorant, and add the Muslim accounts of Muhammad's conflict with the Jews (al-Musayri 1998, 75–81). "Ever since the sun of Islam began to shine and the beginning of the birthplace of guidance, the Jews have plotted day and night against Islam and the Prophet of Islam" (M. 'Arif 1996, 111). Thus, the roots of the conspiracy theory are to be found deep within Muslim historiographic writing and include such nefarious episodes as the Jews' attempted assassinations of the Prophet and their bewitchment of him, and his subsequent temporary impotence (see D. Cook 2000).

It is important to note the anti-Talmudic material at the core of the anti-Semitic conspiracy theory. Christian writers also attacked the Talmud because criticism of the Jewish Bible was impossible. Christianity simply could not be divorced from its Jewish roots in a way that would enable the attacks used by

---

ian sect subverted by the Zionists"; 1995). One wonders what Cotton Mather would have said to the idea that he was a Zionist.

Muslims. However, the Talmud attracted the negative attention first of the medieval polemicists against Judaism, and later of those purveyors of the blood libel and finally of *The Protocols.*[9] The Muslim apocalyptist draws on the latter two sources but is not absolutely dependent upon them because of his relationship to the Bible, which differs considerably from that of the Christian.

It is worth giving a thoughtful writer the chance to explain his perception of the conspiracy:

> The great stratagem that the Muslims face in the world now is the Zionist-Crusader plan, which has no other goal but to uproot the Muslims from the world in stages, until Islam will disappear from it. This is the plotting that would be such as to move the mountains [cf. Qur'an 14:46]. Whoever understands these stages knows that [what will happen in] the immediate future will be in the interest of the criminals and not in the interest of the Muslims, and that is in accordance with the human and material factors in history—in other words, in the case of the neglect of the divine heavenly factors that Muslims believe in—because the present events confirm that those lunatic criminals, the materialists, the infidels, the atheists, and the polytheists, led by the Jews, under their god, the Antichrist, will fulfill what they have planned in ordering humanity into corruption that will not end until the Muslims are totally uprooted from the world.
>
> The Jewish plan led by the Antichrist, which has already reached an advanced stage in the final stages [of realization] at the instigation of the UN and the Security Council, then [will happen] with the announcement of what they call the "new world order," which is preparing people through it to be submissive and ruled by their hidden rule through means of the organizations of the UN and the Security Council. The Jewish Antichrist plan is now having the final touches put on it, which will prepare under it the souls of the people to be rulers and ruled, submissive to the rule of one power, led by one man who is the Antichrist. After that he will be able to appear openly to the public and proclaim himself and his [true] form.

---

9. The idea of "blood libel" was accepted by M. 'Arif (1996, 64, 68, 102–3); M. Da'ud (1999, 227–32); Abu Zayd (1999, 52); 'Abd al-Bar (1987, 3–105); Nawfal (1973, 23); al-Sharbati (1994, 24); and Zaytun (1996, 39–40). M. 'Arif says: "As to the dove of peace, they have slaughtered it and soaked their matzo in its blood for their Passover" (1997, 18). Overall, see al-Sharqawi (1990); Talas (1986); al-Bawwab (1996); and Frankel (1996, 416–18).

This plan, or the final stage of it, is an attempt to take away all weapons of mass destruction from every state other than America, which is 100 percent under the control of the Jews, and Israel, both people and state of which are the family of the Antichrist and his relatives, and then [all] humanity—in the event of this corrupting plan succeeding—will go forward into an age when the Jews will force all of humanity to submit, obey, and bow down to the Antichrist. If not, nuclear-tipped missiles will destroy the city or the state that says no to the Jews and refuses to bow down to the Antichrist. [This is] what happened to Iraq, after having been denuded of its weapons of mass destruction—while Israel still possesses them—and what is happening now to North Korea [1993]—[as the world community] desires to denude it of any nuclear weapons at the same time that America, Russia, China, India, France, and Israel possess them—and all of them are in the orbit of the Zionists. (B. 'Abdallah 1994, *dal-ha*, introd.; cf. M. 'Arif 1996, 119; Nawfal 1973, 32)

This scenario is clear enough and reasonably familiar to any Westerner who has had a marginal acquaintance with the literature of the Radical Right in the United States and its fantasies of UN control under a Zionist occupation government. Obviously, among Muslims the feared control would tend to focus more on Israel, but the common hatred of the international bodies and the "new world order" is striking.

These writers also manifest an incredible paranoia about supposed hidden Jews scattered throughout Muslim society as well as European and American societies. Many great personages of contemporary history are said either to have been Jews or to have had some Jewish connections that automatically tainted them. While one would not want to generalize too much, it is comparatively rare to find a recent (or even an important European historical) leader who has not been a Jew, according to the apocalyptic writers. Most Western leaders, including virtually all of the recent U.S. presidents, are included in this category, as are an astonishing number of Arab and Muslim leaders.[10] Examples include the family of King Husayn of Jordan, who was said to have been a Jew, who was aware of his descent, and who went to synagogue.

---

10. Of recent U.S. presidents, only Jimmy Carter is not characterized in this manner (perhaps because of his obvious sincerity, religious faith, and political even-handedness during his administration and afterward).

> There are in the Levant [Greater Syria] rulers who will have difficulty giving up their thrones because they are agents and aliens toward the community with Arab names, but in truth they have suckled the milk of the Jews, or their original semen was Jewish semen, or they were tempted—and the temptation of power is the most cursed of temptations. (M. Da'ud 1997, 147, 152; cf. Musa 1998, 229; 'Amaluhu 1992, 171)

Even Saddam Husayn of Iraq is said to be tainted because of his connection to Michel 'Aflaq (the founder of the Ba'th party in both Syria and Iraq), who was said by his enemies to have been the son of a Greek Jew who converted to Christianity. Because Saddam has in the past been close to 'Aflaq, not only he but also the entire Ba'th structure in both countries must have been perverted from the beginning (F. Salim 1998c, 136–67).[11] This idea shows that no matter how infinitesimal the connection or how distant the link is to the "Zionist conspiracy," if it is there, then the person (or organization) is automatically entirely blackened. Additionally, genealogical descent (even when it is unknown to the person concerned) or other personal connections automatically are the foremost considerations in ascertaining one's true political loyalties.

Part of the conspiracy is the "new world order." This unfortunate phrase uttered by President George Bush, Sr., in the wake of the Gulf War has entered very strongly into the phraseology of the Arabic-language Muslim apocalyptist. Fahd Salim speaks sarcastically about this idea and asks if we are to believe that this phrase could be anything other than malevolent when the entire Cold War was just an illusion perpetrated by world Zionism. Are we now supposed to welcome this new illusion? "Thus the West plays with the minds of the people" (F. Salim 1998c, 17). And the plan is?

> It is well-known among the Jews that the world Jewish king will not announce [himself] until after the attainment of terrifying [powerful] rule, and that will be the breaking of all the nations, as it says in Psalm 2:7–9: "I will

---

11. During the Gulf War, Saddam was himself the subject of an apocalyptic fantasy: see M. 'Arif (1990), who predicted Saddam's downfall just prior to the extermination of the Jews, which was supposed to happen the following year.

proclaim the decree of the Lord: He said to me, You are my Son; today I have become your Father. Ask of me, and I will make the nations your inheritance, the ends of the earth your possession. You will rule them with an iron scepter; you will dash them to pieces like pottery." Ruling the nations or the world is a foundational belief of the Jews, and this will be [accomplished] through the incitement of a dangerous world war, in which one of the sides will be victorious—a nuclear war. . . . For the reason of this great war, incitement of tribulations and disturbances is completed in the Muslim world, especially in Afghanistan, Somalia, and Algeria, preparatory to the descent of Western forces on these places, and their occupation in the name of international law. This gives those states and others of the terrible murderers' [states] the authority of the secret powers and their ambassadors in the outside world the right to demand international interference between the contending parties in these countries. This means the return of the colonialist, but this time the infidel will return demanding [vengeance?] from the people of the house. This is the treacherous Jewish-Crusader plan, when the West will return in a spirit of hatred, the goal of which is complete annihilation and societal destruction in a nuclear war. (F. Salim 1998c, 196–97)[12]

Thus, any interference in Muslim affairs is immediately demonized with the specter of colonialism, even when the motives are purely humanitarian, as they were in Somalia.

Another part of the demonization of the Jews is a flipping over of their messianic expectations to accuse them of actually expecting the Antichrist instead of the Messiah. In other words, the Messiah expected by the Jews is really the Antichrist, and they are being fooled or they are knowingly deceiving others into worshipping the devil.[13]

12. Note that Arabs, with a touch of irony, sometimes ask for the return of colonialism, because their societies are being so badly run. See al-Ibrahim (1996).

13. Because Muslim apocalyptic writers make this accusation so frequently, it is with some irony that Sa'id Ayyub starts out his book (1987, 9–10) with the comment that Christians had (in the Middle Ages, no less) proclaimed that Muhammad was the Antichrist (see Akhbari 1997). While this may indeed be offensive, it must be difficult for Ayyub and others, who accuse the Jews of expecting the Antichrist as their messiah, to escape from charges of hypocrisy. See al-Bar (1998,

The dwelling place of the Jewish prophet [the Antichrist] will be in the temple in Jerusalem. For this reason they try to burn al-Aqsa [Mosque] sometimes, and try to conduct archeological excavations other times, and even try to buy the ground through the Masons of America.[14]

They [the Jews] became confused about the matter [of truth]. . . . They took a messiah in keeping with their deeds and in accordance with their desires. The false messiah at the end of time is a tribulation, leading armies, spilling blood, and conquering the world. They are in need of an army and land to spill more blood.[15] The Antichrist will conquer, as in the Islamic sources, from sea to sea, and from the river to the ends of the earth. It is said about the messiah expected by the Jews that "his dominion is from sea to sea and from the river to the ends of the earth" [Zech. 11:19]. In the Islamic sources about the Antichrist, "No riding beast will be employed by him except a donkey," and the messiah expected by the Jews "rides a donkey." (Ayyub 1987, 32–33)

The accusation of expecting the Antichrist is taken by the apocalyptist to also demonize all of the Jewish view of the messianic future as well. For example, 'Arif cites the Talmud to say that the Jews will burn the weapons of their enemies for seven years during the messianic age (which would probably indicate a peaceful future; see Ezek. 39:9), and says this:

Consider and think about [the fact] that they will burn their weapons that they gather after the victory, and this means that they know from their books and their beliefs that there will come a day when they will not have any further need for modern offensive types of weapons and that the weapons of combat will be the sword, the arrow, the spear, the knife, and the horses. Their books—even if they are false—their feelings of [impending] annihilation compel them to allude without speaking openly to the truth of the final

---

106); Mabruk (1986, 57–58); Bayumi (1995c, 34); M. Da'ud (1995, 47); 'Ali (1996, 107); and al-Sharbati (1994, 86).

14. Ayyub 1987, 106. See also similar comments in Ayyub 1987, 33, 241–42, 311–12; A. Mustafa 1990, 251; Bayumi 1995c, 34; F. Da'ud 1999b, 16; and M. 'Arif 1996, 133. On the issue of excavations, see al-'Alami (1992).

15. Note Abu Zayd: "The Jew takes pleasure in killing the Arab, and worships by means of the blood of non-Jews" (1999, 53).

end. It is imperative for every Muslim to prepare [for a time when] he and his progeny will be honored with a plunge of exuberance to place his sword upon the sons of Zion and to gain one of the two great things [martyrdom or victory]. For this reason the judgment upon the Jews is a judgment upon re-actionary systems, imperialism, communism, secularism, and the present-day Jahiliyya [non-Muslim society]. Islam will never have a state until the final judgment upon Zionism and its tails, the Jews who pretend they are Muslims, is complete. (M. 'Arif 1996, 170)

The supposed domination of the world by political Zionism is perhaps the cornerstone of the modern Muslim apocalyptic scenario and appears in virtually all of its many permutations, as we will see.

Awe of Modern Science and Scientific Methodology

Although many Arabic-language Muslim apocalyptic writers may hate the West and envy its power, there is no question they are impressed with the success of modern technological societies.[16] Apocalyptists share both this envy and this hatred and seek to explain to their audiences how exactly this awesome power is either going to be nullified in the immediate future or is going to be transferred in its entirety to the Muslims. Their view of Western power does not emphasize technological limitations, as a Western apocalyptic writer would. Apparently, examples of the helplessness of power on the part of the Western powers (in Vietnam, in Somalia, or in Bosnia-Herzegovina) have not been interpreted in terms of the inability of a superpower to actually impose its will upon a recalcitrant population. Instead, Muslim apocalyptists time and again seem to believe that the mere possession of powerful weapons ensures victory, and they do not appreciate that victory is actually achieved by much more mundane factors, such as supply lines, training procedures, command and control structure, innovative military techniques, and good intelligence. Automatically, in the apocalyptist's scenario, the one who has the power not

16. For example, M. 'Arif (1995, 58–59) discusses the qualities of Europeans (Romans) that have enabled them to develop modern societies. He says, "They are cowards, but less cowardly than the Jews."

only can enforce that power but also has the will to do so as well, which is not always true of Western countries. Also the apocalyptist does not look for practical ways to assimilate advanced technology into his society and actually to overtake the West in the same way that Japan or other East Asian societies have done. On the contrary, he relies on one of several events to win the war for the Muslims, essentially without their having to lift a finger.

Overall, the appearance of technology is itself one of the signs of the closeness of the end:

> God most high said: "But when the earth puts on its ornamental garb and is adorned, and its people think they are able to get what they want from it, Our retribution comes upon it" [Qur'an 10:24]. This noble verse is a hint that the Hour will arrive when the earth will be adorned or take on its most beautiful form, and that will be when its people think that they are capable of changing everything in it; in other words, changing its weather, climate, nature, and the ways of living in it. This can only come through scientific development and the technology that aids in the making of these things—and so this is a hint of the knowledge that will bring about the development and the advancement to the point, just previous to the Hour, when people think that they are capable of doing anything on the earth that they want to. Just then the Hour will arrive. The scientific development and the technology that we witness during our time advances with a terrifying speed. Now that genetic engineering has appeared, the people of the world think that they are capable of changing the nature of [God's] creation and the production of new creation never seen previous to now. This is one of the signs of the Hour, just as the noble verse of the Qur'an mentions. ('Abd al-Hakim 1998a, 28–29)

Clearly, this selection represents both a contemporary trend in Qur'anic exegesis and a good deal of horror regarding the pace of modern Western civilization.

The most common method of gaining the West's technology is for God to destroy it, or to cause Westerners themselves to make fatal technological errors and destroy themselves. This last is a particularly attractive option because it both destroys the technology, which is the most visible and irritating evidence of the West's superiority over Islam (when it should be the other way around), and at the same time punishes these people for their godless arrogance by killing them with their own creations—a typically apocalyptic idea of just revenge. Speaking about the vengeance of God upon the world, 'Abdallah cites Isaiah 34:1–8 and then says:

> This is a call and an announcement about the torment of the entire world, and all the nations, and all the peoples without exceptions, that there will be a total destruction, that there will be so many killed that there will be no place to bury them and plagues will be many as a result. All of the planes and satellites will fall, and he likened the falling planes to withered leaves [Isa. 34:4] and the satellites to fig trees [Isa. 34:4]. This will be God's vengeance because of the [false] claims of Zion and its corruption of all of humanity and the great Jewish arrogance. (B. 'Abdallah 1994, 133)

God is also capable of exclusively aiding the Muslims—a much more positive approach. In the final battles, while the advantages are all with the technologically and numerically superior Western forces, the Muslims have the advantage of God's total support. Because part of the final battles will be won with the aid of Jesus and the angels, the technology will simply be ineffective. According to 'Abdallah, "God is capable of destroying their missiles and causing them to fall from their platforms, and it will not matter what they have placed against this, and he is capable of destroying their fleets, their destroyers, their submarines, and their planes, and thus nullifying their cunning" (1994, *waw*, introd.).

Among the apocalyptic writers there is also something of an attitude of having reached a critical mass and overstepping boundaries in the technological society of the West. Although this approach is usually worded in purely Islamic terms, it uses many of the same phrases and ideas as do various ecological and environmental apocalyptic movements in the West. For the apocalyptist, the fact is that Western civilization has reached a critical mass and the planet is simply unable to support more of the same—or sometimes the apocalyptist believes that human beings were simply not designed to reach such a level of achievement and therefore God will judge the civilization; overload has occurred. Apocalyptists sometimes take a long view of history—much longer than their religious beliefs should allow them to take, as a matter of fact, since they believe in a world only seven thousand years old. As part of such a view, they believe that the earth has undergone and will yet undergo a number of cycles of technological advance followed by destruction until it suffers its final, end-time destruction. Those holding this view believe that these cycles have been going on for millennia and represent a constant for God's creation (M. Da'ud 1994b; cf. Hancock 1995, 458–506): God simply does not allow his creation to advance beyond a certain level of technological achievement. Examples given are similar both to the biblical story of the Tower of Babel (Gen. 11) and to several Qur'anic records of destroyed peoples. As Mustafa Murad puts it:

> One who considers the traditions obtained about the Portents of the Hour will see that the world is going to return to the Dark Ages, back before one thousand years, back to very primitive weaponry. This means that the civilization of the twentieth century and the present times is going to go and never return. Everything that we see, nuclear weapons and advanced technology in all different fields, is going to perish and be destroyed, and that destruction and obliteration will not take one day or a month or months, but years and centuries according to laws of God concerning nations and civilizations. (Murad 1997, 54; cf. F. Salim 1998a, 14)

Murad goes on to ask where the evidence is of modern weaponry in the hadith traditions. Of course, it is obvious that he is a very reluctant neoconservative, tending much more toward the conservative camp, because even the conservatives would not hesitate to reinterpret the primitive weaponry described in terms that we would understand today. Either 'Abdallah or Ayyub would say, for example, that swords represent rifles and horses, tanks. Murad, on the other hand, does not take even this elementary step.

'Abdallah, in his predictions of the great earthquake that he believed was due to strike the United States in April 1997, prophesied unusual events in store for its technological society. He stated that warnings, especially in the form of thunder and lightning, would occur before the earthquake struck, followed by a meteor strike.'Abdallah speaks quite knowledgeably about asteroids and meteors striking throughout the world (B. 'Abdallah 1994, 335–41). These are signs from God that the society is to repent. "We shall surely let them taste the nearer punishment, prior to the greater punishment, that perchance they might repent" [Qur'an 32:21–22]. 'Abdallah then cites Revelation 8:10 to show that this nearer punishment will probably be a meteorite.

Overall, comets are mentioned quite frequently in both classical and contemporary Muslim apocalyptic literature (D. Cook 1999). 'Abdallah notes the example of the passing of Halley's Comet in 1986 (which unfortunately was one of the less visible passings of Halley), as do a number of other writers (B. 'Abdallah 1994, 341–42; Ayyub 1987, 217–18; M. 'Arif 1997, 69; M. Da'ud 1992b, 148). Other more recent writers have noted the passing of Comet Hale-Bopp in 1997, which was accompanied by messianic speculation in the West as well (Musa 1998, 183–92; F. Salim 1998a, 34). 'Abdallah's principal point, however, is that human technology will not be able to stop or cope with these events. Satellites will fall, computers will fail, and in general, technological society will be shaken to its foundations. Scientists think that they have the answers; they will be shown up by God himself, as planetary bodies and astronomical objects of all sorts rain down upon the earth, causing the first earthquakes designed to induce mankind to repent.

Nuclear warfare is cheap in the landscape of the Muslim apocalyptist (M. 'Arif 1996, 183–84; M. Da'ud 1997, 37; B. 'Abdallah 1994, za, introd.; F. Salim 1998a, 94). The Jews and their supporters easily make decisions to bomb locations with nuclear weaponry. From a forged letter, supposedly from the Antichrist to his Jewish followers, we read the following:

O brothers, those foolish people describe us as cowards, but they are fantasizing, we are the strong ones today. We will possess the nuclear power in every land that wants it, and the future will reveal that [fact] to whomever called us cowards, that we will labor indefatigably, since the peoples of the world have stolen most of our wealth, we will steal what remains to them with the excuse that we have found it to be reinforcing the economic integration. Know, O brothers, that we have prepared for every eventuality with an overflow of general calumny against Islam, which we have placed in the position of daily prayer for all of humanity—because of how much our broadcasts speak about it—we will soon destroy the nerves of humanity in their entirety. We will focus our efforts upon reminding the people of the expected terrors of wars to frighten them. We will make them eager to avoid them [wars] whenever they occur so that when we appear against them with the idea of a single world government, with the excuse that it is the only instrument for prevention without actually going to war. . . . [17] But our true goal will be the preparation for the removal of racial and religious differences so that the hostile peoples will turn to us away from their surveillance and investigation about our secret plans. (M. 'Arif 1997, 113)

The "letter" then goes on to explain how the nuclear bomb will be used to enforce the One World Government. This document (which continues on) reveals more about its Muslim forgers than it does about any conspiracy. It literally details the way that the apocalyptists themselves would act if they were given the incredible power of the bomb. Da'ud speaks of the fear that the Jews have:

In addition, the era of the Mahdi will witness what has never been taken into account by the Jews, and that is the opening of the restraining barriers of their self-control. In other words, the Jews will take refuge from the pressure of fear and terror of being crushed through the exploitation of [their] nuclear weapons, which will make the [world's] response against them many times greater. Israel during the era of the Mahdi will seek its own destruction and dig its own grave. (M. Da'ud, 1995, 38–39)

God will protect the Muslims from anything that could harm them in any case (something akin to the premillennialist Christian belief that Armageddon will not harm them since they will be raptured). Therefore, nuclear bombs go off regularly and destroy large sections of the earth's population without seeming to interfere with the environment or cause any substantive difficulties to the populations of the surrounding countries. For example, in Da'ud's scenario of the Mahdi fighting the battle of Armageddon, multiple nuclear bombs are detonated in the Valley of Jezreel (Armageddon), a mere sixty miles to the north of Jerusalem. While these bombs do not affect the Muslim inhabitants of the city of Jerusalem or the country as a whole, they kill all the Jewish population of Israel. In the same scenario a disturbance in the Mediterranean Sea (where the American and European fleets are located), probably

17. He does not complete this sentence.

caused by all these explosions, overturns the fleet and kills all of the invaders. However, these events (earthquakes, tidal waves, nuclear fallout, and so forth) have no effect upon any of the surrounding Arab countries. Egypt, for example, would be devastated in such an attack, no matter which way the winds were blowing, and it is very probable that Syria, Lebanon, and Jordan would also be destroyed, not to speak of Israel itself. And yet we find the Mahdi setting up his capital in Jerusalem and rebuilding the country. Da'ud has enough realism to understand that it would be totally destroyed, but not enough to comprehend that it would be uninhabitable just a short time later, before the ground has even had a chance to cool down. One should note that God does not apparently interfere with this scenario at all, except that he causes the nuclear winds to blow the other way so that they do not kill the Muslims. Somehow it is ironical to find a writer such as Da'ud, who frequently proclaims his love for Egypt, advocating nuclear war in Israel, when it is clear that his own homeland would be destroyed as a result of this holocaust.

The only other outside force is the technology of the West itself, which in this scenario, after the battle of Armageddon, is transferred wholesale to the Muslim empire of the Mahdi. It is apparent, therefore, that Da'ud actually believes that it will be the West's free technology that will clean up the whole mess, since God does not appear again in the narrative. Technology is a toy, and because the apocalyptist has only a vague sense of what is really out there, he assumes it is so fantastic that it can literally do anything . . . anything, that is, except defeat the Muslim armies when God is supporting them. This attitude is not uncommon among the Muslim apocalyptists, who have a very superficial grasp of what is within the range of possibility. However, even this superficial grasp seems impressive when compared with the assimilation of pseudo-scientific ideas and the UFO mythology.

Pseudo-science and the Use of UFOs

The search for new materials in modern Muslim apocalyptic includes the assimilation of UFO conspiracy material. One cannot say that the issue of UFOs has been as popular in Muslim countries as it has been in the United States, where it has been widely viewed as an example of the government's perfidy and deception (al-'Urfi 1994; H. 'Abd al-Hamid 1996, 113–16). Although the issue of cover-up has definitely attracted the attention of Muslim writers, it has not reached the proportions found in the Western world. In the realm of Muslim apocalyptic, Muhammad 'Isa Da'ud pioneered the assimilation of this angle of the conspiracy. With his 1992 book *Ihdharu: Al-Masih al-Dajjal yaghzu al-'alam min muthallath Bermuda* (Warning: The Antichrist is invading the world from the Bermuda Triangle), he manages to add a number of exciting elements into the narrative popularized by Ayyub. These include answers to questions about the location of the Antichrist, an explanation of the nature and purpose of flying saucers, and, later on, how they are connected to the Jews, his servants.

In the beginning of Da'ud's forays into the apocalyptic scenario, he proposes the idea that the throne of Satan is in the Bermuda Triangle (M. Da'ud 1992a, 74). In his book *Ihdharu,* he develops this idea into a fully elaborated scenario. The beginning highlights the Antichrist's army of jinn and demons, which kidnap unfortunates who wander into the area of the Bermuda Triangle (M. Da'ud 1992b, 49–50). Those who are kidnapped are taken down into his fortress castle far beneath the waters, where there are all sorts of marvelous inventions and contraptions explained in their totality by Da'ud (52–53). The most interesting part of his theory is the connection with the UFOs. Here Da'ud seeks to explain a number of "mysteries" that occupy Western UFO conspiracy theorists. He is not entirely without critical thought, however, and recognizes that the vast majority of UFO sightings are in fact either the product of overactive imaginations or simply identified objects whose provenance is unknown to the person seeing them. There are according to him those last 5 percent of sightings, however, that do not fall under these two, much larger categories (74). After briefly explaining Einstein's theory of relativity (noting that Einstein was an agent of the Antichrist), Da'ud states in explanation:

> Yes, he [the Antichrist] has subordinated light and understood the secrets of vision and arrived at the secrets of magnetic gravity, and the production of sensitive apparati at a particle level, since they are smaller pieces of matter than an atom, apparati that cannot be seen. Yes, the Antichrist rides particles of light, since this idea did not come first to Einstein, the Jewish thief, who stole ideas, theories, and truths. Yes, the Antichrist has incorporated many

powers together and made the production of gravity a terrifying science through which it is possible to overwhelm [or bring down], meaning metal apparati. Yes, the Antichrist is able to make a new type of artificial light and is able to take advantage of the sea of particle rays falling on the earth like a waterfall. (M. Da'ud 1992b, 85–86; 1999, 470–91)

Da'ud comes to the conclusion that many of the sightings in this last category (the 5 percent category) are really those of the Antichrist's followers, although one must ask how it is, if they are moving so fast that they cannot be seen, that anyone has actually seen them.

Most of the descriptions that have come of the pilots of this unknown aircraft would prove that they are living, thinking [beings], and possessed of the same forms as we have, and physiological characteristics, and the same resemblance that God gave us [to each other]: hands, legs, eyes, nose, mouth, and even sexual organs.[18] The only exception is that the Antichrist uses pygmy sailors, or giants mostly, to put on the clothes of astronauts, super advanced metallic or rubber [clothes], instead of using jinn or demons in most cases. (M. Da'ud 1992b, 87; 1994a, 177–81)

After he kidnaps the people, the Antichrist uses them as slaves. Frequently they are breeding machines for his secret armies, although he can also kidnap children. According to Da'ud, he specializes in kidnapping Muslim children so that they can one day be used against their parents and relatives in a secret, well-trained, entirely brainwashed army commanded by the Jews. After discussing how the Antichrist possesses people's minds, Da'ud claims that the Antichrist

prepares the minds of the children of the world for his ideas, to place an opening in the mind of each of them so that one of his demons can enter, if

18. M. Da'ud (1992b, 88, 94) covers the question of abductions and asks the pointed question of why, if aliens are the abductors, they are able to have sexual intercourse with the abductees; this question is covered more graphically by H. 'Abd al-Hamid (1996, 112), who contends that the former are human agents of the Antichrist.

he wishes, and it goes much further than that—he is training a gigantic army (I still do not know their number)[19] under the earth. Where? Under the al-Aqsa Mosque and [the area] nearby to it. Why has the messiah of error chosen this unique place? Because it became available after the Jewish occupation of Palestine and because he knows that it is the most secure of all places in the world because of its uniqueness and he knows from the Qur'an and the traditions of the Prophet that the al-Aqsa Mosque will never be destroyed.[20] It will stand until the appearance of the Hour. If all of the armies of the world tried to destroy it they could not. He insinuates to his people and his institutions the need to destroy the al-Aqsa Mosque in order to study the temple of Solomon, but his engineers are really building under the earth to collect children and leave legions of Jews as leaders and commanders. The kidnappees are very young and are given a military education. . . . Male and female look alike, like animals. They are educated to hate [male] Muslims and to love the women of the Muslims and the Arabs. . . . [They are told that soon] they will have a life above when the great king, god [the Antichrist] comes to take them out and give them spoils and women. . . . [21] The Jewish call for the destruction of the al-Aqsa Mosque is nothing more than sand in the eyes, since the Jews know that the mosque cannot be destroyed, while the hidden hands dig in secret for other reasons. (M. Da'ud 1992b, 126–27; 1999, 408–21, 524–68)

This, therefore, is Da'ud's apocalyptic vision.

Others have found the Bermuda Triangle's function to be attractive (Musa 1998, 81–82). Among those convinced by Da'ud, however, only Hisham Kamal 'Abd al-Hamid has written a full-scale treatise on the subject, and one must say that it is a good deal more coherent than Da'ud's was (admittedly, *Ihdharu* was one of Da'ud's first apocalyptic tracts):

19. Da'ud's addition.

20. In fact, al-Aqsa Mosque has been badly damaged at least five times by earthquakes (although the Dome of the Rock, located on more secure bedrock just one hundred yards to the north of al-Aqsa, has never been touched), nor have I seen anything in the prophetic hadith that would indicate that it is protected.

21. This theme, of killing the men and taking the women as spoils, is well-developed in the Qur'an; see 2:49, 7:127, 141, 14:6, 28:4, 40:25.

After we have proved that flying saucers are not from other planets (stars) and they do not belong to a group of Gog and Magog, as some have thought, but that they are creatures, they must be from among the inhabitants of the earth, which is inhabited by both humans and jinn. Since these creatures do not have a human description, there is only one possibility that needs to be discussed, and that is the study of the scientific, intellectual, logical, and religious proofs that would establish absolutely that this is the best probability [i.e., that the aliens are demons]—other than the possibility that the people of flying saucers are demons in human form.[22]

'Abd al-Hamid presents several "proofs"—largely, the accounts of eyewitnesses and abductees—that these "aliens" are demons in human form. He usually links each eyewitness account to a Qur'anic verse that describes jinn or other supernatural creatures. The Antichrist uses flying saucers as advanced weaponry to subordinate his foes; however, 'Abd al-Hamid is hard pressed to describe these weapons. In Muslim classical sources the Antichrist is described as riding a donkey (because he is a parody of Christ), and 'Abd al-Hamid tries hard to make that donkey into a flying saucer. This attempt is not as successful as it may appear at first glance, and he mercifully leaves the subject behind (H. 'Abd al-Hamid 1996, 151–56).

After we have proved that the people of flying saucers are none other than demons in human form, and that flying saucers are the flying riding beast or the donkey of the Antichrist, which demons made for him to enable him to gain control over the people of the earth, now we need to recognize the goals of the study and the experiments that the demons perform upon human beings and animals in flying saucers. We will relate these goals to the tribulations and the miracles that the Antichrist will bring [to humanity]. (H. 'Abd al-Hamid 1996, 161)

22. H. 'Abd al-Hamid 1996, 136. The cover illustration of his book shows a Jew, carrying a Star of David, being beamed down from a flying saucer and giving instructions to his black-robed and cowled Masonic acolytes before a golden temple marked "U.N." and decorated with Stars of David.

> We have previously seen how the flying saucers passed through the air-space of the United States and hovered over the city of Washington, D.C., exactly over the Congress and the White House, and that when the American fighter planes tried to get rid of them, the flying saucers paralyzed their movements . . . and forced them to return to their bases. (H. 'Abd al-Hamid 1996, 162)

However, even 'Abd al-Hamid cannot understand what the flying saucers are doing. He does ask the very pointed question, however, whether their appearance is a sign that the Antichrist is really loose in the world and not bound as he was during the time of the prophet Muhammad (see the present book, 202–5, the story of Tamim al-Dari, which is connected to the Bermuda Triangle in contemporary apocalyptic literature). The answer is a resounding yes; these repeated sightings of UFOs must mean that the Antichrist is about to unleash his awesome power upon the Muslims—who ironically have not been troubled nearly as much as the West has been by this phenomenon.

It would appear that part of the reason for using examples of UFOs stems once again from apocalyptists' envy of the West and its technological power, and the desire to find something that can best it. Because UFOs are a mystery that fascinates some of Western society (at least those groups that believe in them intensely), they must by definition be beyond the capabilities of the West. Therefore, it is a comfort to know there is such a technology, even if Da'ud and 'Abd al-Hamid are required to use it to aid Satan and his Jewish Antichrist. Even in their fantasies, however, this technology, while immeasurably more advanced than that available to the West, let alone that which is available to the Muslim world, is not used to harm the Muslims at all. The threat of such harm is present, but it is never actually fulfilled, apparently because God is controlling the course of events to such a degree that a fantasy destruction of Mecca (to postulate one possible example) is never contemplated or even feared. But even in Da'ud's own messianic fantasy, flying saucers are not used by the forces of evil in the battle of Armageddon—not that they would have been much help fighting against God's support of the Muslim side in any case. If there really were weapons of such power available to the Jewish conspiracy, and the level of malevolence present there was as great as Muslim apocalyptists describe it to be, then the latter should be hard pressed to explain exactly why some kind of terrible destruction has not yet been visited upon the Muslims.

Fears of destruction remain quite hypothetical until the equation of dating the end of the world is added. Arabic-language Muslim apocalyptic writers have had to explore this angle of the apocalypse in order to give their fears immediacy.

FOUR

THE CONTROVERSY ABOUT DATING THE END OF THE WORLD

Dates Leading Up to the Year 2000

Since the very beginnings of Islam, Muslims have been tempted not only to predict but to date the end of the world, so much so that the Qur'an warns against the practice. No fewer than three passages state specifically that mankind cannot know the time of the end (Qur'an 7:187, 31:34, 43:85).[1] When one examines the hadith literature, however, it is obvious that interest in this subject was so strong among early Muslims that the Qur'an's warnings and other prophetic bans rapidly fell by the wayside (Bashear 1993). This may have been because it is human nature to try to crack a riddle, and the ultimate riddle is God's plan for the end of the world. Muslims have consistently at-

---

1. Muslim apocalyptic writers are aware of these verses and sometimes cite them, yet this knowledge somehow does not stop them from making predictions, as the verses probably intended. See Jamal al-Din (1998?, 38–44) and Jabr (1993, 112).

tempted to date the end of the world using various methods, first by means of prophetic hadith, then by means of gematrical exposition of the Qur'an and other books (mainly Sufi texts) deemed holy by various groups, and finally by astrological calculations, among other means. To date, these attempts have all failed.

This miserable track record has in no way dampened the enthusiasm of modern apocalyptists, however. If anything, the dating frenzy appears to be growing more intense. It is difficult to say exactly when the year 2000 (by the Western, solar calendar) first entered Arabic-language Muslim apocalyptic literature as a significant date. It is not a year one would naturally expect Muslim believers to regard as important, since in the Muslim calendar it is the year 1421 A.H., a date lacking any natural luster as a round number. However, apocalyptic expectations are sometimes tied more firmly to perceptions and expectations than to traditions or round numbers:

> As Muslims we must acknowledge an important truth, and that is that the people of the West are feeling strongly the closeness of the end more than we do. All of the present-day political, religious, and intellectual theses of the West run in that direction, and prove those violent feelings to the point that the Christian intellect has not sufficed with talk of "the end of history" or "the clash of civilizations" or the great confrontation, the battle of Armageddon. They have even pinpointed the birth date of the Antichrist and said that it is close to the end of March 1968, and they have pinpointed the birth date of the one who will lead the battle against the Antichrist. Some of them have written that the Lord intends to send the messiah Jesus before the end of the year 2001, and others have said that he will come in the year 2016. (F. Salim 1998a, 17)[2]

2. Salim further says that Jesus will return in the year 2000, on January 1, 2000, to be exact (1998a, 81); the Dome of the Rock will be destroyed in the early morning hours of January 1, 1999 (134–35, 141); and the sun will rise from the west (the last event of the world) in the year 2010. However, some proofs of Israel's attaching importance to the year 2000 are bizarre: F. Da'ud (1999a, 15) says that there will be thirteen Knessets—that is, one every four years, making a total of fifty-two years—which, when added to 1948, the year of the creation of the state of Israel, indicates a prophecy of the year 2000 among the Jews.

Any scholar examining apocalyptic beliefs will soon recognize that people believe what they want to believe. Passages like Salim's illustrate this: the fact that the year 2000 and other dates following it should have been irrelevant to Muslim believers has not proved to have much weight. It is apparent that the Christian (and secular Western) hype about the year 2000 influenced Muslim apocalyptists, just as occurred before the year 1900 (for beliefs about 1900, see Guest 1900). One of the first to assert the significance of the year 2000— as he was with so many other ideas—was Sa'id Ayyub: "The building of [the temple] according to their plans will begin after the destruction of al-Aqsa Mosque—and the planned date for this is the year 2000" (Ayyub 1987, 28n. 6). This short comment, relegated to a footnote in Ayyub's book on the Antichrist, shows the direction the whole calculation movement would take. As this book had phenomenal success, it is very likely that this small notice was the catalyst for at least some of the subsequent calculations by other apocalyptists, although it is possible that they would have occurred anyway.[3]

Those promulgating the conspiracy theory believed that important things were destined to occur in 2000 (F. Salim 1998c, 16; F. Da'ud 1999, 28). According to Hisham 'Abd al-Hamid, the chain of cataclysms was to be set off by the planned destruction of al-Aqsa and by the rebuilding of the Third Temple in Jerusalem. He set the date for this at the three-thousandth anniversary of the first building of the temple (under Solomon; cf. 1 Kings 5–6), and cited a wide range of sources (including several Christian apocalyptic writers, the Israeli newspaper *Davar,* and Menachem Begin) that said this structure must be built in the immediate future. "The Jews are planning to destroy al-Aqsa Mosque during the year 2000," wrote 'Abd al-Hamid in 1996, "building on a number of mistaken gematrical calculations of some of the

---

3. See also 'Abd al-Hamid 1996, 180, 190–91; 'Abd al-Hakim, 1998a, 6–7. M. 'Arif predicted that the Jews would explode a nuclear bomb in the year 2000 (1996, 184); he also said that the Antichrist would appear on that date (1997, 9, 31, 35, 53). It is interesting that at the beginning of the century Muhammad 'Abduh (n.d., 9:478, 480) predicted the appearance of the Antichrist in either 1400/1979 (which is understandable because it is a round date by the hijri system), or 1407/1986. Ayyub's book was written during that latter year (although not published until 1987); note that 1986 is the year according to the scheme of Bassam Jirrar in which the domination of Israel is supposed to begin its downhill slide.

prophecies appearing in the Torah, in the book of Daniel, and some of the texts appearing in their Talmud, just as they are planning to start a war with the Islamic nations in the year 1997, preparatory to the revelation of the Antichrist" ('Abd al-Hamid 1996, 228).

Some writers feel that the countdown started in 1978, a date that would make more sense in the Islamic context, since it was the year 1400 A.H. by the hijri calendar.[4] In November 1979 a messianic revolt occurred at the most holy place in Islam: the Haram al-Sharif at Mecca (Ketchichan 1990; also Ahmad 1988). Since the claimant at that time called himself al-Qahtani (the title of a tribal messianic figure mentioned in the classical sources), and this particular figure is supposed to rule for some twenty years prior to the revelation of the Mahdi, the apocalyptic writers Fahd Salim and Mansur 'Abd al-Hakim held that the subsequent two decades were that period of time (F. Salim 1998a, 86–90; 'Abd al-Hakim 1998a, 43–45). Of course, this calculation was somewhat forced, since the classical sources do not say anything about the candidate for the position of al-Qahtani being killed twenty years before the Mahdi's appearance. Those sources state that al-Qahtani will lead the way publicly; they do not depict him as an obscure figure like the 1979 claimant, a figure many now have difficulty even recalling given the Saudi Arabian government's success in hushing up the whole episode. It would seem, therefore, that the need to see fulfillment of prophecy in the November 1979 revolt at Mecca was dictated more by the desire to connect significant events to a apocalyptic countdown involving the year 2000 than by independent calculation. Salim seemed to acknowledge this when he said in 1998 (after telling us that his prediction of the Antichrist appearing in 1999 was based on Nostradamus):

As is well known the Masons have set the year 2000 as the outer limit for the implementation of their great plans, and the first part of it will be the destruction of the mosque of al-Aqsa and the foundation of the Third Temple

4. Hijri years rarely correspond exactly to the Western calendar, and as the hijri calendar is a lunar one, unregulated by the solar calendar, it loses between ten and fourteen days each year when compared with the solar calendar. Hence the difficulties in being exact when discussing the two systems together.

in its place. The West believes in this and aids in its realization, and the Muslims alone do not realize this, since the bearers of enlightenment in Arab and Muslim thought have contempt, if only on the intellectual plane, for everything connected with the traditions of the Antichrist. This is in accordance with the tradition of the Messenger [Muhammad], who said that the signs of the appearance of this traitor, this liar [i.e., the Antichrist] will only appear when he is no longer mentioned from the pulpits of the Muslims. (F. Salim 1998c, 174–75)

Others made equally fallacious predictions. Bashir Muhammad 'Abdallah used the Daniel prophecies described above as the basis for his calculations (B. 'Abdallah 1994, 134; also al-Bar, 124; Tawila 1999, 10–11). For him the Gulf War (1990–91) and the proclamation of the new world order were the key events from which one had to begin to count toward the end: "The proclamation of the 'new world order' was nothing other than a breach into part of the plan of the Antichrist and the Jews to rule the world openly during a time that is known to God. The Masonic and other Zionist organizations—under the leadership of the Antichrist—will try to bring this time to a close and prepare humanity to accept it" (B. 'Abdallah 1994, 136).

As 'Abdallah sought to calculate the exact time of the great Earthquake of the Hour, he based his belief on the prophecies of Daniel 8:13–14, which have inspired so many calculations throughout the ages: "He said to me: It will take 2,300 evenings and mornings; then the sanctuary will be reconsecrated" [Dan. 8:14]. 'Abdallah understood the signs of the end to be noted in verse 13: "How long will it take for the vision to be fulfilled—the vision concerning the daily sacrifice, the rebellion that causes desolation, and the surrender of the sanctuary and of the host that will be trampled underfoot?" [Dan. 8:13]. He believed the sacrifice (for which he used the Arabic *muhraqa*, also meaning "burning") to have been the oil wells set on fire by the fleeing Iraqis in Kuwait, which burned through most of 1991. As for the "surrender of the sanctuary" (reading al-Quds, Jerusalem) and the "host trampled underfoot," 'Abdallah stated that they were

indicators of the liberation of Jerusalem from the hands of the polytheist, idol-worshipping *('abd al-taghut)* [Qur'an 5:60] Jews, for they are defiled

(*najis*) [cf. 9:28] and filth (*rijs*) [cf. 6:25], and the cleansing of Jerusalem
from them, and its purification at the hands of the present-day Nebuchadnezzar and the present-day Babylonian army,[5] will constitute "the host that
will be trampled underfoot" like "mud in the streets" [Isa. 10:6], and will
occur twenty-three hundred mornings and evenings after the Kuwait War.
(B. 'Abdallah 1994, 474)

Furthermore, after dismissing ideas that these 2,300 mornings and
evenings could mean 1,150 actual days (instead of counting them separately),
he explained, "If this period is of 2,300 days—in other words about six and a
half years—then the year of the entrance [i.e., the invasion of the Iraqis] upon
the Banu Isra'il would be 1997, about halfway through it, and so probably the
great earthquake [of the Hour, the subject of his book] would be during that
year, during the first half of it. But if it is the second possibility, then the period
would be 1,150 days, and the entrance would be in the year 1994" (B. 'Abdallah 1994, 476).

He then explored the month in which this was likely to happen and concluded that it had to be 10 Dhu al-Hijja [falling on April 19, 1997], a calculation based on Qur'anic sources (Qur'an 89:1–14). It is curious how he
switched back and forth between biblical and Muslim sources and dates; at the
very least this gave him an easy escape if his predictions did not come true, as
they were based to such a substantial degree on non-Muslim materials.

'Abdallah's reliance on Daniel as a base for his calculations has been emu-
lated by Safar al-Hawali, the well-known Saudi radical, who states:

The final, difficult question remains to be answered: When will the Day of
Wrath come? When will Allah destroy the abomination of desolation [Israel]?
When will the chains of Jerusalem be broken and its rights returned? The answer has already been implied. When Daniel specified the period between its
distress and relief, between the era of anguish and the era of blessing, he put
it as forty-five years! We have already seen that he specified the time of the establishment of the abomination of desolation as the year 1967, which is what
in fact occurred. Therefore the end—or the beginning of the end—will be

---

5. Although 'Abdallah has not always favored Saddam, one would assume that it is he who
was meant by this statement.

1967 + 45 = 2012 or in lunar years 1387 + 45 = 1433." (al-Hawali 2001, 122)

In addition to such calculations based on foreign material, modern Muslim apocalyptists have given weight to several corresponding Muslim calculations. One source is the important treatise *Kashf 'an mujawazat hadhihi al-umma al-alf* (in al-Suyuti n.d.[b] 2:86–92), written by Jalal al-Din al-Suyuti about one hundred years previous to the year 1000/1591, when Muslims were preparing for the expected end of the world at that time. This treatise was designed to put off speculation about the subject. In this attempt it succeeded; unfortunately it put off the speculation until our own time by suggesting that the end of the world would occur in the year 1500/2076, a prediction adopted by many modern apocalyptists. Since the events forecast by al-Suyuti to signal the coming of the end of the world are expected to occur over a period estimated at between forty to eighty years, we should be seeing the beginnings of the end. In addition to this classical treatise, several modern calculations are available.

Virtually all of the apocalyptists cited in this book have made predictions at one time or another. Muhammad 'Isa Da'ud, for example, predicted in 1997:

The *sahib al-amr* [a messianic title] will emerge at the festival of the Hajj in 1419 [1998–99], and in Muharram 1420 [1999–2000] he will proclaim the return of the caliphate. If the issue is delayed, it will not be beyond 1425 [2004–5], as the exact people tend toward [i.e., those people calculating the end exactly], and a personage whose *kunya* (patronymic) is al-Sufyani will precede him, destroying the Gulf and striking at Israel[6] . . . and in 2000 there will be the battle of the Mediterranean and in 2001 will be Armageddon, which will be preceded by or be close to a great nuclear battle between

6. Muhammad 'Isa Da'ud (1997, 129–32) believes that Saddam Husayn was the Sufyani; see also 'Abd al-Hakim, who says that Yasir 'Arafat is the figure known in classical sources as al-Abqa' (an idea repeated by F. Salim [1998c, 137]), Hafiz al-Asad was the one known as al-Ashab, and Saddam was probably the Sufyani ('Abd al-Hakim 1998a, 28–31).

France and America in which Paris will be destroyed, and the sea will swallow up New York. (M. Da'ud 1997, 56)[7]

Predictions Concerning the Year 2000 or Leading Up to 2076

Some of the most impressive calculations about the date of the end of the world have been undertaken by the Egyptian writer Amin Muhammad Jamal al-Din in his series of books on the subject. In his first book, he attempted to calculate the time of the battle of Armageddon. To illustrate its imminence, he used hadiths, above all those of the a'maq tradition ("The Byzantines will make a secure treaty with you"), which he identified as treaties made between the United States and various Arab countries (cf. Abd al-Hakim 1998a, 71) and treaties made between Russia and China. Assuming that the 1996 election of Benjamin Netanyahu as prime minister of Israel would inevitably lead to war with Israel, he regarded it as a clear sign that the end was near. While Jamal al-Din has the honesty to admit that no one knows exactly when Armageddon will occur—probably thinking of the Qur'anic verses mentioned above—he did state that the Jews were expecting their messiah to appear in April 1998, fifty years after the foundation of the state of Israel.

It is interesting that Bashir Muhammad 'Abdallah also used this figure, only to reach a date for Armageddon one year earlier, noting the conjunction of a number of holidays during that year (the Passover of the Jews, the 'Id al-Adha of the Muslims, the Easter of the Christians) in that month. As a result of this coincidence, 'Abdallah said that the Christians were expecting Jesus to return in the fall of 2001 (since that would happen three and one-half years after the revelation of the Antichrist) (see also Jamal al-Din 1996, 61–63).

It is in his 1996 book that Jamal al-Din introduced the first of many methods he devised to calculate the date of the end based on a Christian text. This first method paraphrased the parable Jesus told in Matthew 20:1–16,

---

7. Note how in the midst of a paragraph, without any explanation, Jamal al-Din changes between *hijri* and Christian dates.

known as the parable of the workers.[8] According to Jamal al-Din, this parable tells the story of a master (God) who hires a number of different groups throughout a given day to work for him. There are those who come in the morning (the Jews), those who come at noon (the Christians), and those who come just before sunset (the Muslims). At the close of the day (the end of the world), the master pays them all the same wage, much to the irritation of those who had toiled throughout the entire day. The point of the parable in the New Testament is eschatological and somewhat ecumenical, but it focuses on God's bounty toward his servants rather than on the relative times within the chronological sequence that these things were due to occur. Indeed, Christians would have had difficulty doing anything else with the parable, since there are a number of groups mentioned in it; any other interpretations would have invited later revelations (such as Islam). Because of its eschatological content, this parable was assimilated into the hadith literature quite early, in classical times—a fact apparently unknown to Jamal al-Din (al-Mawsili 9:343, 10:208–9; see Tawila 1999, 277). He concentrated on the calculations obtainable from the parable, and, after taking the relative proportions from the time sequence (i.e., morning, noon, and night, relative to a day) and citing several Christian authorities (Richard Nixon, Billy Graham,[9] Jerry Falwell,[10] Hal Lindsey,[11] and Pat Robertson), he asserted that the Antichrist should appear in April 1998 (Jamal al-Din 1996, 50–52; 1998?, 12–17).

In this particular book, Jamal al-Din refused to give exact dates beyond the expected appearance of the Antichrist. However, he did finish his exposi-

8. In his third pamphlet, Jamal al-Din details six additional methods of computing the end; I am listing them in the order in which he does.

9. Billy Graham is extensively quoted by Musa (1998, 44ff) and Tawila (1999, 269), among many others.

10. Falwell is popular among Muslim apocalyptic writers and is frequently cited as an authority who knows something about the end of the world: e.g., by F. Salim (1998a, 71); F. Da'ud (1999, 20); Tawila (1999, 270); M. 'Arif (1997, 24); and M. Da'ud (1999a, 401–2). In addition to the above names, Caspar Weinberger is cited as a source by F. Salim (1998a, 84–85, 96) and H. 'Abd al-Hamid (1998, 9–21), and a number of Christian personalities (Jimmy Swaggert, Jimmy Baker, Pat Robertson, Oral Roberts, Kenneth Copeland, Richard De Haan, Falwell, Billy Graham, and Ronald Reagan as well as the Scofield Bible) are cited.

11. Hal Lindsey is cited extensively by al-Hawali (2001).

tion (under the heading "What Do the Muslims Say?") by pointing out that the Muslims' expectations are very closely tied to those of the Christians and the Jews, being in many ways the inverse image of them. But signs of the impending end are everywhere:

> When we look at the present situation we see that there is no one on the face of the earth who can be called a caliph, other than the people of the Arabian Peninsula (Saudi Arabia), who allow their king to be called a caliph. Supporting our statement that all of the pointers indicate that the end is near—it is remarkable that the health of the present caliph (King Fahd) has declined very much during the recent past to the point where he has named a regent to look after the affairs of state for the long term. . . . Is it possible that he is the caliph whose death will be a sign of the appearance of the Mahdi? (Jamal al-Din 1996, 64)

Jamal al-Din was severely attacked for these remarks by several faculty members at al-Azhar, who must have been intensely embarrassed that he splashed their institution's good name on the front of his books to signal his own credentials. In 1997, Mustafa Murad wrote *Mata taqum al-sa'a?* (When will the hour appear?) as one of several responses to Jamal al-Din—and probably to the radical school in general, which had been throwing out dates over the previous years with increasing promiscuity. As usual with the neoconservatives, Murad granted a great deal of the radical argument, accepting that the Hour was near, but warned that it was just not as near as they would like us to think. He also made judicious use of the relevant Qur'anic passages, noting that only God knows when the end is going to occur. While Murad named no names, he employed the following arguments:

1. If the Antichrist were to appear in 1998, the Mahdi would have appeared already.

2. The a'maq tradition of the truce and treachery of the Byzantines was clearly being fulfilled, but as of the time of writing the Western countries had not attacked the Muslims nor made any hostile moves (for a response, see Tawila 1999, 281).

3. A number of signs have not yet appeared.

Murad poured scorn upon the exact and round numbers used by Jamal al-Din. For example, he asked how it was that the period of time allotted to the Jews was *exactly* 1,500 years or *exactly* 2,000 years? What if it were really only 1,632 years (for which he claimed to have proof from Muslim classical historical texts)? Or what if it was 1,925 years? Murad displayed a number of different calculations, showing a range of predictions all the way up to 2500 A.H., all based on Jamal al-Din's figures (Murad 1997, 56–61; also al-Barak 1999, 98–99; al-Harbi 1998, 35–81). In short, he showed just how many random assumptions were being made by those apocalyptic writers seeking to date the end of the world.

Not all neoconservatives were as hostile to Jamal al-Din as Murad, however. In 1999, for example, after publication of a third book by Jamal al-Din containing most of his calculations, Tawila responded by conceding that the calculations might be right. However, Tawila continued, there was no way of knowning for sure: there was simply not enough information available to come to a conclusion (Tawila 1999, 275–79).

Apparently Jamal al-Din was not impressed by these criticisms of his thesis; in response he blasted his opponents by offering no fewer than six additional ways of calculating the end of the world that would yield dates close to the year 2000. While some of these methods might seem to be a little ludicrous and all of them use circular reasoning, they are nevertheless worth examining.

Jamal al-Din's second method of calculation depended on the words of al-Suyuti, who stated that the community of Islam would not pass the year 1500/2076, since the life span of the world is seven thousand years and the prophet was sent in the last part of the sixth millennium. If one adds up all the events due to take place before the end, he argued, there must be at least 120 years of apocalyptic events before the final apocalypse, proving by simple mathematics that the end times have begun (Jamal al-Din 1998, 19–27; see also F. Salim 1998a, 52–56).

Jamal al-Din based his third method of calculation on that of the classical scholar Ibn Rajab al-Hanbali, citing the tradition that says, "Your [the Muslims'] stay [i.e., your length of time upon the earth] in relation to those who were previous to you is like that which is between the late afternoon prayer and the setting of the sun." Taking the mathematical proportions implicit in this statement (and with the background of the seven-thousand-year length of the world), he concluded that three thousand years had passed between the

advent of Adam to that of Moses and the development of the three monotheistic faiths (Judaism, Christianity, and Islam) accounted for another three
thousand years.

He calculated that Judaism had been alloted a period of fifteen hundred
years and Christianity, six hundred years. As for Islam, he figured that although it had originally been allotted nine hundred years, God had added on
"half a day" (that is, five hundred years, since a day is a thousand years in the
sight of the Lord [Qur'an 22:47]), bringing us to 1400/1979 (Jamal al-Din
1998, 27–29).[12]

Jamal al-Din's fourth method of calculation was based on the method of
"the half of a seventh," which relies on the tradition that says "I [Muhammad]
was sent together with the Hour, just like these two, and pointed with his two
fingers" (usually considered to have been his pointer and his index fingers).
Taking the relative lengths of these fingers and calculating on the basis of the
seven-thousand-year length of the world Jamal al-Din came up with a date of
approximately 1560 A.H. (or about 2134 by the Western solar calendar)
(Jamal al-Din 1998, 30–33; see also 'Ali 1996, 179). While this method
might sound a little ridiculous, it in fact was the one that attracted the least
criticism, if only because it seemed to indicate a date far in the future. Tawila,
for example, accepts it.

Jamal al-Din based his fifth method of calculation on the calculations of
Ibn Hajar al-'Asqalani, together with a tradition that says, "There is nothing
remaining for my community in the world other than the length of when the
late afternoon prayers are prayed for me [Muhammad]." Working from this
statement and other descriptions of how long this particular prayer took in relation to the day, the author again arrived at the date of 1400 A.H. (Jamal
al-Din 1998, 33–34).

Jamal al-Din also used another method of Ibn Hajar al-'Asqalani for his
calculations, seeking to harmonize a certain tradition that speaks of the rela-

---

12. See Abu Da'ud (1998, 5:61, nos. 4349–50) for the classical traditions; Jabr (1993,
122–23), who had already proposed this argument; and F. Salim (1998a, 57–60), who, while accepting the argument, notes that those five hundred years have been nothing but disasters for the
Muslim community, and so he really cannot understand why God did not finish off the world in
the year 1500, because the Muslims were in a good position at the time.

tive lengths of the time allotted for the Jews (usually, as above, estimated at fifteen hundred years) with the time allotted to the Muslims. Muslim tradition allots the Jews a longer span on earth than that given to the Muslims; therefore, the Muslims cannot be allotted much more than fourteen hundred years or they would overtake the Jews (Jamal al-Din 1998, 34–35).

Finally, Jamal al-Din created a new rationale for his predictions through a synthesis of all the methods of calculation described above, arguing that the fact that all of them—proposed by different sources and different writers at different times—produced dates for the apocalypse very close to one another constituted an absolute proof of their accuracy insofar as Muslim tradition is concerned.

> It is clear that all of the methods of calculation agree approximately in their results and swirl around the year 1500 [2076]. It does not matter to us a little here or a little there when exactly. However, we can gain something of an idea when the end of the world will be and that it is close, and it is not thousands of years off, and not hundreds, as the lovers of this world would claim. We can gather that the end will be preceded by tribulations and apocalyptic wars and conflicts already clarified in this book. This necessitates preparation for the Day of Mutual Calling [of Resurrection, cf. Qur'an 20:124] with repentance and returning to God, and preparation of hearts for the advance of the unknown in the world, and the remembrance [of God] and asking [him] for forgiveness to obtain the favor of the Great, the Forgiver. (Jamal al-Din 1998, 37)

It is difficult to tell whether Jamal al-Din persuaded his opponents with these calculations. Most probably not, because the stakes are simply too high for the conservatives and the neoconservatives—among whom, ironically, Jamal al-Din must be numbered in everything he writes other than these calculations—to concede on this point. No other apocalyptic writer has made such a blatant attempt to undercut their authority, and the fact that Jamal al-Din is himself a graduate of al-Azhar has only made the fight more bitter. Dating and calculating the end is perilous, since such a prophecy must be close enough to impel urgency if it is to draw adherents, yet if it is are too close, the person making the prophecy risks failure when the date comes and goes without event, followed by ridicule and abuse, or the humiliation of having to admit to error and adjust the prophecy.[13] Obviously, with the passing of the year 2000, some of the writers discussed in this chapter have already suffered this fate. However, it does not seem to have affected them as much as one would expect. We will have to see, for example, what justification Muhammad 'Isa Da'ud, part of whose prophecy about the battle of Armageddon has already been discomfirmed, and Bashir Muhammad 'Abdallah, who predicted that the Earthquake of the Hour would strike the United States on April 19, 1997, will produce for this collision with reality.

A great many of the calculations of the date of the end of the world are tied to the expected end of the state of Israel. Therefore, we must examine the predictions concerning this event more closely.

13. Note the detailed predictions of F. Salim (1998a, 145–47), who says that on July 14, 1999, a nuclear missile will be fired at the Vatican, apparently from the area of the Gulf; on August 1, Iran will conquer the Gulf states; during the months of September-November there will be major apocalyptic wars in Syria and Israel; on November 23, 1999, the Antichrist will openly proclaim himself; and on "Friday, January 1, 2000, which is 15 Ramadan 1420, the world will be blinded by the light of the great prophet and messenger Jesus, as he descends upon Jerusalem, and upon the Muslims under the leadership of the Mahdi, as the Antichrist is besieging them" (147). Since the failure of these prophecies, Salim has not published any books on apocalyptic subjects.

FIVE

QUR'AN 17:4–8—FROM BANU ISRA'IL TO THE STATE OF ISRAEL

Introduction to the Changing Exegesis of Qur'an 17:4–8

There is a common misperception that interpretation of the Qur'an has changed little since the early compilations such as those of al-Tabari (d. 923). Although in general changes have been few and plagiarism from predecessors has been widespread, there have been and continue to be developments in the field of *tafsir* (Qur'anic exegesis) that are visible over the long run. Dramatic changes can and do occur very suddenly, particularly so during the recent past, and thus the field should be watched carefully by those interested in apocalyptic interpretations of Islam. One of the most outstanding examples can be observed in common interpretations about the group known in the Qur'an as the Banu Isra'il.[1] Western

1. The term *Banu Isra'il* appears in the Qur'an approximately forty times.

scholars identify this group with the biblical Israelite people, the ancestors of the Jewish people, but for theological reasons most classical Muslim commentators have tried to avoid making this connection,[2] pointing out that references to Banu Isra'il in the Qur'an are usually favorable, while those to the Jews are not.[3] Nevertheless, some Muslim scholars contest this position, finding evidence supporting the view that the Jewish people constitute the Banu Isra'il.

Immediately following the verses describing the Prophet's Night Journey (17:1–2), Qur'an 17:4–8 provides a description of the Banu Isra'il that is far from favorable. The verses thus raise a question as to which of the two groups is intended. The exegesis of these verses has changed through the centuries. We will examine what relevance this has for contemporary Muslim apocalyptic literature. The verses read as follows:

And We decreed for the Children of Israel (Banu Isra'il) in the Book: "You shall make mischief (or corruption) in the land twice, and you shall become very haughty." (4)

And when the punishment for the first [making of mischief] became due, We sent forth against you servants of Ours possessing great might who went after you in your country. Thus Our threat was accomplished. (5)

Then, We gave you back your turn against them and aided you with wealth and children and increased you in number. (6)

[And We said]: "If you do good, you do good for yourselves, and if you do evil, you do it for yourselves too." And when the punishment for the second [making of mischief] became due, [We sent Our men again] to afflict you, and to enter the Mosque *(masjid)* as they entered it the first time, and to utterly destroy that which they conquered. (7)[4]

2. See S. D. Goitein's entry, "Banu Isra'il" *(Encyclopedia of Islam,* 2d ed., 1960–2002).

3. One Muslim writer who disagrees with these classifications is Tantawi. He points out quite accurately that Qur'an 2:40–41 and 2:211 seem to necessitate a change in the dogma that Banu Isra'il does not mean the Jews, since those verses are clearly addressed to the contemporaries of the Prophet (Tantawi 1987, 57–58). One should say, therefore, that Banu Isra'il can also mean the Jews, but the reverse is never the case.

4. The *masjid* is understood to be the Second Temple.

It may be that your Lord will have mercy on you; but if you go back [to mischief], We shall come back and make Hell a prison for the unbelievers. (8)

Upon initial examination these passages are a typical selection of Qur'anic "sign" passages, where the people involved are warned against a certain action, do it anyway, and are punished by God for their disobedience. In this particular case, the punishment is actually twofold, since this people, the Banu Isra'il, is given a second chance and yet needs to be punished again. It is very likely that the Qur'an had in mind the historical situation of the Israelites and the Judeans during the destruction of the First and Second Temples in Jerusalem (586 B.C.E. and 70 C.E.) and is trying, like so many other classical compositions, to draw a moral from the story. This chapter examines how these verses were interpreted during the classical stage of Muslim exegesis, both Sunni and Shi'i, and how they are interpreted by contemporary Muslim scholars in light of the existence of the modern state of Israel and the apparent realization of the verses by its appearance. As could be expected, most commentators concentrate on the judgment that is to befall Israel. I also draw attention to the change in interpretation from the idea in classical exegesis that Banu Isra'il cannot be the Jewish people to the contemporary interpretation that it must be.

Classical Exegesis I: Sunni Historical Interpretations

The earliest Muslim commentaries—that of Muqatil b. Sulayman (d. 762), the *tafsir* ascribed to al-Hasan al-Basri (d. 728), and that of Sahl b. 'Abdallah al-Tustari (d. 896)—interpret this selection in terms of the historical experience of the Jewish people, although al-Tustari is terse to the point of difficult comprehension (al-Basri 1997, 2:78; Muqatil 1983, 2:521–23; al-Tustari n.d., 86).[5] Of these writers Muqatil is the more detailed. He states that the first captivity under Bukhtnassar "al-Majusi" (Nebuchadnezzar the Babylonian) lasted for seventy years, that the Jews were permitted to return to Pales-

5. This material has been admirably summarized by Busse (1996); the material found here has been cited solely for the purpose of introducing the passage within its exegetical context; further in-depth comment can be found in Busse.

tine by Karwas (that is, Cyrus) b. Mazdak al-Farisi, and that their reconstituted state flourished there for another 210 years. There is some confusion about the text describing the next conquest, which mentions destruction by one Antibakhus b. Sis (probably Antiochus son of Selucius) al-Rumi, who is said to be king of Nineveh. Although technically speaking there was no actual destruction of the temple, it was considered to have been desecrated during the time of Antiochus III Epiphanes, such that it had to be reconsecrated by Judah the Maccabee in 132 B.C.E. This was followed by another destruction, that of the Second Temple, by Titus b. Astanus (Titus, son of Vespasian), because of the murder of John the Baptist. All in all, 180,000 Jews are said to have been killed for these offenses. This is quite a detailed historical account and, within the limitations of a classical Muslim writer, reasonably accurate.

Such accuracy is not the usual case. Hud b. Muhkam al-Hawwari, who died around the ninth century, maintained that the first destruction was visited by Jalut al-Jazari (Goliath, who is said to have been from al-Jazira; 1 Sam. 17), and that the second one was accomplished by Bukhtnassar because of the murder of John the Baptist (of which he gives an account entirely parallel to Mark 6:14–29) (al-Hawwari 1990, 2:408–10).[6] There is no mention of the Romans or the Second Temple destruction. Al-Qushayri (d. 1072) does not mention any historical material (n.d., 4:8–9). Al-Tabari (d. 923), as usual, is the most detailed. According to al-Tabari, the first of the two corruptions was apparently the murder of the prophet Zechariah (cf. Matt. 23:35). That punishment was inflicted by the king of the Nabateans or by Sapur Dhu al-Aktaf (i.e., Shapur II, 309–79 C.E.), the king of the Persians. Tabari then includes numerous descriptions of the temple and its magnificence, followed by an account of the desecration by Antiochus III. Titus's destruction of the temple is also recounted in detail, although it is not clear how it fits into the scheme of the two destructions in the Qur'anic text (17:5, 7). Many biblical accounts of prophets (including stories about Isaiah and Daniel) and their unfriendly reception at the hands of the people of Israel appear in the commentary to these verses. Others say that Bukhtnassar was the first to punish Israel and that Titus was the second (Tabari 1954, 15:20–43).

6. Note that Ibn al-Munadi (1998, 44) states that Bukhtnassar was punishing the Banu Isra'il for their murder of John the Baptist.

Several Andalusian (Spanish Muslim) exegetes also deserve to be mentioned. Al-Qurtubi (d. 1272) relates the verses regarding the first destruction to the sufferings of the prophet Jeremiah. The second series of judgments was brought about by the murder of John the Baptist, whose killer was said to be a person by the name of Lakht (a shortened form of Antiochus?). Most important, al-Qurtubi mentions the artifacts of the Second Temple, which were transported to Rome and left in the "Church of Gold, where they are to this day" (1986, 3:110–12). He goes on to say that the Mahdi will return them to Jerusalem at the end of time. This is one of the few notices in the classical Sunni tradition in which the historical interpretation of these verses is connected with the messianic era. However, it is not surprising that it should happen in an Andalusian context; after all, when the peninsula was conquered, relics from the temple were said to have been recovered from various sites (Ibn Habib 1989, 141–43).

At least one exegete considered the prophet Muhammad's treatment of the Jews in Medina as the fulfillment of these verses. But since at all times versions of the historical First and Second Temple accounts were prevalent, it was difficult to fit that episode into the verses exactly (al-'Uqayli 1994, 2:307–11 at 308). There were, after all, only two corruption/destruction sequences to be filled; with both of them taken by the two destructions of the temple, there was no room for other later punishments of Jews to fit into this scheme. However, it is significant that already in classical times, the Banu Isra'il and the Jews were occasionally identified with each other on the strength of these verses. Later medieval Sunni exegetes usually summarize the same points of view, rarely adding anything of note.[7] However, al-Balanisi (d. 1380) adds a note of confusion when he says that King Herod murdered the prophet Jeremiah at the instigation of a woman named Jezebel, which happened together with the murder of John the Baptist (1991, 2:123–28).

Despite the overwhelming tendency of Sunni commentators to view these verses historically and not with an apocalyptic perspective, certain apoc-

---

7. See, for example, Ibn Kathir 1983, 3:24–25; al-Suyuti n.d.{a}, 4:163–66; al-Brusawi 1984, 2:332–333.

alyptic writers managed to unite the two genres. The early Iraqi apocalyptic writer Ibn al-Munadi (d. 947) uses these verses to introduce a lengthy Muslim Daniel apocalypse (Cook 2002a). He says that the first judgment was at the hands of Goliath and that the second happened during the time of King David. This latter infraction was the one punished by Bukhtnassar (Ibn al-Munadi 1998, 22–24). Curiously, Ibn al-Munadi was not confined by the apparent two periods of corruption and destruction described in the Qur'anic text. He views this sequence as an ongoing experience (although he very carefully neglects to say exactly which group is indicated here, the Banu Isra'il or the Jews) and says, "Then the end of it all was that [God] sent this tribe of Arabs [Muslims] against them, and so they are being punished until the Day of Resurrection" (Ibn al-Munadi 1998, 23). Apparently, then, although he does not say specifically that this is the case, we are to assume that he viewed the Arab Muslims as God's servants in oppressing the Jews for their corruption. In the writings of the Andalusian apocalyptist al-Dani (d. 1053), we find mention of the historical events surrounding the destruction of the Second Temple as in the commentaries above. However, in addition, we find the apocalyptic promise that the Jewish ritual objects stolen by the Romans at that time and afterward taken to Rome will be returned to Jerusalem during the messianic age by Muslims. It is perhaps significant that this theme is for the most part brought out only by Spanish apocalyptists, such as al-Dani and later al-Qurtubi, for whom this messianic theme would already be familiar (al-Dani 1995, 5:1102 no. 596; al-Qurtubi n.d., 704–5; al-Sulami 1989, 266).

Classical Exegesis II: Shi'i Apocalyptic and Supercessionist Interpretations

Shi'i traditions about the Banu Isra'il verses took a considerably different turn. Usually Shi'i writers interpret the term *Banu Isra'il* as a code word for the Prophet's family. However, there are difficulties with such an exegesis because in the verses the Banu Isra'il are clearly being punished by God for a variety of sins, and their oppressors have the sanction of the deity. It is unthinkable for this to be true of the Prophet's family. Al-Qummi (fl. ca. 919) is the earliest commentator who mentions this theme; he says that at the beginning of the verses in question, God ceases to speak of Banu Isra'il and turns to the family of Muhammad:

"You shall make mischief [corruption] in the land twice"[8]—meaning *fulan* and *fulan*[9] and their companions, and their breaking of the vow—"and you shall become very haughty"—meaning that [monstrous] claim of theirs to the caliphate. "And when the punishment for the first [making of mischief] became due"—meaning the Day [Battle] of the Camel [658]—"we sent forth against you servants of ours possessing great might"—meaning the Commander of the Faithful ['Ali] and his companions—"who went after you in your country," searching for you and killing you; "thus was our threat accomplished"—meaning that it is finished and it will be. "Then, we gave you back your turn against them"—meaning Banu Umayya over the family of Muhammad—"and aided you with wealth and children and increased you in number" [over] . . . al-Hasan and al-Husayn and the sons of 'Ali and their companions, and they killed al-Husayn b. 'Ali and took the women of the family of Muhammad captive. "If you do good, you do good to yourselves, and if you do evil, you do it for yourselves, too. And when the punishment for the second *(al-akhira)* became [*sic*] due, "the Qa'im and his companions [will return] "to afflict you," to blacken their faces "and to enter the mosque as they entered it the first time"—meaning the Messenger of God, his family, his companions, and the Commander of the Faithful and his companions— "and to utterly destroy what they conquered"—meaning he will overcome you and kill you; then he turns to the family of Muhammad and says, "It may be that your Lord will have mercy upon you"—meaning give you victory over your enemy—and then, speaking to the Banu Umayya, "But if you go back [to mischief], we shall come back"—meaning, if you return with the Su-

8. It is obvious that even though the commentator is reading the same Qur'an as we are, he is reading the word *li-tufsidunna* in the passive, as *li-tufsadunna*, so that the "Banu Isra'il" of the verse (i.e., the Prophet's family), rather than causing corruption, are being corrupted by an outside force (meaning that their rights to the caliphate are not being given to them).

9. These euphemisms indicate Abu Bakr and 'Umar, the first two caliphs, who usurped 'Ali's rightful place: see Amir-Moezzi (1994, 87–89).

fyani, we will return with the Qa'im from the family of Muhammad. (al-
Qummi 1991, 13–14)[10]

This is a very interesting example of Shiʻi allegorical interpretation. It is
clear that there is an element of supercessionism vis-~-vis the Banu Isra'il (and
it is not easy to pick out who the characters are in the many switches among
pronouns and objects of speech). This, of course, is not the only Shiʻi interpretation of this Qur'anic selection. Early commentators such as al-Tusi (d.
1067), al-Maybudi (d. 1126), and al-Tabrisi (d. 1153) never deviate from the
earlier Sunni historical interpretation.[11] Other, later Shiʻi commentators, such
as al-Bahrani (d. 1696), al-Fayd al-Kashani (d. 1660), and al-ʻArusi (d. 1701),
however, go even further than al-Qummi, saying that the "two times" of corruption mentioned in verse 4 are, first, the murders of ʻAli and al-Hasan, and,
second, the later murder of al-Husayn.

But since Shiʻi exegesis is oftentimes multilayered, there is also an apocalyptic stratum to these verses. In apocalyptic terms, they are said to refer to
the coming of the Qa'im (the messianic figure) at the end of time, and the
second appearance of al-Husayn and his seventy companions, who were all
martyred at the Battle of Karbala' in 680. The Qa'im will be one of their
party, and eventually al-Husayn will in fact bury him.[12] Later Shiʻi scholars,
such as al-Kashani and al-Mushhadi (d. 1714), mention these affinities and
make an effort to concentrate on the cyclical nature of the history of the suf-
fering messiah juxtaposed with the victorious messiah at the end of time
(Muhammad al-Mushhadi 15:472–79 at 476). However, the comparison is a
little forced because the identification of the personalities breaks down no
matter how one tries to construe these passages. One who makes a valiant ef-

10. On the Sufyani, who is the apocalyptic opponent of the Mahdi (Qa'im) at the end of the
world, see Madelung (1986b).

11. See, for example, al-Tusi 1957–65, 6:447–49; al-Maybudi 5:504–25 (Persian);
al-Tabrisi n.d., 3:397–400; and Ansari 1428–29 (2:563).

12. See al-Bahrani (1996, 3:502–3); al-Kashani (1982, 3:178–80); and al-ʻArusi (n.d.,
3:138–41), who merely summarizes previous commentators. See also al-Majlisi (1983, 51:45,
273; 52:89, 143; 53:60, 76, 82, 105, 132).

fort is al-Lahiji (d. ca. 1689), who cites part of the above tradition from al-Qummi and develops it much further (1961, 2:774–82). For Shi'is, therefore, the dominant reading was as an historical allegory equating the Banu Isra'il with the imams.

Modern Exegesis: The Return of the Jews, the State of Israel, and Apocalyptic Expectations

Many modern Muslim commentators—at least those writing after 1948—have asked rhetorically whether the state of Israel is the fulfillment of the second return of the Banu Isra'il, as provided in the Qur'anic verses. This question, of course, does not imply any love for the modern Jewish state, since many of the commentators so patently hope for the very destruction promised at the end of the verses. Let us examine the transition from Banu Isra'il as the Qur'anic people to Banu Isra'il as the modern state of Israel. The earliest modernist commentators, such as al-Qasimi (d. 1914), while aware of the relevance of the verses to the Jews who were then beginning to dominate in Palestine, did not emphasize this connection. Al-Qasimi is far more interested in what modern historians have to say about Jewish history than he is in what the Muslim commentators say (Qasimi n.d., 17:3902–7). Muhammad Hasanayn Makhluf (b. 1890), another modernist, does not even relate the verses to the historical context of the Second Temple, let alone the modern Jewish people; he maintains that the whole section should be interpreted in the light of the prophet Muhammad's relations with the Jews of Medina (Makhluf n.d., 1:450–51), which is the way that Ahmad Mustafa al-Maraghi (writing just prior to 1948) understands the verses as well (1946, 15:13–16). Even those commentators writing just before the Six Days' War of 1967 do not mention this interpretation (Hijazi 1967, 15:7), and still much later, al-Tantawi, who is associated with al-Azhar, avoids the whole issue altogether (1971, 15:38–41; also al-Jammal n.d., 3:1714–15).

One of the most decisive modern commentators is 'Abd al-Karim al-Khatib (n.d., 8:442–57), who does not shy away from the total identification of Banu Isra'il with Israel.[13] A number of his comments are worth trans-

___

13. For example, al-Khatib speaks of *kiyan bani isra'il* (the entity of the Banu Isra'il) instead of the usual *kiyan sihyawni* (Zionist entity; 442); and of *wa-qad zalla bi-aydihim ila an dakhalahu*

lating in full because of their definitive nature for the upcoming discourse. He is familiar with the range of classical Sunni interpretations of this passage, expanding upon them greatly; he adds a range of historical knowledge about the fate of the First and Second Temples. He has difficulty with the idea that the biblical Banu Isra'il could be punished by God for their behavior if they were *ahl al-kitab* (lit., people of the book; either Jews or Christians). An answer, however, is forthcoming: they were really just as bad as the idolaters and could not legitimately be called *ahl al-kitab* (Khatib n.d., 8:447). He quickly moves to the modern period, however:

> Has the promise of the end come, meaning the second time? And if it has not, when will it, and what will be the preconditions pointing it out? The answer is, first, this promise, the promise of the end, was not fulfilled at the time of the revelation of the Qur'an; it was yet in the future, either near or far. [He points out that the difference in the phrasing between the two phases is that one is past and that another is in the future.] Thus the mention of the temple as a "mosque" *(masjid)* is a clear indicator toward the second time, when the corruption of Banu Isra'il will happen, which can only take place during the Islamic period, during the time when inside Jerusalem there is a mosque for the Muslims. (Khatib n.d., 8:448–50)

In light of the discovery that the verses concerning the second corruption are part of the future of the Muslims, his conclusions are startling:

> Thus the Banu Isra'il who have come for the promise of the end and are gathered today in Palestine, and who established the present state under the decree of God (who foreordained about them that the day of their end would come)—these Banu Isra'il have come from every one of the horizons [and are] being led to their deaths, called to their predestined fate according to the word of God most high. (Khatib n.d., 8:456)

This understanding of the God-ordained nature of the state of Israel, albeit with the shadow of God's righteous judgment hanging over it, is a new

---

banu isra'il fi hadhihi al-ayyam min 1387 hijri (meaning the Six Days' War of 1967; 451); and he believes that the very name of the state was chosen because of the prophecy of this verse (455).

theme in Muslim apocalyptic interpretation of these verses. It has proved to be a very fruitful line of discourse because the wars with Israel consistently have not favored the Arab interpretation of the prophecy.

The Egyptian radical leader Sayyid Qutb (executed in Egypt in 1966) likewise felt that these verses had relevance to the Arab-Israeli conflict and that God has had to punish the Jews continually throughout history:

> For they [the Jews] returned to corruption and so God gave them into the power of the Muslims, and they [the Muslims] expelled them from the Arabian Peninsula entirely. Then they [the Jews] returned to corruption, and God gave them into the power of other servants, until during our own time he gave them into the power of Hitler. They have returned today to corruption in the form of "Israel," which has caused the Arabs, the possessors of the land, to taste woes, and God will give them [the Jews] into the power of someone who will impose upon them the worst of torments. (S. Qutb 1996, 15:16)

Muhammad Jawad Mughniyya's interpretation is closely related to that of Qutb. He says about the Jewish people:

> The intention by their corruption is not the general corruption that encompasses unbelief, lying, and taking of interest, preparation of conspiracies, and the like, even though this is their natural disposition in every age and epoch, and in every phase of their existence. "The Jews say: Allah's hand is tied; may their own hands be tied, and may they be damned for what they say. His hands are rather outstretched; he grants freely as he pleases. And what has been sent down to you from your Lord will certainly increase many of them in arrogance and unbelief. And we have cast in their midst animosity and hatred until the Day of Resurrection. Whenever they kindle a fire for war, Allah extinguishes it; and they go about spreading mischief, but Allah does not like the mischief makers" [see Qur'an 5:64]. . . . The intention is not the general corruption, but the intention is the specific [present-day] corruption, which is [their] ruling and domination, and their rule is by its very essence corruption. (Mughniyya 1981, 5:15–16)

After describing the stories of the conquest of the land of Palestine by the Israelites under the leadership of Joshua (see Josh. 6–11), Mughniyya notes that it is "not an innovation that the colonialist Zionist state should cut up the bellies of the pregnant women in Palestine, bury the young men alive, open fire on prisoners, throw napalm bombs on the helpless, and destroy homes with the families yet inside" and that in this manner history proves the point of the Qur'an (Mughniyya 1981, 5:16). His discussion on the applicability of the verses to the present time is worth quoting; responding to a discussion in an Egyptian newspaper in January 1969 about this selection of verses, Mughniyya says that there are several possible interpretations:

> The first group says the first of the two strikes against Banu Isra'il occurred at the hand of the Muslims during the days of 'Umar b. al-Khattab [d. 644], when he conquered Jerusalem and the Muslims stormed through the Palestinian lands. This group interprets the second corruption of Banu Isra'il in the light of what the fanaticism of the Zionists did during June 1967 and what they are doing now, and interprets the second strike in that God will make the Zionists helpless before the Arabs and the Muslims in the future, and thus they [the Muslims] will recover from them [the Jews] the stolen land they grabbed under the guardianship of colonialism. . . . As for the other group, it says that the two corruptions of Banu Isra'il have both passed and the two strikes passed with them before Islam, and the first strike was previous to Islam by over one thousand years, and it was at the hand of Bukhtnassar, the king of Babylon, or his father, Senacharib, who destroyed Jerusalem [*sic*] and burned the temple, and killed a huge number of Jews. (Mughniyya 1981, 5:19–20)

After this passage, Mughniyya describes Titus's destruction of the Second Temple and then elaborates on the view of the second group described above by saying that because Israel is neither a religious state, nor a political entity, nor a real state, it cannot be the intended Banu Isra'il of the verses.

> These [people] who have invaded our land with the weapons of colonialism and the wealth of the Zionists are not of the descent of Isra'il [from Jacob] the son of Isaac, and do not believe in his faith nor in the faith of Moses, but

are a new creation, a strange wonder, which has no like previous to it, because it is made of scattered fragments that have absolutely no connection and no commonality of land or languages or any principle other than the principle of working to strengthen the powers of the evil of colonialism. (Mughniyya 1981, 5:20–21)

The problem is that he wants to have it both ways:

The interpretation of his word, "Enter the Mosque as they entered it the first time" [Qur'an 17:7]—its interpretation is that God has predestined and ordained the expulsion of the Zionists from Palestine . . . for God has not and will never forgo the war against Israel, nor the war against colonialism and Zionism, even if we prayed and hoped for it from him, because the most meritorious form of worship in his eyes is the sacrifice with all of our energies and abilities against unrighteousness, tyranny, corruption, and aggression. (Mughniyya 1981, 5:21)[14]

The reader is left confused: does Mughniyya believe the modern state of Israel is that of the Banu Isra'il mentioned in the verses? It would seem that he reads in some undefined way that the end of Israel is being prophesied here, even though he has already denied the identity of the Banu Isra'il with the modern state.

The contemporary Shi'ite commentator al-Taba'taba'i exercises much more caution concerning the relevance of the verses to the modern state. He has almost entirely abandoned the traditional Shi'i interpretation but does not use the new paradigm to the full. It is clear that he is aware of this line of thinking but shies away from saying more than that "the outer *(zahir)* meaning of the verse is that for Banu Isra'il domination will return over their enemies after the promise of the first time, and they will overcome them and conquer them and free themselves from their enslavement to them and bondage to them"

---

14. Some of this confusion is also reflected by Tantawi (1987, 631–52) in his exegesis of these verses, in a section titled "The Threats and Punishments of God Against the Banu Isra'il." Although he admits the identity of Banu Isra'il and the Jews, and even though he seems to be speaking about the future, he never makes the connection between the verses and a future destruction of the state of Israel.

(al-Taba'taba'i 1972, 13:39–43 at 40; al-Husayni is more cautious; n.d., 7:329–30). Other Shi'is go further. The contemporary *Tafsir-i namumeh* says that there is "a group of Jews, the Zionists, who have taken the land," and it continues along lines already familiar to us (12:25–34 at 33). However, many Persian and Urdu writers appear to ignore entirely the connection to the modern state.[15]

The Syrian radical writer Sa'id Hawwa has taken a slightly different direction in exploring the meaning of the verses. At first he takes a purely supercessionist view, that "the corruption and injustice that happened to the Banu Isra'il have already happened to our community [the Muslims]: the *shari'a* of God is inactive, and his punishments *(hududuhu)* are inactive as well, other than a few" (Hawwa 1985, 6:3038–40 at 3038). But he is also convinced that the present times are the fulfillment of these verses. He notes that during the 1980s and 1990s threats against the state of Israel came from the direction of Iraq (especially during the Gulf War, 1990–91), which is the same direction from which the previous destructions of the Banu Isra'il came. Thus, it is likely that God will send his final judgment upon the state of Israel from that location as well (6:3040), and Hawwa is concerned that Muslims prepare themselves properly for the liberation promised in the verses.

Do the verses point out what is appropriate to do in order to liberate Jerusalem and Palestine? That the Muslims should tackle the battle courageously when they have combined worship of God with "great might" [Qur'an 17:5] . . . "If you go back [to mischief], we shall come back"—this is a threat from God to them that he will dominate over them every time they cause corruption in the land, and that they will conquer the al-Aqsa Mosque. But from this it is appropriate that we give the Muslims a definitive warning: that this conquest of the al-Aqsa Mosque will not be continual until the Hour arrives, as some have understood it from the Messiah's [Jesus'] killing of the Jews when he descends. Those whom the messiah will kill on that day are those who come with the Antichrist. The texts inform us that at that time

15. See, for example, M. 'Ali (n.d., 1:844–45); 'Ali (15:42); and Ahmad (4:299–301).

al-Aqsa Mosque will be in the hands of the Muslims and Jerusalem will be the capital of the caliphate, all of which is incompatible with the present situation. (Hawwa 1985, 6:3041; see also the leader of the Palestinian Jihad al-Islami, Fathi Shiqaqi, in R. Ahmad 1997, 1:437–39)

Hawwa concludes that the liberators will probably be the Iraqis, who are descended from the peoples chosen by God to punish the errant Israelites: "The first overlords are also the second overlords" (1985, 6:3042).[16] In other words, history is cyclical, and God always uses the same peoples to accomplish his ends in history. Other more recent writers, such as Shaykh Husayn Fadlallah, the spiritual leader of Lebanon's Hizbullah, find the ambiguous position taken by previous Shi'i writers to be frustrating. On the other hand, Fadlallah says that it leaves open the possibility that the verses do not relate to the earlier two destructions of Jerusalem but portray the Arab-Israeli conflict in its ups and downs, with the Muslims eventually to stand victorious and totally destroy Israel (Fadlallah 1986, 14, 41–42; but see Atat 1992, 43–44).

Very frequently the commentators take the word *masjid* in verse 17:7 to actually be the present-day mosque of al-Aqsa, so that even those writers who do not identify the Banu Isra'il with the modern state of Israel clearly place their exegesis within a contemporary framework (Ibn 'Asakir 1995–99, 31:403–4). Therefore, it is difficult to believe that a Muslim reading their commentary would not come to the immediate conclusion that the two peoples are identical. However, there is a great deal of anachronism in the use of the term "al-Masjid al-Aqsa," and one finds that modern writers use this in connection with the temple, apparently believing that the two are identical. Whether for political reasons (i.e., to strengthen the Muslim connection to

---

16. Hawwa rejects other possible interpretations of this verse (1985, 3042–44); he is concerned that people might identify the overlords of the Israelis with the Romans, who historically destroyed the Second Temple in 70 C.E. He says that it is impossible that God meant the Romans, because they were idol worshippers (3043), seemingly overlooking the fact that the Babylonians were also.

the area of the Temple Mount/Haram al-Sharif) or through sheer ignorance, this anachronism can lead the researcher astray.

Muslim Apocalyptic Writers and the Interpretation of Banu Isra'il

Because Israel, together with the anti-Semitic conspiracy theory, is so central to modern Muslim apocalyptic literature, it is hardly surprising to find that predictions about its end are constantly appearing and are frequently dated. These predictions are sometimes keyed to the sequence of the year 2000, since the basis for that year's apocalyptic significance is indeed the rebuilding of the temple (which Ayyub had predicted would occur in the year 2000). Because this action is so inextricably tied in with the appearance of the Antichrist and the downfall of Israel and the "Zionist world government," it is obvious that there is a connection to the previous calculations (see this book, chap. 4). However, Israel's end is most commonly dated to a number during the first decades of the twenty-first century. Many Muslim apocalyptic writers cite this verse sequence in support of their theories; only a small number of them are discussed herein. Muhammad 'Izzat 'Arif has written a great deal on the subject of apocalyptic. His *Nihayat al-Yahud* (The end of the Jews) is representative of his larger body of work, which comprises some twenty volumes on various subjects. This volume, as one could suspect from the title, is a vituperatively anti-Semitic book and employs the verses discussed above as the centerpiece of the author's thesis. According to 'Arif, the Jews will be finished off in their entirety, and he goes to great lengths to explain exactly how God has foreordained this.

'Arif divorces the passage entirely from the historical context of the destruction of the two temples in Jerusalem; he proposes that the first "corruption" happened during the time of the prophet Muhammad. Therefore, the first destruction of the Jews occurred in Khaybar, which Muhammad captured and subdued in the year 8/629 ('Arif refers to Khaybar as the "Jerusalem of the Jews"; 1996, 111). As he writes, "From this point the conspiracies proceeded and the vipers of the sons of Zion marched, since it [Khaybar] was the brain plotting the devices of the Jews against Islam then" (1996, 111). He then connects this history of conspiracy to present-day events:

These Israelis have never ascended in the land since God created the creation [of the world] like this ascension.[17] They rule the world through the political economy and the Masonic intellectual hegemony, which is their hidden face, polarizing the states, subjecting the peoples and playing with the [people's] minds—events and documents attest to this. The ascendancy of the Jews is built on the exploitation of the sunset of the rightful caliphate, and the absence of [true] Islam. But there is no escape from the return of the servants of the Merciful, who will extirpate them, destroying [with them] their gold with which they have bought the world. (M. 'Arif 1996, 202)

'Arif goes on to prove that according to the logic of the verses, the words "Our servants" must mean the Muslims and cannot mean the historical Romans or the Babylonians as previous commentators had assumed:

"And this is a promise performed," thus the repeat of their entrance a second time into the mosque as they entered it the first time—this means that they are a group of Muslims who are the servants of the Merciful. The end of the Jews at the edge of the sword will be at their hands, and this is the end: "And when the punishment for the second [making of mischief] became due, [We sent Our men again] to afflict you and to enter the mosque as they entered it the first time."[18] These are the followers of Muhammad, since the *sura* began with the traditions of his Night Journey from the Masjid al-Haram to the Masjid al-Aqsa [17:1–2] . . . attesting that the end of the Jews will be at the hands of an army of the followers of Muhammad [Muslims], and God most high spoke truly. (M. 'Arif 1996, 202–3)

From this group of verses, 'Arif builds up an entire scenario about the end-time destruction of the Jews. (Although he does not say how Jews outside of Israel will be destroyed, apparently they will be murdered together

17. Throughout this book 'Arif usually refers to "Jews" (as in the title of the book); only here does he seem to make an absolute identification between Banu Isra'il and the Jews and Israel.

18. Although 'Arif clearly has a bloodbath in mind for this future entrance into the city of Jerusalem, it should be noted that this would not be "as when they entered it the first time," when, in 636, the city was taken by the Muslims without bloodshed (as he himself notes when he describes the earlier conquest; see M. 'Arif 1996, 114–15).

with other followers of the Antichrist when his downfall occurs.) Some writers (notably Bassam Jirrar, below) have seen in these verses such a strong prophecy that they incline toward fatalism. 'Arif definitely seeks to deny this.

> Our expectation that the *sunna* of God will be fulfilled in them with annihilation should not allow us to let them ravage corruption in the earth. No, never!! But it is necessary that we have our strikes against them in battle and that we cut off a snake's head from them and that we fight the Jews in every arena, every place, every time. We should seek for types of challenges between us and them, since the Jews are destroyers, corrupters, who do not deserve a truce because they are the evil that corrupts life, all life. (M. 'Arif 1996, 152)

'Arif's book is not intellectually deep, nor does it explore all the ramifications of these verses. For this we must go to Bashir Muhammad 'Abdallah. 'Abdallah paints a powerful description of the alleged Jewish corruption of the world, and these Qur'anic verses serve as his principal, although by no means only, mainstay. One of his opening salvos, as a matter of fact, deals with another Qur'anic passage:

> "You shall find the most hostile people to the believers to be the Jews and the polytheists" [Qur'an 5:82]. The meaning of these two groups being the strongest in enmity toward the believers is that there is an eternal conflict between the community of the Messenger [Muhammad], the seal of the prophets, and the infidels, the polytheists, and the idolaters and all of the other religions and sects led by the Jews and Christians, since the Jews are fiercer in enmity even than the Christians. The Jews are the leaders of evil and the planners of destruction, enmity, and corruption in their fight against the people of truth and belief, the community of God. (B. 'Abdallah 1994, 94)

After he cites verses 17:4–8, he explains how they are to be interpreted. Prophecy is placed eternally within the descendants of Abraham; any other prophets are to be rejected as impostors from the start. 'Abdallah sees the struggle over the land of Israel-Palestine as a microcosm of the battle between good and evil, truth and falsehood. Although his argument is circular (since he relies upon the Qur'an to prove his point), and he of course has already decided that the Jews and Christians are evil by nature, he comes the closest to a mystical understanding of the Arab-Israeli conflict on its deepest metaphysical plane. In truth, two views of history are at war here, Jewish and Muslim, since his view of the Bible is entirely dictated by a Muslim vision of what that past should have been. Therefore, according to this view, the building Solomon built on the Temple Mount was indeed a mosque (according to the common reading of the text), and the kingdom that he established was a caliphate. The past should be seen through this lens, stripping the Jews of their own history in the process, which now becomes the legitimate property of the Muslims.

These views of biblical and prebiblical history, which present the Palestinians and the Jews endlessly struggling since the dawn of time over the land, are common in Palestinian literature, where the representation of Canaanites as Palestinian Arabs (and even sometimes as Muslim Arabs) is an oft-repeated refrain.[19] For the most part, however, Muslim apocalyptists have not emphasized this element very strongly, since their concern with Jerusalem and its history relates to a broader pan-Muslim plane rather than the narrower Palestinian one.

'Abdallah's points concerning the nature of the Jews' "making mischief in the land" are worth summarizing:

1. In a general sense, the corruptive nature of the Jews has persisted throughout history and is not localized to any one historical point. Ever since they abandoned monotheism and belief in God, "they became the most evil of creation, and the most full of enmity toward those who believe, and in truth this has happened numerous times," and one cannot isolate merely one occasion.

2. In some way, this particular corruption must be connected with arrogance in the land, according to the Qur'anic verses. Therefore, the verses cannot point to the period of the conflict between the prophet Muhammad and the Jews during the seventh century, since the land was not an issue then (according to 'Abdallah).

19. See, for example, A. Mustafa (1990, 47–48, 57); Baydun (1993, 8–10); Abu Ghazala (1994, 5–7); and Rababi'a (1993, 9–13). 'Arif says that the inhabitants of the area were Palestinian Arabs when the Muslims conquered it in the seventh century C.E. (1996, 115, 126). Some of these ideas have also penetrated Western scholarship; see Provan (1997).

3. The corruption leads inexorably to arrogance.

4. One of the two corruptions and its attendant punishment by God preceded the revelation of the Qur'an (17:5).

5. The first corruption was not necessarily punished by men of great might (17:5), but the second one will be; obviously, the author is angling for "the men of great might" to be a description of contemporary Muslims.

6. This judgment and God's revenge upon the Jews will occur at the end of time.

7. No one doubts that the Jews have not had an independent state in the land between the destruction of the Second Temple and 1948. Therefore the second corruption must be the contemporary state. By this analysis then the issue of the First Temple or the first corruption is moot (B. 'Abdallah 1994, 96–98).

Throughout this close analysis of the text he persists on referring to the Jewish people as "Banu Isra'il," but when he finally discusses the modern state, he then refers to them as Jews, without any explanation as to the reasons for the change.

'Abdallah goes on to detail Jewish world domination and then shows how Jews secretly control all Muslim societies as well, through Masonic orders and their control over the oil market. Finally, he comes to the crux: the proclamation of the state of Israel is God's sign that the end is near, because the judgment of the Jews must take place close to the end.

> There will be at the most one or two generations and not very much time between them. This shows clearly that the period of the present state of Israel will be very short—in relation to the life spans of states—and not only that, but that its proclamation was in a very real sense a declaration of the proximity of God's vengeance upon them by gathering them into it [the land]. (B. 'Abdallah 1994, 103)

Therefore, according to this interpretation, God has gathered the Jews into the land of Israel in order to take his righteous vengeance upon them, something that could not have happened previously because the Jews were scattered throughout the nations. Judging them at that time would have meant by necessity judging their innocent neighbors. God's strategic move, therefore, was to draw them into this land as a trap, from which they can be excised from the world.

'Abdallah has also taken the trend begun by the commentator Sa'id Hawwa and expanded upon it. Apparently forgetting that he has to deny one or the other of the two punishments in order to come to his conclusions, and he has already ignored the First Temple destruction (586 B.C.E.)—which was the one actually accomplished by the Babylonians—he says that Iraq [the Babylonians] was the direction from which the previous punishment came; therefore, this will be the case yet again:

> Israel has more than two hundred nuclear bombs on the tips of missiles pointed toward the great Arab cities. How can it be in the shadow of this nuclear fear that the present-day men of great might will be able to enter into the mosque, as they did the first time under the leadership of Nebuchadnezzar? But God is dominant in his rule, and he is in control of their cunning, which would move mountains [Qur'an 14:46], and from there will be the entrance of those rough-hearted servants against them after the great earthquake by several weeks, before those criminals can place their missiles and prepare them for launching in order to prevent the men of great might [i.e., the Muslims] from entering upon them. They will enter with the permission of God and will utterly destroy what they [the Jews] raised. This will be, in measurement of the human factors of human history, among the most amazing events of history. I mean by this the event of the destruction of the Jews in Israel and the slaughter of tens of thousands of them, maybe even hundreds of thousands, while they are at the peak of their great corruption upon the earth. (B. 'Abdallah 1994, *za*, introd.)

Many other writers, especially Egyptians, follow these two analyses of the verse sequence. For example, Muhammad 'Isa Da'ud says, "There is no fleeing from the Muslims' fighting the Jews, and there will be no return from the Muslims' conquering the world after that, because this is a command of God and a fulfillment of divine law" (1997, 34). He states further:

> Egypt will always be against Israel from the beginning to the end of Israel; there will be no agreement with them other than a temporary truce, which

Israel will utilize by tearing the Egyptian people apart morally in the dissemination of fornication, adultery, corruption, drugs, urging women to have
contempt for chastity, modesty, married life, and God's laws *(hudud allah)*.
This is to help the Israeli over-all plan without military battle, so the victories
are numerous; the victory of 1967 was a victory of treason, without battle, in
the sense of being without true confrontation under any circumstances [cf. F.
Salim 1998c, 135–37]. Egypt will continue to be the greatest cause of fear
for the Jews until their end after 2033, because the Egyptian, when he approaches the battlefield, believes that he will gain one of two good things, either meeting God and his pleasures [martyrdom] or the victory, and that the
truth will dominate in the world. But as for the Jews, they and anxiety are the
same [i.e., they are possessed by anxiety]. "Say: O you who have adopted Judaism; if you claim to be Allah's friends, apart from other people, then do
wish for death, if you are truthful" [Qur'an 62:7]. (M. Da'ud 1997, 155)[20]

Again, there does not seem to be any consciousness on the part of this
writer that he is making a substantial leap both from the traditional exegesis
and from the literal text of the passage.

Likewise, the author Hisham Kamal 'Abd al-Hamid, whose book *Halak
wa-damar Amerika al-muntazar* (The expected ruin and destruction of
America) is something of a plagiaristic spin-off of Bashir Muhammad 'Abdallah's volume, has this to say about the verses, after explaining that the Jews are
guilty of murdering the prophets and of general corruption:

There cannot be the slightest doubt that the Jews have reached this great arrogance now [referring to Qur'an 17:4] through the Zionist world government, which governs the entire world, and through the blind support that
the Zionist American government gives them in thought and in tendency,
and through the United Nations and the Security Council, which are both
under the control of the American government and the Zionist world gov-

20. M. Da'ud also said, "But I believe that before the curtain falls on the year 2000 one will
appear who will destroy the rule of Israel, and at the latest five years from then. This is what the
Torah says, what Revelation says, what the prophetic tradition relates, and what the indicators are
in the Qur'an about the arrogance of Israel and its end and destruction" (1997, n. 36).

ernment, which are managed from behind the curtain by the Antichrist and Satan, just as the book of Revelation points out. (H. 'Abd al-Hamid 1996, 64)

Far removed from this vituperative spirit, although much closer physically to the country of Israel, are the writings of the Palestinian Hamas leader Bassam Jirrar, who heads an organization called Nun li-l-Abhath wa-l-Dirasat al-Qur'aniyya in Ramallah, north of Jerusalem.[21] This organization is dedicated to the gematrical interpretation of the Qur'an in order to find computer-generated mathematical proofs for the inimitability of the Qur'an. The use of Qur'an 17:4–8 for polemical purposes was very appropriate for Hamas, and these verses are cited in some of its earliest leaflets.[22] While these early notices are naturally very warlike (dating from 1988–89), Bassam Jirrar, writing while exiled from his home in Lebanon in 1992–93, interprets the verses in a considerably different manner. He reads the Qur'an in a gematrical fashion, trying to find meaning behind a pattern employing the number 19,[23] and while exploring these verses comes to the conclusion that God has foreordained that the state of Israel will exist for a total of seventy-six years divided into four periods of nineteen years (breaking points at 1967, 1986, and 2003, with the end occurring in 2022).[24] Jirrar's interpretation is almost entirely free of classical exegesis, as he states baldly, "Reality is the true exegete of correct prophecies" (1995, 21; see also Jirrar 1994; and Dibaja 1999). His calculations have been widely publicized, and even *al-Rabita*, a conservative mis-

21. The apparently odd name of his organization comes from the *nun* (one of the mysterious letters) in front of Qur'an 68, which according to tradition was the first *sura* revealed. See Jirrar (1998).

22. See, for example, Mishal and Aharoni 1994, 216–17 (leaflet no. 8, dated Mar. 13, 1988).

23. For other Muslim responses to calculations based on the number 19 (which ultimately is based on Qur'an 67:30), see Hashimi (1981); Phillips (1988); and, overall, Ibn al-Rawandi (2000, 201–22).

24. Since Jirrar is calculating in the *hijri* calendar, the numbers do not add up properly in the Christian calendar.

sionary magazine associated with the Saudis, has featured an article using them (Abu Zayd 1997).[25]

Jirrar himself is not very polemical and is not given to offensive anti-Semitic statements. He is well acquainted with Jewish history and does not take any liberties with the historical facts (similar to A. Mustafa 1990, 68, 73). Overall, his solution to the problem of Israel supposes that the Jews will eventually convert to Islam. With this peaceable solution he precludes the type of slaughter fantasies one can become accustomed to while reading this material. However, because of his desire to interpret the verses in accordance with contemporary history, he finds himself forced to combine the destructions of the First and Second Temples. He answers the implicit question immediately:

> Why has this prophecy happened another time, after its first occurrence in the Torah, prior to the *Isra'* [the Night Journey of the Prophet] by approximately eighteen hundred years? I say: If the prophecy had been fulfilled in its entirety previous to Islam, we would find it difficult to understand the connection [between the Night Journey and the judgment on Israel]. But if the first time was fulfilled previous to Islam—which is what happened in reality—[then] the second must be fulfilled in the future of the Muslims, and the issue becomes completely understandable, especially since we are living in the time of its fulfillment. (Jirrar 1995, 25; cf. 'Ali 1996, 305–18; Faraj 1993, 145–53)

Jirrar then plays with the verses and explains what would happen if each of the possible interpretations detailed above were to be accepted. Finally, as he has already stated, he accepts that the verses relate to the modern state of Israel. However, he does not deal with the thorny issue of how Banu Isra'il suddenly became the Jewish people after so many years of exegetical denial. This is a curiously missing point, particularly because Jirrar strikes the reader as intellectually honest enough to have dealt with it forthrightly and not glossed over it. His basic desire is to return the verses to contemporary reality, and he

---

25. See also "The Termination of 'Israel': A Qur'anic Fact," www.islam.org.au/articles/20/termination.htm.

does not have any difficulty dismissing the weight of thirteen hundred years of commentary about these verses.

In recent years Jirrar's predictions have been modified somewhat by Hamas leaders. Shaykh Ahmad Yassin, the spiritual leader of Hamas, has stated on a number of occasions that the true date of the end of the state of Israel is either 2026 or 2027, basing his prediction on a modified version of Jirrar's exegesis. Most recently the daily *al-Bayan* (based in the United Arab Emirates) cited him as saying that "the *hudna* [truce] is just a tactical move. . . . Hamas still believes that Israel will disappear by 2027" (October 7, 2003). It remains to be seen whether this prediction will be modified as the date approaches.

Others have polemicized with Jirrar, such as Khalid 'Abd al-Wahid, who wrote after the year 2000 but still used gematrical calculations based upon the Qur'an, although without the focus on 17:4–8. Instead, 'Abd al-Wahid uses sura 18, *al-Kahf,* from which he derives the following calculations:

1. 2001–2 will be the end of Israel.

2. 2003–4 will be the end of the United States.

3. 2009–10 will be the time of the appearance of the Mahdi.

4. 2016–17 will be the time of the appearance of the Antichrist and the descent of Jesus to fight with him ('Abd al-Wahid 2001, 247–54 at 254).

Interestingly enough, 'Abd al-Wahid predicts the troubled end of Israel during the time period between September 23, 2001, and March 13, 2002, during the course of which the United States began its "war on terror" and Israel suffered a large number of terrorist attacks ('Abd al-Wahid 2001, 252).

Finally, there are those who deny entirely the connection between Banu Isra'il and the Jews and yet still cite the verse while speaking polemically about the Jews. Fahd Salim (see this book, chap. 10, for further material), in his volume *Kashf al-sirr al-ta'rikhi: Yahud al-yawm hum Yajuj wa-Majuj, wa-iq-taraba al-wa'd al-haqq* (Revelation of the historical secret: The Jews of today are Gog and Magog, and the promise of the truth is approaching), tries to prove that the present-day Jews are actually identical to Gog and Magog (F. Salim 1998b, 21–23). This he accomplishes by referring to a number of ethnographic studies deriving from the ahistorically based premise that most modern-day Jews are descendents of the Turkish tribe of the Khazars, who converted to Judaism in the tenth century. Among his Muslim proofs, however, is the idea that both groups are described as "causing corruption" (*fasad;* cf. Qur'an 18:94 for Gog and Magog). Although he cites 17:4, referring to the Jews, he is clearly in a quandary because the beginning of the verse speaks of "Banu Isra'il" as those who cause the corruption, and he has already denied the mutual identification of the two groups (F. Salim 1998b, 10, 116). In the end he simply does not quote the entire verse, apparently relying on his readers' ignorance of the Qur'anic text in order to prove his point.

Conclusions

Although the exegesis of these verses has always had an apocalyptic tinge, even in classical exegesis, recently the eschatological flavor has become much more pronounced and has even filtered into the political writings of non-Islamists seeking Qur'anic backing for their positions (Akram 1995). The reasons for this are the exigencies of the modern world, primarily the conflict with Israel.

In general, Muslim apocalyptic literature is overwhelmingly based on texts other than the Qur'an (see Cook 2002c, chap. 6, for a full discussion). Although a few Qur'anic verses attract the apocalyptic attention of classical exegetes, this has not been the norm; the Qur'an is rarely cited in apocalyptic traditions or even books (with the notable exception of Ibn Kathir's *al-Nihaya fi al-fitan wa-l-malahim*). It seems that modern radicals are uncomfortable with this calculated neglect of the Qur'an, although in truth there are few verses that can be pressed into service. This is in sharp contrast with the Bible, in which whole chapters and even parts of books are apocalyptic sequences. The re-creation of Israel—according to the Muslim interpretation of the above verses—provides exactly such an apocalyptic sequence, with a beginning and an end, God's intervention and judgment, and a theologically acceptable reason for the Muslims' failure to win their wars with Israel. God's decree, as set down in the Qur'an, provides Muslims with a powerful explanation for this frustrating fact, and it supplies them with the promise that God will change this negative course of events within the future.

Therefore, it is no wonder that many Arabic-language Muslim apocalyptic writers and exegetes have actually abandoned the classical exegetical traditions on this selection of verses and even overturned the previous identification of Banu Isra'il with a group other than the Jewish people. This new exegesis is in the interest of the higher goal, that of finding a satisfying prophecy in the Qur'an. With the use of these verses, we have the creation of a historical apocalyptic sequence where previously there was none. Qur'anic exegesis previous to 1967, or at the very earliest 1948, had always favored a historical reading of these verses in accordance with what was known about Jewish history of the First and Second Temple periods and the attendant temple destructions. Shi'i exegetes were divided between this historical approach detailing the history of the Jews and an allegorizing approach that interpreted the verses in a historical fashion but focused on the tortured history of the Imams rather than the plain meaning of the text. With this new tendency toward apocalyptic predictions, we can see how Shi'i writers have abandoned their own heritage in favor of the politically and socially expedient interpretation of the apocalyptic significance of the state of Israel. Few Sunnis or Shi'is deal with the question of the plain meaning of the text or address the question of how Banu Isra'il all of a sudden became Jews once again, in Israel, after such an association had been denied for so many centuries.

There is the additional question of whether this identification is in fact a positive step for Muslim apocalyptists to take, since the Qur'anic prophecy, if taken at face value, is a very clear one and may therefore lead to a complacent attitude. Only Muhammad 'Izzat 'Arif and Bassam Jirrar of all of the apocalyptists surveyed above seem to be aware of the dangers inherent in a definite prophecy concerning an enemy. Both of them understand that if one is inclined to be passive, then the prophecy encourages passivity. In no way does it encourage Muslims actually to take action against Israel, because it is apparent that when God wishes to, he will raise up an army to punish the Zionist state. To fight actively against it now is to fight against God's will, since it is obvious that no force is being presently raised up. Concerned about this passive tendency, Mustafa, in his book on the future destruction of al-Aqsa Mosque, says:

The first Muslims, when they were told that God would break the dominion of Caesar at their hands, did not sleep on their beds waiting for the fulfillment of the prophecy and the occurrence of a miracle. Instead they got to work and removed the sword from its sheath and went forth to the land of God, fighting in the name of God whoever denied him, until the dominion of Caesar had fallen and the enterprise corresponded with that which was predestined . . . but some Muslims today say, "No, the fighting of the Jews will not happen until the Antichrist appears, and probably it is all part of the tribulations the Antichrist inflicts upon the world." This fatuous statement has deceived sections of Muslim youth, and they have refused to accept any responsibility from their elders toward [the mosque of] al-Aqsa, just as many were deceived previously by an even more fatuous statement than that: the idea that the Islamic state and the caliphate will never arise until the Mahdi appears! (A. Mustafa 1990, 277)

Thus, while this prophecy gives radical Muslims hope for the indefinite future and allows them to find solace in making gematrical calculations after the fashion of Jirrar, it does not give any practical tips on how to defeat Israel, and in the short term at least it promises the survival of Israel. The conquest cycles of the Mahdi, however, give us another method by which Israel could be defeated.

SIX

THE MAHDI AND WORLD CONQUEST

The Mahdi's Appearance and Personality

Like that of the Antichrist, the Mahdi's personality, is difficult to grasp. In essence he is a projection of the powerful, dominating, messianic personality that the Muslim apocalyptist feels is most lacking in the world. This personality is the epitome of what the true Islamic ruler should be; he is the person who will set things right. His personality is subject to the endless changes happening in the world because, in the end, his personality is the product of those occurrences. Fahd Salim, when he dedicates his book *al-Sharr al-qadim* to the Mahdi, says this about him:

> To my lord *(sayyid)*, the great leader whom God will cause to appear after clear signs in the heavens and on the earth, to put out through him the fires of blinding temptations. To that one whose personality I do not know, and [even] he does not know

126

himself, and none of the people know him, but he is the pure and inspired one, who will appear pure and will not be mixed up with political calls or intellectual or sectarian creeds. To the expected divine deliverer, who will have the caliphate delivered to him while he is sitting in his home, who will not call [people] to himself, and no one will call to him. To the helper of the faith and the unifier of the Muslims against the enemies of Islam at the end of time, to the arising of my noble lord I dedicate this humble work. (F. Salim 1998c, dedication; al-Atat 1992 makes a similar dedication)

According to Salim, even the Mahdi himself is not self-aware. However, 'Abdallah gives a list of events, paraphrased here, that are due to occur before the Mahdi's revelation and immediately following it:

1. The Sufyani will appear, to reconquer Israel for the Muslims and kill many of the Jews.

2. The Mahdi will reestablish the caliphate. 'Abdallah, in his use of the Bible, relates this to the reference to the Ancient of Days (Dan. 7:9, 13, 22), who is the new caliph.

3. The Mahdi will conquer Constantinople and Rome and all of Europe as the Antichrist openly proclaims himself.

4. Jesus will come down from heaven and defeat the Antichrist (B. 'Abdallah 1994, 155–56).[1]

As 'Abdallah's list of events indicates, the Mahdi will thus be the central figure in the unfolding of the drama of the end of the world. He will put everything the way it should be and conquer most of the world for Islam.

The opening scenes of the Mahdi's appearance are dominated by the "truce and treachery" scenario of the a'maq (described in this book, chap. 2, sec. 4), where the "Byzantines" (glossed as the United States) first join with the Muslims and then betray them. It must be noted that although the Mahdi is coming to deliver the Muslim world from the evil and tyranny of the West and its Jewish overlords, and to finish off the Jews entirely, his primary enemies will be those Muslims who resist his rise to power for their own selfish ends. The Muslim community must be purged of these negative elements. There-

1. Ayyub also gives the matter some thought (1987, 307–18), but he simply cites the traditions and does not comment on them or build a scenario.

fore there will be a period of judgment and vengeance prior to the final establishment of the Muslim empire and the renewal of the caliphate. The Mahdi's
appearance is described in the following terms by Tawila, a neoconservative:

> The Mahdi is a man from the family of the Prophet, and his name is Muham-
> mad b. 'Abdallah of the progeny of Fatima, the daughter of the Messenger of
> God, through the descendants of al-Hasan—he is the Alawite, the Fatimid,
> the Hasani, whom God will straighten [make right] during a single night,
> and he [God] will give him success, cause him to understand, and guide him
> rightly and give him the expanse of the world in knowledge and the ability to
> actualize justice, after it not having been like that. He will appear when cor-
> ruption has passed all boundaries, and people will swear allegiance to him as
> the commander [of the faithful] between the *rukn* (corner) and the *maqam*
> (the standing place of Abraham) at the Ka'ba, hoping that the straightening
> of the situation will be through him, and he will accept it [the rule] reluc-
> tantly. He will not know, and they will not know, that he is the expected
> Mahdi, and previously there will be no calls for him to be Mahdi, and he will
> not even know himself, but God will choose him, and the people will choose
> him suddenly.
>
> When the swearing will have finished and he seeks to go about his task,
> an army will come from Syria to fight him. The army will arrive at the *bayda'*
> [the wasteland], where God will cause it to be swallowed up.[2] Then [those]
> both far and near will know that he is the Mahdi, and delegations will come
> to swear to him, and God will support him with people from the east who will
> aid him and establish his government and strengthen his supports. Their flags
> will be black, which is the dress of sobriety, and they will overcome the pow-
> ers of evil that surround him, and he will fill the earth with justice as it was
> filled with injustice. (Tawila 1999, 65)

One can easily see that the ideal of the Mahdi as a reluctant leader, first
chosen by God, after which the choice is apparently spontaneously confirmed
by the masses of Muslims, is a highly attractive one (as an alternative to methods of selection that involve violence and coercion). This reluctance on the

---

2. Despite the fact that today the *bayda'* is a topographical location near Medina, in the classical texts the meaning of this term is indistinct.

part of the Mahdi is presumably designed to preclude the ambitions of those who would otherwise struggle for the title. Further confirmations will follow after he has to face his enemies (who will be swallowed up in the wasteland), and when he finds supporters; by the end of a short period he will have gained the allegiance of the Muslim world. Muhammad Isa Da'ud, the radical writer who has developed the most complete Mahdi scenario, said in 1997:

> The Mahdi will return balance to the globe and honor to the servants of God. He will finish off the monstrous lies of America that the globe has grown old and that there is no further way to restore the atmosphere and clean up the pollution. The Antichrist—curses upon him—has men spreading the idea of invading the cosmos to search for another planet, which will not be like the world, in other words will not be ruled by death, destruction, and pollution. (M. Da'ud 1997, 39–40)

He predicted that the Mahdi would appear at the Hajj around the year 2000 or shortly thereafter:

> The *sahib al-amr* [a messianic title] will emerge at the festival of the Hajj in 1419 [1998–99], and in Muharram 1420 [1999–2000] he will proclaim the return of the caliphate. If the issue is delayed, it will not be beyond 1425 [2004–5], as the exact people tend toward [i.e., those people calculating the end exactly], and a personage whose *kunya* is al-Sufyani will precede him, destroying the Gulf and striking at Israel[3] . . . and in 2000 there will be the battle of the Mediterranean and in 2001 [the battle of] Armageddon,[4] which

---

3. M. Da'ud believes that Saddam Husayn was the Sufyani (1995, 129–32). See also 'Abd al-Hakim (1998a, 28–31), who states that Yasir 'Arafat was the figure known in classical sources as al-Abqa'; this idea is repeated by F. Salim (1998c, 137) and 'Abd al-Hakim (1998b, 171–72). For 'Abd al-Hakim, Saddam was the Sufyani (174), Hafiz al-Asad was the figure known as al-Ashab, and Saddam was probably the Sufyani. See F. Salim (1998a, 128–33), except that he does not know who the Sufyani is, not accepting the Saddam Husayn interpretation, saying that this figure must appear in Jordan. Salim says further that there will be a civil war among Palestinians between al-Ashab (he identifies this figure with 'Arafat) and Shaykh Ahmad Yasin, whom he identifies with another minor figure called al-Mushawwah (138–40).

4. Note how in the midst of a paragraph without any explanation he changes between *hijri* and Christian dates.

will be preceded by or be close to a great nuclear battle between France and America during the course of which Paris will be destroyed and the sea will swallow up New York. (M. Da'ud 1997, 56)

While he is in the Haram, next to the Ka'ba, Da'ud continues, an unknown person will shout out, "Here is the Mahdi!" At once people will notice his incredible God-given gifts, and *'ulama'* (the Muslim religious leadership) will come rushing to him to see whether he is really the one. Everyone who is in the city will swear allegiance to him, and the whole city will ring with cries of joy (M. Da'ud 1997, 65–67).

Road to Conquest and Empire

Not everyone in the outside world will be filled with joy at the Mahdi's appearance. Immediately following the Mahdi's proclamation, a gigantic army will descend upon Mecca to suppress the new movement, but according to the scenario, this army will be swallowed up in the wasteland by God (most of these troops will be non-Muslim, probably American). Since Egypt will be the first country to swear allegiance to the Mahdi, the following will ensue, according to Muhammad 'Isa Da'ud:

> The king of Egypt during that time will be the man who devastated the Jews in the Sinai and exiled their remnants from it and let in the forces of the [foreign] agent the UN, which removed weaponry from most of the Sinai and stayed to guard the illusions of peace or the deluded peace. . . . So the king of Egypt will proclaim the union of Egypt with the caliphal state, and the Egyptian armies in expectation of the Mahdi will combine together to aid the religion of God. (M. Da'ud 1997, 114)

The entire Arabian Peninsula will be aflame with news about the Mahdi, and many delegations will come to visit him and swear allegiance to him. In order to further confuse matters, opponents of the Mahdi will light up oil wells all over Saudi Arabia, and the blaze will be such that it fulfills another prophecy (fire will glow until one can see the castles of Bostra in Jordan; M. Da'ud 1997, 68–71; 'Abd al-Hakim 1998b, 202–4; 1998a, 47–50, 83–84).

Egypt will be the first to swear allegiance, and its ruler will be one of the few who will willingly abdicate their power and place their armies under the control of the Mahdi. Other countries will send willing followers (Afghanistan, Pakistan, and Sudan), but many will need to be coerced.

After this point, the story of the Mahdi is more or less a long series of conquests. He is always provoked and always victorious—a perfect record. Most fortunately, he has to confront each of his enemies singly; they never seem to ally against him or attack him from a direction he does not expect. The first group of countries to receive the Mahdi's attentions will be those of the Persian Gulf, where Kuwait will resist, being supported by the United States. This generous offer on the part of the Egyptian ruler to amalgamate Egypt with the state of the Mahdi, however, will conflict with American interests in the area, provoking a brief first battle, resulting in the defeat of the American troops in the Sinai desert. Initially, the Mahdi merely gains the allegiance of the Muslim countries around him, many of which fall into line fairly quickly; however, several do not. Kuwait, for example, apparently cognizant of its dependence upon American arms, chooses to resist and rely upon its powerful ally. "Quickly the Islamic armies belonging to the caliph of the Muslims will surround the land of Kuwait, and [take possession of] the keys of entering and departing [i.e., besiege it]. The foreign presence [of the American troops] will be obvious, clear to the eye, and cowardly!" (M. Da'ud 1997, 132). The Americans, unsurprisingly, will lose the battle in Kuwait this time around. This will be judgment day for those oil shaykhs:

> The tyrants of that time and the corrupters, and all of their sons around them, will try to flee with all of their special and not-so-special planes and yachts and their fast cars, with what is easy to carry and of great value.[5] But the issue is not the burning of the gasoline or tanks or gas pipes or the oil wells. This is the day of the nearer punishment, which precedes the greater punishment. "We shall surely let them taste the nearer punishment, prior to the greater punishment, that perchance they might repent" [Qur'an 32:20]. The revelation of the final accounting has come, and the divine decision has

5. This image is obviously taken from the pictures of the Kuwaitis fleeing the Iraqis in the aftermath of the Iraqi invasion of Kuwait in August 1990.

been announced: annihilation for those who loved this life and were satisfied with it and who humiliated the Muslims, and made their bodies heavy above their thrones of money and gold, of those who were pretend Muslims or hypocrites. (M. Da'ud 1997, 105; cf. 'Abd al-Hakim 1998a, 85)

The American forces protecting Kuwait and the other oil shaykhdoms will be defeated and destroyed. Then, "the entire Arabian Peninsula will be turned into a very great armed camp for Arab and Islamic armies. Even the Christian Arabs, who come with the other Arab armies, will convert to Islam when they see the divine miracles that fulfill the prophecies of Muhammad" (M. Da'ud 1997, 112–13). The Mahdi will then issue a statement to the Muslim world.

He will announce that the Islamic caliphate has been established to fulfill the truth and to destroy wrong, and that anyone who is not satisfied with it is fighting God and his Messenger, or [anyone who] wants peace with those who desire to fight us.[6] The entire Muslim world, whether its leaders submit their authority in the oath of allegiance to the caliph of the Muslims, or whether the Islamic armies are compelled to take possession of every inch [of their territory], its people will submit to the laws of God without spilling blood—if the surrender is to the will of God; if not there is nothing wrong in the legal fighting for the realization of the truth and the raising of God's word [to the highest, cf. Qur'an 9:40]. There can be no restraint in war with infidels, even if they wear the clothes of belief or of Islam. (M. Da'ud 1997, 113)

Most of the leadership of Muslim countries will resist in some way; their people, however, will respond fervently in favor of the Mahdi:

Millions carrying the black banners from Iran and from the independent Islamic states of the collapsed Soviet Union will descend to the Arabian Peninsula in bunches of cars, which no one will expect, to swear allegiance to the Mahdi personally, hand in hand [see Khalidi 1985 for this process], without

6. In other words, those who want to be at peace with the countries actively fighting the Mahdi will be considered hostile. There will be no neutrals in this war.

an intermediary. . . . Despite the fact that the people of Iran have an incorrect view of the Mahdi, this view will be straightened out, since the true Mahdi with divine signs and proofs will have appeared. There has been no one else for whom God has done what He has done for him [the Mahdi], and the swallowing up by the earth will be the great material sign after which there can be no argument [about the truth of his claims]. The people of Iran are possessed of strong belief and a living consciousness. (M. Da'ud 1997, 130; cf. H. 'Abd al-Hamid 1998, 55–57)

Among those resisting the Mahdi will be Turkey, which will call upon its allies in NATO, but the Western armies will be defeated by the Muslim armies, and once again Constantinople will be conquered (as in 1453). Muhammad 'Isa Da'ud says that Turkey will be conquered before Israel—not afterward, as some have imagined and as would be the best strategic move on the part of the Mahdi, since Israel and the other Levantine countries are left in the middle of his fledgling empire. "The Mahdi will call the ruler of Turkey to an announcement of the oath of allegiance and unconditional surrender, but among the rulers of Turkey at that time are true [Muslims] and agents, and among the [latter] are Jews of the Donmeh [sect] and Masonic agents—and the greatest Mason is the Antichrist" (M. Da'ud 1997, 133).

The fact that Constantinople has to be reconquered—because its conquest is one of the signs that the Antichrist is about to appear—is something of a problem for modern apocalyptists; some solve this difficulty by seeking to deny that the original conquest in 1453 was actually accomplished by (true) Muslims so that it can be "reconquered" at the end of the world. Others, such as Tawila in the following quotation, simply blame Kamal Ataturk, the founder of modern Turkey, who is usually characterized as a Jewish agent for turning Turkey into an atheist country under the ideological occupation of the West, from which it needs to be freed by a new conquest: "Constantinople came under the rule of the atheist Mustafa Ataturk, a creature of Zionism and imperialism, and affairs in Turkey have gone from bad to worse, until they have made a pact with the Jews and opened their land to them and fallen in love with them" (Tawila 1999, 81).

Others, such as Jamal al-Din, have concentrated on the mutual defense pact between Israel and Turkey, together with Turkey's pro-Western policies. When this is coupled with the training that the two countries' armed forces do together, and the threat of Turkey's controlling the water sources of the Euphrates and Tigris Rivers, the nature of the Jewish control of this country becomes clear. "The immediate future will reveal Turkey's true face, and then we will say that the Messenger of God said truly, 'You will conquer Constantinople.' Yes, they deserve a conquest" (Jamal al-Din 1996, 74).[7] The method of conquest is that described in the classical sources (cf. Josh. 6):

> The Messenger of God said: You have heard of a city where one side of it is on the dry land and the other on the sea [i.e., Constantinople]? They said: Yes, O Messenger of God. He said: The Hour will not arrive until seventy thousand of the Banu Ishaq [interpreted as the Muslims] will raid *(yaghzu)* it, and when they have come to it, they will camp and not fight with weapons and not fire arrows. [They will say,] "There is no god but God!" and "God is great!" and one of the sides [of the walls] will fall down. (Jamal al-Din 1996, 75)

Clearly this tradition is brought to show the future conquest of Turkey by "true Muslims."[8]

As the Mahdi's empire grows, it will attract the attention of the United States. It is surprising that the conquest of the Arabian Peninsula, Egypt, Iraq, Iran, Afghanistan, Pakistan, and the Central Asian republics, Turkey (a member of NATO), Malaysia, and Indonesia would not have caused the United States to act previously, especially since a number of these countries are closely allied with the United States, not to mention the destruction of the American garrison in Kuwait. Muhammad 'Isa Da'ud says that the stratagems of the United States will be undone by the Mahdi and thus all of Muslim Asia will be

---

7. Compare Jamal al-Din (1997, 113–14); Bayumi (1995a, 27); al-Faqir (1995, 68–69); M. 'Arif (1996, 191; 1997, 99–100); F. Salim (1998a, 120–21), although Salim says that the West will occupy Constantinople in 1999 and the final plans for this are in place (125); H. 'Abd al-Hamid (1998, 117–18); and 'Abd al-Hakim (1998b, 196; 1998a, 23–26). Ayyub (1987, 197 no. 32) has a different solution (his book preceded the Turkish-Israeli alliance): Constantinople is really Rome, and that is the city that will be conquered at that time.

8. See also Owadally (1997, 15), who shows a map of Turkey and states, "Turkey will be conquered by the Muslims without arms."

united. However, Muslim Africa is another matter. At this stage, the Mahdi's empire on the African side of the Suez Canal will include only Egypt. Interestingly enough, the Mahdi will not be greeted with open arms in the Muslim countries of North Africa. Da'ud sees them as countries totally controlled by the Zionist world conspiracy, and he regularly refers to their rulers as *hakhams* (rabbis). Mu'ammar al-Qaddafi, the ruler of Libya, will resist for a time because he is said to be a messianic candidate himself (being equated with an obscure figure called al-Barqi, from the town of al-Barqa, in the classical literature; see al-Qurtubi n.d., 694; Ibn al-Munadi 1998, 80–1). From there the Mahdi will go to the Sudan, which will surrender without a fight. Like dominoes, the whole area of East Africa down to Mozambique, even Christian Ethiopia, will in one spasm swear an oath of allegiance to the Mahdi. As this is happening, the United States will proclaim that the Mahdi is a world dictator and a tyrant, saying that he is just like Saddam Husayn or Hitler (M. Da'ud 1997, 141). However, he will not respond to these insults, choosing instead to bide his time. After conquering all the rest of North Africa, the Mahdi will then turn his attention to the central areas of the Levant: Syria, Jordan, Lebanon, and Israel, which are much more problematic and are all ruled either by hidden Jews or by open servants of the Antichrist, according to Da'ud, who details the "hidden Jewish" nature of the Hashemite dynasty of the Jordan (1995, 147–53).

Throughout the Mahdi's rise to power he will continually be confronted with opposition on the part of Western countries, which are all, according to Da'ud, ruled by Jews. For example, France will interfere with his conquest of North Africa (understandably), and we have already noted the initial battles with the Westerners in their puppet states of Kuwait and Turkey. However, essential Jewish interests are at stake as the Mahdi moves toward the area of Israel, and therefore much larger armies will appear on the scene to oppose him. It is by no means clear why Da'ud thinks the Mahdi's enemies will allow the Mahdi to deal with them piecemeal, since according to Da'ud they are aware of his power and his eventual goals.[9] It seems that were this scenario actually

9. The most likely reason for this oversight is that the battle of Armageddon must be fought in Israel, but there will be no Muslim side to fight the battle if the Muslim countries are not all united previously. Therefore, according to the logic of the apocalyptic scenario, the Mahdi is re-

to take place, Israel, and probably Turkey as well, would attack the Mahdi's rear while he was occupied in North and East Africa, and they probably would be able to conquer a substantial piece of territory before he could do anything about it. But suffice it to say that Da'ud leaves realism by the wayside. From the very beginning the Mahdi's enemies are obvious, and most Muslims (even when their governments are hostile) will want to follow him. His enemies move slowly, are naturally incompetent, and do not seem to make the defensive alliances or strategic moves necessary to win their war against him.

The process of his conquest is a broad circle, starting in the country of Jordan, where the Mahdi removes the "Jewish" royal family ("hidden Jews," according to Muhammad 'Isa Da'ud) and then goes to Syria.[10]

> The Mahdi and his armies will close in on the Syrian borders. The Syrian ruler will gather his armies on the borders and plan a simple battle—what is known as a "vicious fight," in which planes and armor will work jointly. So the Mahdi will be forced to put aside [Islamic] prohibitions because of necessity—the necessity here is not eating or drinking the forbidden [foods or drinks], but the necessity is to return to God a land called Muslim and that it be submissive to the rule of God embodied by the Mahdi through his practices.[11] This necessity is stronger than the necessity of life or death, because the entirety of existence is subject to God's laws, from the throne to the mat [i.e., from the highest to the lowest], both humanity and jinn. Therefore, just war is at the command of God, by a man empowered by God to perform the task. This means one thing: that the Mahdi is the man of the Lord at the beginning of the end of time, not a prophet and not a messenger, but a servant whose path God has straightened and whom he has made responsible for the

---

quired to leave Israel and the other Levantine countries alone and go about the torturous process of uniting all Muslims under his control previous to the occurrence of this final battle.

10. According to Muhammad 'Isa Da'ud, the late King Husayn and his family are completely Jewish and have regularly attended the Jewish synagogue in Jordan because "they suckled the milk of Jews or perhaps their original sperm was Jewish sperm" (1997, 147–48).

11. What he means by this statement is that, because Syria is a naturally Muslim country currently ruled by non-Muslims (the 'Alawites), it must be returned to Muslim control, which the Mahdi will accomplish.

matters of the Muslims, whether he [the Mahdi] wanted it or not—since he wanted to flee from [taking] the oath of allegiance. So God's subordination of this rule to him was without his personal desire, but he was obedient to the desire of God. (M. Da'ud 1997, 157; cf. Mustafa 1998, 80–86, F. Salim 1998a, 122–24)

Having clarified that matter, Muhammad 'Isa Da'ud would have the Mahdi defeat the Syrian leaders by an uprising of their own people, and he would then proceed toward Lebanon, where he would find that the Western powers threatened him.

When the Mahdi attacks Lebanon, "America will forget its sufferings and announce that it will not remain quiet if the armies of the Mahdi enter Lebanon" (M. Da'ud 1997, 167). This will be announced by the American president, who is said to be a "rabbi who hides in Christian Torah garb." However, Da'ud is puzzled as to why anyone would be afraid of the Mahdi:

Why is there this fear of Islam? The Mahdi will not force anyone to convert to Islam, because God has set down the law, "There is no compulsion in religion" [Qur'an 2:256], and his armies will not touch anybody hurtfully unless they lift up arms against them. The return of the Islamic caliphate is a return of the truth to its people, and a calling of things by their [proper] names. But blind hatred has no logic, and oppression and tyranny have no intelligence. (M. Da'ud 1997, 168)[12]

Muhammad 'Isa Da'ud attributes the negative American attitude toward Muslim unity under the Mahdi to America's desire to stand as the only power on earth. The government of the United States apparently will have some difficulty deciding how much force it wants to use against the Muslims. Since the United States already lost a flying saucer in the failed previous nuclear attack, perhaps it would be wise not to use flying saucers again? However, the policy of fighting the Muslims is really that of the Antichrist, who controls the Amer-

12. Likewise, 'Abd al-Hakim says: "This will be the Islamic Army of Salvation—this name is ours because the goal of the Islamic Army will be to save humanity in its entirety during the age of the Mahdi from error and tyranny into right and justice" (1998a, 87).

ican government entirely, and this policy is not designed to be beneficial to the Americans themselves.

Thus, as American fleets come toward the Levant, God will judge the sinful nation of America by totally destroying New York City in a nuclear conflagration, which will be one of the worst disasters to hit the country. No one will know exactly what happened, since Da'ud proposes that perhaps the French will have bombed New York—although he does not clarify what precisely will have led to this exchange, he does mention that the Americans had previously bombed Paris—or perhaps that it was one of the Antichrist's flying saucers that did the job (this book, chap. 3). From this point forward, America will be increasingly beset by disasters that will at least partially distract it from the momentous events occurring in the Middle East. "No one can fight God, no one is powerful enough to do so. God fights tyrants with what they deserve because of their arrogance, and they will be despised and humiliated" (M. Da'ud 1997, 161). After conquering Lebanon, the Mahdi will advance upon Israel from the north, which is the most unexpected way available to enter the country with a vast army. One wonders at this point whether Da'ud is acquainted with the geography of the area of southern Lebanon and northern Israel and whether he understands the practical difficulties of military advance in such a mountainous region; perhaps he simply looked at a map and decided that was the best way to go.

The Mahdi will make the following statement as he is marching toward the battle of Armageddon:

Jerusalem is truly the city of peace, God is peace, and Islam is peace. The mobilization of America and the West here is a war against the Lord of Peace, and they are the aggressors under the flag of the Jews, just as the Jews were the aggressors under their flags previously. Jerusalem is Arab Muslim, and Palestine—all of it, from the river to the sea—is Arab Muslim, and there is no place in it for any who depart from peace or from Islam, other than those who submit to those standing under the rule of Islam. They will have to pay the *jizya* if they wish peace or life under the shadow of Islam keeping their own religions, or submit to God, loving what was before it [i.e., the previous faiths], or fighting will decide between us, and God will judge in our dispute—God is the best of judges and we are marching on Palestine. (M. Da'ud 1997, 179–80; cf. H. 'Abd al-Hamid 1998, 56–58)

When the Western powers realize that the Mahdi's eventual aim is the conquest of Israel and the annihilation of all of the Jews in the country, they will send a very large force to prevent him from accomplishing this aim. The Western army will vastly outnumber that of the Muslims, but the Muslims will be totally united by their belief in God, and God will be literally on their side. Not all Western countries will participate in this adventure: Australia and New Zealand are specified as having refused, and Austria, which will be ruled by a man who is openly Muslim, likewise will not join the EU and the American army (M. Da'ud 1997, 184). The end result of this war will be a massive victory for the Muslims, who will be aided by the sea rising against the enemy Western fleet, overturning it and drowning the vast majority of the Christians. A Palestinian fighter will attack the Western fleet in the Mediterranean Sea, committing suicide with a nuclear weapon and destroying the fleet. Still, the Mahdi will be conciliatory. "The Mahdi does not wish to destroy anyone; he was forced to fight and to defend against aggression. He is a conqueror *(fatih)* and not an occupier" (M. Da'ud 1997, 200).

At every point the Westerners will try to use their superior numbers and weaponry, but God will cause the weaponry to backfire on them. Nuclear missiles will blow up as a result of accidents, and the radioactive winds will blow the wrong way afterward and end up killing the Christians, while enemy chemical weapons will be effective only against their possessors.

As for the camp of the Muslim powers, God desires that the wind be from the [direction of the] attacking army of God, and some of them will be from the defending army of God. Whoever attacks will die [i.e., the enemy], and whoever defends will be safe. The nuclear winds will blow toward wherever God desires, destroying and ruining the enemies, and then will go with the rest of the dust to whichever countries or lands God wishes. The sides of the camps of the Muslims will shake with cries of *Allahu akbar,* and his unity—yes, there is no God but him, he has the dominion, the praise, and he makes whomever he wishes to live and to die!! (M. Da'ud 1997, 222; cf. 'Abd al-Hakim 1998a, 89–95; Owadally 1997, 39–44)

In the final scene of this futile fight against God's will, the Western fleets anchored out in the Mediterranean Sea will be wiped out in their entirety as a result of the violent nuclear explosions happening in the battle of Armageddon. These explosions will be triggered by a suicide attack upon one of the ships in the center of the fleet. Part of this conflagration will occur close to Jerusalem, and much of the city will be burned, together with its Jewish population (the Muslim Arabs living there will be saved, however; M. 'Arif 1996, 126). In light of this situation, the Mahdi will announce to the people of the world that he is entering Jerusalem and that Palestine will be Muslim once more. Da'ud says: "We would not exaggerate if we say that despite their fear and apprehensiveness most of the Europeans and Americans, even most of the people of the world, will be overwhelmed with joy and happiness, thanks to the removal of this thing, the claimed state of Israel" (1995, 224). At this time most of the Jews of Israel, and indeed of the entire world, will have been killed (224–26; 85 percent of world Jewry will have perished and the "ground will be soaked with their blood"; 226), and the Mahdi will purify Jerusalem from any buildings of Jewish vintage that remain and begin to establish his own capital there—after a major nuclear war just two hours' drive away to the north. From there, he will begin to reorganize and reorder the Muslim empire, as is implicit in his titles (from the classical literature it is said that "he will fill the earth with justice as it has been filled with injustice").

After the end of the Jews or at least of those in Israel, many Westerners will fundamentally reappraise the situation, and many Europeans will convert to Islam. American and Western ambassadors will sue for peace and try to make treaties with the Mahdi, who will busy himself rebuilding the ruined city of Jerusalem in preparation for its becoming his capital. Only those Jews left scattered around the world, primarily in the United States, will have any real desire to fight after this long series of disasters that will have left the Western countries militarily indefensible. Certain European states, such as Sweden, will openly ally themselves with the Mahdi and convert to Islam in their entirety, and Da'ud says that an army of Muslim thinkers and *'ulama'* will descend upon them to lead them in their new faith. "But as for Europe and

America, there will be varied reactions, and the idea of a Satanic vengeance will begin to dominate them, with the Antichrist stoking the flames, but still the fear of the great power of the Mahdi will rule the hearts of these countries" (M. Da'ud 1997, 236).

There will be tentative peace overtures, since many of the countries—at least on the outside—will want to make peace with the Mahdi and join the "new world order" (Da'ud apparently delights in using that particular phrase for the Mahdi's state), so that the Mahdi will not try to conquer them. Many American and European youth will come to Jerusalem to see the Mahdi and breathe in his superior spirituality. It will be an age of technological wonders because one of the planks of the peace negotiations with the defeated West will be a massive technology transfer from Europe and the United States to the Mahdi's empire, and "the United States of America will never again be able to do anything against him" (which is not strictly speaking true in light of following events). None of the delegations that visit him will depart without declaring their conversion to Islam.

The Mahdi will allow the West to keep none of its technology; it is all given to the Muslims. The Westerners henceforward have to fend for themselves in a hostile world, just as they supposedly forced others to do before the beginning of the Muslim messianic empire. Now it is they who will be constantly subject to famines, plagues, and other natural disasters, in addition to violence building up inside their countries and revenge attacks from the outside world.

> America and the Western world will be wailing alone [hopelessly, without anyone listening to them], and America the humiliated will bewail its difficult portion in the time of the Mahdi, especially after New York is swallowed up and [after] the destruction of Florida and a number of other states. Its internal problems will increase dangerously, and there will be many civil tribulations. The country will sink to the ground under the pressure of poverty, famines, drugs, prostitution, floods, and earthquakes. (M. Da'ud 1997, 239–40)

All of the peoples of the world will be looking to the Mahdi as something of a pope or a Dalai Lama—the very epitome of spiritual greatness in the world, and many of the people in the West will convert to Islam, taking the oath of allegiance.

Of course, the Antichrist and his Jewish minions will not be pleased with this turn of events. In all of the countries of the West there will be mass conversions to Islam as a result of the Muslim victories, but even some of those Christians who do not convert to Islam will realize that the real responsibility for the extermination of the Jews in Israel lies with the Jews themselves, and thus they will be favorable to the new world order established by the Mahdi:

> Since the Jews deceived the Christians and caused them to fall into the trap of Jew-loving and mutual help against the common enemy [Islam], the just Christians will proclaim that this war was the greatest deception of the Jews, [intended] gradually to bring the Western Christian world, under the leadership of America, to fight the Muslims, led by the Arabs, without intelligence or sound logic, other than the hopes of the Jews to destroy the community of Islam. (M. Da'ud 1997, 226)

However, many others in the West will come to the conclusion to which the Antichrist wants them to come and will desire a war of revenge.

> The war of the Mahdi against America and the Jews of the West is a war against a case of blind fanaticism and hidden hatred toward Islam and the Muslims. The Mahdi, when he defeated and annihilated their armies, annihilated the branch of hatred and the sprout of malice. . . . The plan was [for the Antichrist] to appear after the annihilation of the Mahdi's armies at Armageddon, but the opposite happened, and that is what frightens and terrifies him [the Antichrist]. (M. Da'ud 1997, 226)

Because the Jews and their Antichrist control the Catholic Church—remembering that according to the apocalyptic scenario set down by Ayyub most of the popes have been Jewish—they will send Catholic saboteurs throughout the Mahdi's empire to destroy the society that he is in the process of building (or rebuilding). When they are caught and brought before the Mahdi, they will confess to their crimes, and a curious scene unfolds:

The Mahdi decides the matter in a speech directed to the entire world, that this dramatic satanic plot is a device of the pope, with the agreement of the Italian government to the stratagem. He declares the protection (*dhimma*) of those who have sought asylum with him [who confessed to the plot], and the protection of their loved ones in Rome. If any of those who have entered into the Mahdi's and the Greater Islamic State's protection are hurt or something happens to them, then the Islamic armies will advance by land, sea, and air, since the protection of a *dhimmi* [a non-Muslim living in the lands of Islam] is like the protection of a Muslim. The Mahdi will grant the governments of the Vatican and Rome a grace period of twenty-four hours to bring out the families and children of those who sought asylum. But the sword preceded the warning [given by the Mahdi], and they [the Italians] had already taken vengeance upon some of the families by killing them. (M. Da'ud 1997, 239)

This papal provocation will necessitate the conquest of all of Europe and its subordination to the caliphal Muslim empire. The Western world will look on helplessly, "just as the Muslims did during their days of weakness and humiliation" (M. Da'ud 1997, 239). Technically speaking, since the provocation was made only by the Vatican and the Italians, they are the only ones who should have to face the Mahdi's righteous wrath. However, the Mahdi's advisors will tell him that this would be a perfect opportunity to achieve a grander plan and conquer the entire continent. Not all of Europe will actually resist this invasion, since many will have already converted to Islam (M. Da'ud 1997, 237; cf. 'Abd al-Hakim 1998b, 212; 1998a, 95–96), especially in Scandinavia and in Austria—whose rulers will be openly Muslim, and Da'ud says that their peoples will have conducted a complete purge of all of the Jews in these lands after the battle of Armageddon. At the opening of the invasion, the Mahdi makes the following statement: "Islam is the final word of God, and the final word of God to his creatures is the Qur'an, and his final word should be generally [accepted] throughout the globe. War is the final solution, but he will send ambassadors to all the non-Muslim countries of Europe [to persuade them to accept Islam peacefully]" (M. Da'ud 1997, 241).

Most will initially refuse this offer. However, as the Mahdi's army descends through Europe from (Muslim) Scandinavia, many will reconsider. In Germany, according to Da'ud, there will be many who will have an intense desire to convert to Islam. Russia will convert completely, along with all of Eastern Europe. However, both Great Britain and France will fight the Mahdi, as will Serbia and Greece. Da'ud is realistic enough in that; both of these latter countries would know that their traditional anti-Muslim stance would not win them any real place in the Mahdi's empire and that it would be better for them to go down fighting. "The Mahdi's power with all of its trappings will dazzle the West, even before they comprehend the particulars of the orthodox law of God [i.e., before they convert to Islam], just as previously the Arabs would gaze dazzled toward the West. The matter will have turned around entirely, and the West will be dazzled by the Muslims and their leadership, and at their head, the Mahdi" (M. Da'ud 1997, 272).

Once again, just as with the battle of Armageddon, the Mahdi will favor an attack from the north, not the expected direction. Sweeping down from his allied states in Scandinavia—who will support him actively as well—he will advance through Germany toward France. He will then order the two countries of France and Great Britain to surrender to him within twenty-four hours or they will be bombarded with nuclear weapons. Both will refuse, and so the Mahdi will order the nuclear holocaust of London, Paris, and Washington, D.C. (the Americans would not stop helping their allies in Europe, and had to be taught a lesson).

> The twenty-four hours have passed, and only minutes remain before the terrifying explosions will reverberate in the three capitals, which have turned to ruins: Paris, with its iron Eiffel Tower turned to a heap of destruction and ruin everywhere. London, the capital of whoredom and hypocrisy vis-à-vis America, has been wiped out. The miserable and antiquated crown [of England] will fall in the mud and ruin that swallow the city. Washington, the city of the White House, where the policies of Satan [are laid out], and the cursed Congress, whose decisions are led by the devil and are carried out by the Antichrist, will be swallowed by fires and will become past tense. (M. Da'ud 1997, 273)[13]

13. According to M. Da'ud (1997, 56) the United States had already destroyed Paris (just previous to the French nuclear attack on New York). It is thus quite remarkable that the Eiffel Tower would have survived to be destroyed in this second nuclear attack.

In the end the two reluctant countries will take the oath of allegiance and become fully Muslim. The Mahdi then will continue on with his advance. Most other southern European countries will accept Islam without a fight and will take the oath of allegiance. Finally, the Mahdi will conquer Rome and destroy the Catholic Church utterly (M. Da'ud 1997, 276; Tawila 1999, 84–86; 'Abd al-Hakim 1998b, 210–11).[14] He then can prepare to build the messianic kingdom. There can be no question but that Da'ud's messianic scenario is supposed to be a payback time for the West, in which it gets a dose of its own medicine.

This interpretation of Muslim, Christian, Gnostic, and pseudo-scientific materials, combined with an immense hatred of the West and envy of its power, forms a complete apocalypse in the sense of future history. While it can be criticized on many grounds, not the least of which is plausibility—and one should not forget its weak connection to the original Muslim sources as well—it still has the power to give hope to a group of people otherwise lacking in hope. Muslims do not see much hope in the modern world: their culture and values are irrelevant, their opinions and positions are ignored or ridiculed, and many of their best and most promising people either emigrate to the West or take on its culture wholesale. This fantasy provides a hopeful future in which the world will finally be righted. Islam will be generally accepted, rule will once again be in the hands of the rightful caliph, and the technology that should have been Muslim will be returned to the reconstituted Muslim empire. The lands of Islam will be peaceful, and people will convert to the true faith on a consistent basis. The hated powerhouses of the West, led by the United States, will be humiliated and recognized to be false and anti-God, and the Jews, the most malevolent of all the enemies of Islam, will be wiped out entirely or converted to Islam.

The Messianic Age

It is unfortunate that Arabic-language Muslim apocalyptists lavish so little time elaborating the messianic age—the last part of humanity's history. After

14. See also the popular preaching of Yusuf al-Qaradawi, Muhammad b. 'Abd al-Rahman al-'Arifi, and others on this conquest of Rome and the destruction of the Vatican at Special Dispatch no. 447 (Dec. 6, 2002), memri.org.

so much negative comment about what is wrong with the world today, it would be pleasant to conclude on a positive note, even if this can only be accomplished by the extermination of the Jewish people and the emasculation of the Western world. However, the visions we are granted of the messianic world are curiously undefined and principally taken from the West itself; Tawila, for example, cites Isaiah 11:1–6 (1999, 242–43). It is rather ironic that in many ways the apocalyptic writers' envy of the West is essentially a desire to have what the latter has, not to replace it with a fundamentally different order. As noted, at the end of the battle of Armageddon the Mahdi orders the West to be stripped of its technology and for all of it to be shipped wholesale to his empire; bizarrely he does not seem to care much about the technological knowledge retained by Western people—the knowledge that would enable them to rebuild everything even if all of the products were forcibly removed. This massive infusion of technology enables the Mahdi to create a world of wonders, at least for that portion of the world under his control.

> European and American youth will come, immigrating to see the Mahdi, dazzled by his personality, and will come to Jerusalem to meet him, and the meetings will be safe havens in which there will be discussions at a high level of thought. Thought is the most important weapon, and the thinker is the greatest doctor for the spirit and the engineer for the mind, and the artist for the personality and its reformation. Not a single one of the delegations will leave these discussions without converting to Islam. . . . The United States of America will never be able to do anything because the Mahdi will rule the entire world, and the technology is the main thing.[15] Most of the miracles that he will accomplish will not be divine miracles but very advanced scientific miracles that stupefy the people and make them happy at the same time. The youth will work with him to make the world into a vision that he sees— those sciences of Islam that make the people happy and not make them frightened as happened at Hiroshima and Nagasaki. (M. Da'ud 1997, 237; see also M. Da'ud 1997, 41)

15. This is not strictly true, since even in M. Da'ud's own fantasy the United States is the leader of the Antichrist's final invasion of the Mahdi's empire, and thus is indeed "able to do something."

Da'ud's vision of the messianic future is that of a benevolent dictatorship. His world is one of technological wonders, food for the poor, full employment for everyone, ecological and environmental sensitivity, and the spread of Islam.[16] There is no democracy, and the Mahdi rules the entire world—although he does not appear to have conquered it all; perhaps certain parts are ruled through indirect control—as an absolute, albeit benevolent, dictator. Thus, in essence the Mahdi has achieved the one-world government that supposedly the Jews and their Antichrist aspired to previously. The only real difference is that the Muslims are ruling it. This is an entirely Western-based fantasy, and there is no real Muslim part to it at all, with the single exception of domination and rule on their part. No classical Muslim society has ever looked like the Mahdi's empire nor has one ever even aspired to look like it.

> There is no doubt but that the Mahdi will start from the principle "Man is brother to man," [17] and his battle will be principally a battle of consciousness and enlightenment. But [this will be] with God's will and in accordance with God's will, and by attacking the principles of ignorance that are foundational for the custodians of the politically autocratic centers [of the downfallen West], the repressive economic domination and intellectual stagnation, and the appearance of secret plans and discussion about assumed [positions].[18]

16. In reality, of course, the assimilation of modern technology has been difficult for Muslim society; see Khader (1982); such a massive transfer would have immeasurably greater consequences.

17. "Man is brother to man" was a principle of the Enlightenment; the comparable Islamic principle is found in Qur'an 49:10, "Surely, the *believers* are brothers" [emphasis mine]. For Muslim attitudes toward the subject, see al-Shaybani (1976) and Shaqiq, who cites the above verse (1990, 110) and says that it is the foundation of Muslim society. See also Shaqiq 1992, 123–39; al-Muhadhdhabi (1993); Mufti and al-Wakil (1992, 94–96); Salih (1988, 87–102); al-Zayn (1994); and Bahlul (1993).

18. One would assume that here Da'ud is speaking of the "conspiracies of the Jews" (or of the West). Thus the end to conspiratorial thinking is also a messianic desire, as Muhammad 'Amaluhu says in his conclusion: "O youth! In our battle with Zionism, our guiding principle is the good of humanity, and the propagation of the flag of just peace, without aggression, without hatred, without killing, destruction, and without *The Protocols* being composed on the sly to finish off the humanity of a person in his morals, religion, values, and principles" (1992, 179).

The conquests of the Mahdi do not mean the destruction of the dominating conventions, but simply returning those conventions to their virtue or returning virtue to the conventions, just as the conquests of the Mahdi do not necessarily mean the destruction of the cultural heritage totally, to the extent that it displays the true heritage and discovery of wisdom and its dissemination, and the propagation of the pure Islamic belief to instruct souls and return the people to God, elevating them and opening them to the gifts and the intellectual senses in order to [come to an] understanding of God. (M. Da'ud 1997, 287)

In other words, culture will be preserved in the Mahdi's empire to the extent that it serves the purpose of disseminating Islam and not for its own sake. This is a Marxist, or even fascist, ideal and one that is hardly likely to attract large numbers of non-Muslims.[19]

There is a complete and total divorce between this Mahdi fantasy and the classical sources, with one major exception.[20] In the Mahdi's empire there is no real freedom of religion—only the traditional Muslim conception of what constitutes this freedom. That is, Islam has the right to grow, and other faiths have the right to shrink and eventually die out. "He will not allow anyone to stop the propagation of Islam, and war will be for anyone who attempts to put out the light of this great faith or tries to stop it" (M. Da'ud 1997, 284–85). In a certain way it all sounds very communistic, since there is no system by which all of these things will happen, it is just assumed that they will happen. People will want them to happen, so they will. The Mahdi wants everybody to

19. Some writers do embrace the Marxist theme thinly veiled in Islamic terminology. For example, Sharfi starts by stating: "A specter is haunting the globe, the specter of Islam" (1985).

20. The question of Muhammad 'Isa Da'ud's sources is one that has been covered elsewhere; see Cook (2002b). But it is striking that he cites no sources of any kind for this element of his fantasy—a few Qur'anic verses illustrate what he wants to say, but there are no Muslim sources of any kind here. The most probable reason for this fact is that the Muslim vision of the messianic age did not involve a millennial kingdom of the type described in Isaiah 11:1–6 but was a fighting fantasy of continuous war against the infidel. Therefore, there is simply nothing upon which Da'ud can base his ideas, and he does not even attempt to bring out his dubious "new manuscripts." Perhaps even he realizes that this messianic future cannot be attached to classical Muslim sources, even questionable ones.

be technologically advanced, so they will be. Nobody should be poor or miserable, so they will not be. This is strikingly similar to the Qur'anic fiat of creation: "Indeed, when We want a thing to be, We just say to it: Be, and it comes to be" (16:40). There are no practical insights about how humanity will change, nor how exactly Islam could do a better job at ruling than the West has done. It is simply that it is Islam's place to rule, not the West's place, and so once this rule is returned to its rightful possessors, then human civilization will be rectified and the messianic age will be achieved.

Da'ud does not assume there will be any opposition to Islam after the Mahdi's conquests, another Marxist-like fallacy. He appears to assume that other countries and other faiths will want to join in this vision, without giving credence to the reality of their beliefs or feelings. Nor does he take into account the power of resentment and vengeance, even after a victory in battle. The Mahdi, during the course of his path to power, has murdered millions of people (even if this was accomplished with benevolent and good intentions) and even exterminated whole nations—since in this messianic vision, Da'ud recognizes that this step would be necessary. One must ask honestly: would that legacy of murder and the accompanying hatred really just disappear because the Mahdi is a marvelous ruler and the most tolerant and scientifically minded potentate that Islam has ever produced?

In the scenarios of Da'ud and the other Arabic-language Muslim apocalyptic writers, the United States is a distant place. The United States is attacked on a regular basis, punished for its sins, and yet still seems to have an inexhaustible supply of soldiers to send all over the world. This objectification of the United States in contemporary apocalyptic literature needs to be explored in further depth.

SEVEN

PROPHECIES OF AMERICA, THE SECOND 'AD, AND ITS DOWNFALL

The Importance of America in Muslim Apocalyptic Literature

The dominance of the United States in the modern world and the pervasiveness of its influence in the Middle East have given it a parallel prominence in Muslim apocalyptic writing. This chapter, therefore, examines how popular Muslim apocalyptic writers have approached what they see as the problem of the United States, what prophecies are at their disposal for this purpose, and how and to what degree U.S. power and domination in the world have provoked a reinterpretation of verses in the Qur'an. An example of such reinterpretation can be found in the work of Hisham Kamal 'Abd al-Hamid, who wrote an entire book anticipating the downfall of the United States. In his book, entitled *Halak wa-damar Amrika al-muntazar* (The expected perishing and ruin of America), he asks, "Why did God not mention America

in the Qur'an, and the Prophet not mention it in the prophetic hadith?" He
then goes on to answer:

> This is a question that every Muslim has asked himself, and has been con-
> fused in finding the answer to it. . . . God pointed to America in the Qur'an
> when he told us of the first 'Ad [Qur'an 53:50], and the Prophet pointed to
> it in the telling of tribulations and apocalyptic wars and the signs of the Hour,
> just as the Torah and the Gospels bring a separate mention of America, and
> its characteristics and actions, and the time of its appearance and its end on
> the tongues of the prophets of Banu Isra'il. (H. 'Abd al-Hamid 1997b, 5)

Negative feelings about the United States are not lacking in modern Muslim apocalyptic literature. Sa'id Ayyub, one of the most prominent of Muslim
apocalyptic writers, writes: "[The United States] is now the principal center
for the Jews. History bears witness that the United States of America, which
has been occupied in all areas by the beliefs of the Antichrist, is the chief
enemy of Islam in every place" (1987, 64). Earlier chapters of this book have
cited many similar passages from other writers.

These prominent apocalyptic writers show the importance they attach to
the United States and the concern Muslims have felt about the apparent lack
of material about the United States in the traditional hadith literature. Essentially, the Muslim traditions touch upon every area of the world known during
classical times. Extensive references to Europe reflect Europeans' longstand-
ing importance as the Muslims' greatest and most dangerous enemy, even as
long ago as thirteen hundred years. These references can be pressed into service whenever a conflict arises with that region of the world. The Muslim traditions also place within the apocalyptic world many other nations and peoples;
Turks, Indians, and various African peoples, among others, are mentioned either as destructive agents or as objects of conquest. In the same manner as in
modern Christian Catholic or evangelical apocalyptic scenarios, reinterpretation of names is common among Muslim apocalyptists. For example, since
Gog and Magog are given prominence in Muslim apocalyptic literature but
are nowhere to be found in the modern world, these names are reinterpreted
to mean either Russia (because of its repeated attacks on Muslims in
Afghanistan and Chechnya) or perhaps China, which also has an apparently

inexhaustible supply of people (H. 'Abd al-Hamid 1997b, 120–31; chapter 10 of this book).

Naturally, the United States does not have an apparent place in the classical schemes. This would not ordinarily present a problem if it were not for the fact that the United States so clearly affects the Muslim world that a vast range of issues cannot be satisfactorily explained without reference to it. For example, one of the most pressing issues for the Muslim apocalyptist is how to deal with the state of Israel and to answer the question of how it will be overcome and defeated close to the end of the world. This is not something that can be pushed to the back burner, since it is of major concern for vast numbers of Muslims, who look to the future to bring them some hope concerning this issue.

We have already noted that the apocalyptists' view holds that there is a worldwide conspiracy of Zionism, which controls a large part if not the whole of the Western world, and through this the rest of the world as well.

> America before its independence was a peaceful, neutral state, but after its independence Zionists dominated it, and since its independence it has become a completely Zionist state, especially after the Jews emigrated to it and the number of Jews in it became more than that in the state of Israel. The principal concern of America became the tending of the interests of the Zionists, and the state of Israel in Palestine became an American state. For this reason the end of the Jews is interconnected with the end of America, and the end of America is interconnected with the end of the Jews. (H. 'Abd al-Hamid 1997a, 64)

This theory of a Zionist conspiracy and the United States' involvement in it has fostered a range of bizarre corollaries disseminated by Muslim apocalyptic writers. One popular Palestinian author, Fa'iq Muhammad Da'ud, asserts, for example, that support for Israel is mandated in the U.S. Constitution and that it is legally impossible for a U.S. president to be elected without swearing to abide by Israel's dictates (1999, 28–29).

The overwhelming power held by the Western world over the destinies of both the larger Muslim world and the lesser Arab world within it gives impact to such beliefs. So, too, do the more subtle effects of Western political and economic power, particularly the intrusion of Western (and most especially American) cultural norms into Muslim society. It is for these reasons that Muslim apocalyptists cannot simply ignore the United States in their predictions but must somehow explain its position at the end of times. As the apocalyptic writers ask: "How could it be that God did not relate in his Qur'an, or the Prophet in his hadith, about the tribulation of the age and the greatest power known to the history of humanity, at the same time as God says in the Qur'an: 'We have not left anything out of the Book' [Qur'an 6:38]?" (H. 'Abd al-Hamid 1997a, 96). To get around this problem, the apocalyptists turn to the various peoples that are mentioned in the holy book and then use them to draw parallels with the society of the United States. Azad and Amina, for example, have put forward a gematrical interpretation of the Qur'an based on the number 19 to demonstrate that the end of American power is near (2001).

"The Second 'Ad"

The people of 'Ad are mentioned in the Qur'an twenty-four times.[1] Unfortunately, the vast majority of these references do not convey much information to a reader not already somewhat familiar with them. The Qur'an's style makes certain demands on its audience, one of which is familiarity with a pool of common knowledge often not shared by later exegetes.[2] Some of the relevant verses dealing with 'Ad are the following:

> And remember the brother of 'Ad [i.e., the prophet Hud], when he warned his people upon the sand dunes, warners having gone before him and after him, saying, "Do not worship anyone but Allah. I fear for you the punishment of a great day." (21)

---

1. These are Qur'an 7:65, 74, 9:70, 11:50, 59–60, 14:9, 22:42, 25:38, 26:123, 29:38, 38:12, 40:31, 41:13, 15, 46:21, 50:13, 51:41, 53:50, 54:18, 69:4, 6, 89:6; and see material about *Iram dhat al-'imad* in 89:7.

2. Most of the relevant information is summarized in *Encyclopaedia of Islam,* s.v. "'Ad" (F. Buhl), and "Iram dhat al-'Imad" (W. M. Watt); see also 'Abd al-Mun'im (1994).

They said: "Did you come to divert us from our deities? Bring us then what you are promising us if you are truthful." (22)

He said: "Knowledge is only with Allah and I am conveying to you the message I was charged with, but I see that you are an ignorant people." (23)

Then, when they saw it as a cloudburst coming toward their valley, they said: "This is a cloudburst raining upon us." No, it is what you sought to hasten, a wind wherein is a painful punishment. (24)

Destroying everything at the behest of its Lord. Then when they woke up, there was nothing to be seen except their dwellings. Thus do we reward the criminal people. (25)

We had established them firmly in a manner We did not establish you, and We gave them hearing, eyesight and hearts; but their hearing, eyesight, and hearts availed them nothing, as they repudiated the signs of Allah; and so they have been overwhelmed by that which they used to mock. (26) (Qur'an 46:21–26)

According to the early commentary of Muqatil b. Sulayman (d. 762), the 'Ad were a nomadic people.[3] They are said to have lived in Dakk al-Ramal in the Yemen near Hadramawt. While the commentaries are quite indistinct about the time frame of their existence, apparently it was shortly after the Flood, since both Noah and Idris [Enoch] are said to have been active among them; in fact, they are described as being Noah's in-laws. Their prophet, however, was Hud, a nonbiblical figure still revered in the area of Hadramawt (Serjeant 1954). He ministered to the people of 'Ad in a fashion reminiscent of Elijah, speaking to them about God's judgment upon their sins, bringing natural disasters for a period of time and finally a devastating flood of rain and a wind lasting seven days that completely destroyed the area.

The location most closely associated with 'Ad is the mysterious Iram dhat al-'imad (Iram of the columns; Qur'an 89:7). Early commentators explain the "columns" or poles mentioned in the name as simply those used by the tribe of 'Ad as tracking devices in the shifting sands of the desert—something akin to the snow poles common in areas known for deep snow. Gradually, from the time of al-Tabari (d. 923) onward, the mysterious Iram dhat al-'imad became

---

3. See also Muqatil 1983, 3:273–74 (on Qur'an 26:126–29), 4:23 (on Qur'an 46:21–26), 687–88 (on Qur'an 89:7–8).

ever more prominent in the imagination of the commentators. Great cities such as Damascus and Alexandria vied for the name, although most serious commentators dismissed these claims (Tabari 1954, 5:664; 6:674–78; 7:620–24; and see also Ibn 'Asakir 1995, 1:216–18; Ibn Hammad 1993, 124, 171–72; and al-Majlisi 1983, 52:274). By the period of al-Khazin al-Baghdadi (d. 1324), the commentators were in possession of detailed "knowledge" about the city, including descriptions of its large and impressive buildings (al-Baghdadi 1995, 5:445–47; 6:419–21; see also al-Dimashqi 1998, 15:59–63, 404–13; 20:315–20; al-Brusawi 1984, 4:67–69; and the Shi'i al-Bahrani 1996, 5:46–47).

Some commentators then began to wonder whether there was not some connection between these extensive building projects and the judgment inflicted on the unfortunate city. The Shi'i commentator al-Fayd al-Kashani (d. 1679) cites the following tradition to explain the punishment: "Every building being built is a curse *(wibal)* upon its owner *(sahib)* on the Day of Resurrection, other than that which is strictly necessary" (al-Kashani 1982, 4:45; cf. al-Majlisi 1983, 76:3, 13; and Wensinck, s.v. *"wibal"*). Traditions of this sort, condemning the building of fancy mosques or other places of worship, belong to a leveling strain in apocalyptic literature that has its roots in early Muslim expectations of the imminence of the Day of Resurrection. Since the final hour is close at hand, there is no point in investing one's time and energy in the works of this world; one's actions should instead be focused on the next (Kister 1962). In his commentary on the destruction of 'Ad, for example, Ibn Kathir (d. 1372) cites a *ma'wiza* (hortatory sermon) put into the mouth of Abu al-Darda' (an early companion of the prophet Muhammad):

When he saw the new buildings that the Muslims had built in the Ghuta (the valley of Damascus) and the trees that they had planted, he rose in the mosque and said: "O people of Damascus! Are you not ashamed, are you not ashamed that you are collecting wealth you cannot eat, building what you cannot dwell in, hoping for what you will never attain. Before you there were ages [of civilizations] that collected and contained [water and so forth], built and were certain [about the future], hoped and lengthened [their time on earth], and their hopes became illusions, their collection was destroyed, their dwellings graves. 'Ad ruled what was between 'Aden and 'Uman with horses and riders, and who [today] would buy the inheritance of 'Ad from me for two dirhams?" (Ibn Kathir 1983, 3:294; see also 4:142–44, 443–45; for a considerably different version, see Ibn 'Asakir 1995–99, 33:400)

The apocalyptic sense of these verses is still quite strong; even in classical times they were associated with the idea of judgment on a (supposedly) advanced society that sought to go beyond the limits placed upon it by God. This idea is strikingly similar to that of the biblical judgment of the people of the Tower of Babel (Gen. 11) and of other stories in the Qur'an featuring God's judgment on a civilization. In this regard, the story of 'Ad is one that is ripe for use by modern apocalyptic writers.

Apocalyptic interpretations are currently coming into vogue as a secondary sort of Qur'anic commentary. Bashir Muhammad 'Abdallah, the writer who popularized the interpretation of 'Ad as America is aware that this exegesis is new. "What is the certain foundation for our saying that the United States is the most deserved land for the punishment of God encapsulated in the Earthquake of the Hour and the Western swallowing up [in the earth]?" (B. 'Abdallah 1994, 193). He begins with a review of the Qur'anic view of warning and punishment by God after being warned by prophets (mostly biblical, albeit as viewed through the Qur'anic interpretation). Moses' mission to Pharaoh is a good example; Pharaoh was arrogant and refused to listen to God's message to him, and so he was punished.

In his analysis, Bashir 'Abdallah asserts that these qualities are true of the United States. He then gives reasons for God's judgment, paraphrased below:

1. The polytheists and idolaters have arrived at a deep level of essential error by doubting in the existence of God. These atheistic groups have publicly confronted the proclamation of belief [Islam] upon which the messengers and their followers stand, saying: "We disbelieve in what you have been sent forth with, and we are certainly in disturbing doubt regarding what you are calling us to" [Qur'an 14:9]. This doubt they manifest publicly is doubt in the existence of God. This is the furthest that a man can go in the stages of essential error.

2. Denial of [God's] messages and calling the messengers liars, which is necessary because of their despicable anti-God beliefs. These atheistic beliefs were propagated by Jewish Zionist groups as part of the disgusting Jewish

plan in every area—what they call "freedom of thought" and "belief in secularism," and what is known as relativism in contemporary modern philosophy.

3. Harming messengers and their followers—the scholars, missionaries,
and fighters *(mujahidin)* in the path of God most high—and expelling, tor-
turing, and killing them in an attempt to wipe them off the face of the earth.

4. The final stage is exemplified by terrifying plans to wipe all the believers
off the face of the earth and to make the world entirely empty of them. This
will be accomplished by [forcing upon the believers] the choice between two
possibilities: Either they enter the infidel community—the atheism and the life
of lust in accordance with the manner of the good life as the infidels and atheists practice it—or [they will] be expelled, killed, and annihilated.

5. When the situation reaches this level, then God comes to the aid of the
oppressed believers by the destruction of the oppressors, with a chastisement
of complete uprooting [from the earth], or a partial chastisement to destroy
their power and their authority as judgment against their attacks [upon the
believers] and their arrogance upon the earth [cf. Qur'an 28:83].

6. The establishment of the Islamic caliphate will follow this, together
with the believers' inheritance of the earth [Qur'an 7:137–38]. Then God's
word will be the highest [Qur'an 9:40] (B. 'Abdallah 1994, 195–96; cf. 'Abd
al-Hakim 1999, 71–73; H. 'Abd al-Hamid 1997a, 200).

The choice for the apocalyptic Muslim believer is clear: submit to the evil
atheistic world order or be killed. Bashir 'Abdallah feels that the annihilation
is taking place this very minute under the guise of what "they" (his euphemism for the larger world conspiracy) call "ethnic cleansing" and the "war
against terrorism." In his view, God's judgment must inevitably fall on the
United States because of its excessive immorality, economic and fiscal crimes,
and political tyranny. Moreover, the entire idea of "freedom" offends 'Abdallah: "The proclaimed and practiced freedom in America especially and in the
Western world in general is not freedom from slavery of a man to a man . . .
but it is freedom from the worship a human being owes the Lord of Worlds"
(B. 'Abdallah 1994, 214). For this reason, freedom in the American sense
cannot be accepted; indeed, it must be fought against at all costs, because it is
essentially against the nature of man as God created him. (For Muslims, man
is not fallen by nature but is a Muslim by nature; it is a man's environment that
changes him for the worse). In a later passage 'Abdallah expands on this idea,

contending that the entire new world order is an attempt to nullify the *sunna* of God (B. ʿAbdallah 1994, 230).

The United States' alleged economic crimes are equally serious. Colonialism stole the wealth of the world and took it back to Europe and the United States. Jewish banks control and manipulate the world's finances in such a way as to ensure that no one but they themselves have any money, and they place impossible demands upon those countries in need of loans from the supposedly Jewish International Monetary Fund. It goes without saying that this usurious banking system is against the principles of Islam to begin with (al-Faqir 1995, 34–35). But "probably the greatest theft, swindle, and fraud in the history of humanity is what the Zionists have done secretly in the United States of America—the swindling of the Arab Muslim oil wealth—because they [the Zionists] determine the price and the amount of oil produced in such a way as to return the greatest profit and benefit to the Jews and the least little bit to the possessors of the oil" (B. ʿAbdallah 1994, 202; cf. al-Faqir 1995, 39).

American political crimes are literally innumerable. In this Bashir ʿAbdallah compares the democratic world order to that of Thamud mentioned in the Qur'an (Qur'an 7:73–79; 11:61–68), preparatory to his exposition of America as the second ʿAd. Thamud was a group (anachronistically called "democratic" by ʿAbdallah) warned by God, which stands in contrast to the warning given to Pharaoh (Qur'an 28:4–6) alone as a single dictator. Thus, ʿAbdallah compares two types of systems: the dictatorial and the democratic, and shows how God judges each one. Whereas Egyptians as a whole are not said to be responsible for Pharaoh's evil, in the case of both ʿAd and Thamud the entire group participated in the rejection of God's message. Thus, when Pharaoh was judged, he alone received the punishment. ʿAbdallah sees the Western democracies as more culpable than Third World dictatorships, since the former have the capacity to change and repent whereas the latter do not, and their sins are the responsibility of one man (or a small group) alone (B. ʿAbdallah 1994, 205–10). What are the factors that enable a nation to be judged by being totally uprooted?

1. Freedom of choice (such as in a democracy); as noted God does not judge dictatorships like this;

2. The relative absence of Muslims inside the society, except those few who can leave in the event of the judgment; and

3. Arrival at a level of error that causes other nations and peoples to go astray (B. 'Abdallah 1994, 211–12).

If there is a possibility that part of the society will eventually believe in Islam, as Bashir 'Abdallah says there is with Christians, then God will not judge them with a complete uprooting, but with a partial uprooting. "Therefore we can say that the *sunna* of God as regards a complete uprooting is not absolutely necessary upon the community of Christians, who the Zionists have worn [like a shoe], and evil and corruption in the land have been realized because of them" (B. 'Abdallah 1994, 213). He forecasts a partial uprooting that will also hit Europe and Russia in judgment for their crimes, and at the same time there will be another partial uprooting, but more severe, that will focus on the principal guilty parties: Israel and the United States.

Bashir 'Abdallah then begins to compare the United States to 'Ad.[4] According to his description, 'Ad was an advanced society with amenities. The people of 'Ad could predict the weather (Qur'an 46:24), and they possessed other advanced technology.[5] They had advanced weaponry and organized sports and cultural events (Qur'an 26:127). These, however, were merely for pleasure, not for the purpose of glorifying God. Their advanced weaponry included nuclear weapons (Qur'an 26:129), similar to those of the United States. And they had a secular humanistic culture together with public approval of sexual perversions (B. 'Abdallah 1994, 216–19).[6]

Regarding the capital of 'Ad, Iram dhat al-'imad (Iram of the columns, in

4. Muhammad 'Isa Da'ud also subscribes to the idea of 'Ad being the United States; see M. Da'ud 1997, 109–10. He cites an unidentified "new manuscript" as his source for much of the information allowing to identify America as 'Ad—which he quotes as saying, among other things, "The battle days of God during the time of the Mahdi will be like those during the time of 'Ad" (212). For more on Da'ud's sources, see Cook (2002).

5. One should note that this is one of the five things that God says humans cannot know, according to Qur'an 31:34; for this reason weather forecasting has occasionally been curtailed in Muslim countries by the very conservative. See Hoodbhoy (1991, 46–47).

6. B. 'Abdallah is referring here to homosexuality, about which he says, "and they even call this act 'gay' (*mazh* or *mazih*)" (B. 'Abdallah 1994, 225). 'Abdallah also is familiar with the AIDS

Qur'an 89:7–8), there are numerous comparisons to be made with the city of New York. Both of these cities were dominated by skyscrapers ('Abdallah anachronistically interprets the "columns" of Iram as skyscrapers; B. 'Abdallah 1994, 220), and in their own time they were the capitals of godlessness in the world:

> The similarity between 'Ad the perished and present-day New York is also that both of them were tyrannical, oppressive, haughty, world-class cities imposing their rule by means of unjust force to divide the rest of the peoples and nations of the world. Everything that happened in 'Ad of old has happened in America, just as God said: "As for 'Ad they waxed proud in the land unjustly and said: 'Who is superior to us in strength?' Did they not see that Allah who created them is superior to them in strength? And they used to repudiate Our signs" [Qur'an 41:15–16]. (B. 'Abdallah 1994, 220–21; cf. M. 'Arif 1995, 52–53)

Thus, the arrogance of 'Ad was also equal to that of the United States:

> America has proclaimed a "new world order" after the collapse of the Soviet Union, and announced the imposition of submission and the necessity of obedience upon all of the peoples and nations of the world to the Security Council and the General Assembly of the UN, which it rules openly and the Jews [rule] in secret and in reality. She [America] does not conceal her rule over the Security Council. . . . America says openly, "Who is superior to us in strength?" [Qur'an 41:14]. The president of America, Bush [Sr.], openly proclaimed this after the end of the Kuwait War, saying, "The twenty-first century is the century of the United States of America." (B. 'Abdallah 1994, 221)

America is to be judged, therefore, not for the power it has amassed, but for the attitude that power has engendered in its rulers, as in this passage by Bashir 'Abdallah: "This is America's unlawful arrogance in the world. If it had proclaimed that it is the most powerful country ruling countries and nations,

---

virus and uses it to prove the degeneracy of the West (315–16); see also M. Mahmud (1993, 107).

and done justly and ruled with righteousness, and taken what was deserved from the powerful [and given] to the weak, and preserved peace righteously between peoples, it would not have been like the first 'Ad" (B. 'Abdallah 1994, 222).

But since it attacked Iraq on the pretext of the invasion of Kuwait, ganging up on it with thirty other countries, and since it ignores the alleged evil of Israel and the actions of the Serbs in Bosnia, it has not done justly and must be punished for its arrogance.[7]

> Therefore, America deserves now, according to the *sunna* of God regarding the punishment of nations, a partial chastisement [like that] which caught 'Ad, and it is only because of the spread of Islam among millions of people in America, and God's knowledge that from the loins of the Christians of America there are those who will believe in God and his prophet [convert to Islam], and his final book at the hand of the messiah Jesus, the son of Mary, that this partial strike coming upon the second 'Ad is not a total uprooting. (B. 'Abdallah 1994, 223)

Bashir 'Abdallah's analysis of the Qur'an is a new one—it has internal coherence and power, and there are no obvious inconsistencies in it. For the most part it is too soon to say whether this analysis will pass into the mainstream of Muslim apocalyptic literature, but those writers who follow 'Abdallah chronologically speak of him with respect and often parrot his views (see, for example, M. Da'ud 1999, 186; both 'Abd al-Hamid and 'Abd al-Hakim frequently cite

---

7. Note that in the Palestinian daily newspaper *al-Nahar* for December 15, 1990, the following apocalyptic prediction appeared: "Believing tongues these days are passing around an unknown tradition, whether it proceeded from the great Messenger [Muhammad] or not. An examination of [whether] the source is trustworthy and the transmitters reliable has occurred, and until now a large number of religious authorities have refused to confirm or deny the reliability of this tradition, [that it] came from the Messenger [of God] Muhammad. The tradition says: 'The Messenger of God said: The Banu al-Asfar [whites], the Byzantines, and the Franks [Christian groups] will gather together in the wasteland with Egypt[ians] against a man whose name is Sadim [Saddam Husayn] none of them will return. They said: When, O Messenger of God? He said: Between the months of Jumada and Rajab [mid-November to mid-February], and you will see an amazing thing come of it.' Most probably this originated with Saddam Husayn's propaganda machine."

him; and Mustafa 1998 is largely built upon his work). From the aesthetic point of view, he is far more pleasurable to read than most Muslim Arabic-language apocalyptic writers since he eschews the bombastic and bloodthirsty style they favor. His book tends to be more analytical and measured.

Predictions for the Future: The Antichrist and the Earthquake of the End

Predictions for the United States can be divided into several different groups. First of all there are those apocalyptic scenarios that present the country as functionally ruled by the Antichrist, through the "world Zionist conspiracy." Opinions frequently differ regarding the unholy alliance between the United States and Israel with respect to the question of whether Israel is in control of the United States or vice versa. This question is not merely academic because the correct answer will also indicate where the Antichrist currently resides. The Antichrist's personality is nebulous, and it is frequently difficult to get a firm picture from Muslim apocalyptic sources as to whether he is a person (that is, an identifiable living person), a group of people (the Jews), a country (usually either Israel or the United States), a tendency (such as Westerniza-tion), or the collective mind of the world Zionist conspiracy (see chapter 9 of this book). In this chapter we focus on those who tend either to see the United States as the Antichrist or to interpret him as residing there; the following chapters will explore the other options.

Identified figures for the position of Antichrist are not lacking; however, many writers are reluctant to name names. Most recent U.S. presidents have qualified for the title "Antichrist" (with the noted exception of Jimmy Carter) at one time or another, or at least for being an agent of the Antichrist (like Ronald Reagan or George Bush, Sr.).[8] The sources are divided about Bill Clinton: is he the Antichrist or an agent?[9] The citations from Bashir 'Abdallah

8. See Ayyub 1987, 166–67; F. Da'ud 1999, 20; and F. Salim 1998c, 186–87. Salim states that many Masonic agents are named George, such as George Washington and George Bush, Sr. (188).

9. F. Salim (1998c, 180) says that Clinton is the president who will preside over the battle of Armageddon.

indicate that he sees Clinton as the personification of evil in the United States; however, Clinton's exact relationship to the evil Antichrist is left unclear. Biblical verses are cited for his punishment; his given name is connected to Jeremiah 50:2, where the figure of Bel (a Babylonian god) appears (also to Jer. 51:44; "I will punish Bel [Bill Clinton] in Babylon"; B. 'Abdallah 1994, 449–51). This dovetails perfectly with 'Abdallah's scheme of things because he regards America as the modern Babylon (such as in Rev. 17:3–4; B. 'Abdallah 1994, 182–23, 406–9). Many other distinguished figures have also qualified for Antichrist status, notably Henry Kissinger (al-Hawali 1992) and a number of actors or cultural figures, including Clint Eastwood, Burt Lancaster, and the magician David Copperfield. Muhammad 'Isa Da'ud is obsessed with David Copperfield, whom he is convinced is demon-possessed (M. Da'ud 1992, 117, 131).

At the end of the Antichrist scenario, concurrent with the appearance of the Mahdi, who will liberate the Islamic world from the current American occupation, there will be an enormous earthquake that will "totally uproot" the sinful American nation: "And the results of the general earthquake are a total uprooting for some of the infidels who have penetrated deeply into evil and tyranny, being arrogant in the land. God said: 'O people, fear your Lord. Surely the clamor of the Hour is a terrible thing' " [Qur'an 22:1] (B. 'Abdallah 1994, 377–78).

However, this earthquake will be unusual because it will strike down all the enemies of Islam, whom Bashir 'Abdallah lists. In addition to Christians, there are Buddhists, Hindus, Chinese, and the "sun-and emperor-worshipers in Japan" (B. 'Abdallah 1994, 382). A series of *khasf*s (swallowings up by the earth) will precede this event. One will occur in the Arabian Peninsula, where 'Abdallah asserts that the rich Gulf Arabs will be swallowed up and judged for their arrogance and waste of resources. Another will take place in the Far East, in either Russia or Japan, the two most evil countries in the area. He does not preclude, however, the possibility that the Hindus may receive a similar judgment: he states merely that no final conclusion has been reached on the matter (B. 'Abdallah 1994, 392–95).

On the matter of the Western "swallowing up" there is more certainty. America will be targeted, most specifically New York City (called the "great Babylon" of Rev. 18):

God's punishment falls on the evilest of his creation, and the more evil, the more intense the punishment. Since America is now the chief and first Zionist power (the dragon [of Rev. 12]) and the strong arm of the Antichrist (the false prophet), and the first head of the beast that leads the other six heads, so the punishment will be more intense upon it than upon others. Since in New York especially there are more Jews than in other places, and in it is their wealth, their banks, their political foundations that control the entire world (the UN, the Security Council, the International Monetary Fund, the World Bank, and the principal media networks), so there is no evil in any other place on the inhabited earth greater than in New York, and for this reason their portion of the punishment will be greater in measure, and it will be a total uprooting. (B. 'Abdallah 1994, 395–96; cf. M. Mustafa 1998, 70–71)

A great many pages of Bashir 'Abdallah's book are devoted to proving that New York is the Babylon the Great of Revelation 18, and to detailing its trade and the evil practices of its inhabitants (B. 'Abdallah 1994, 419–20, 440–49).

His Word: "And one of the seven angels who had the seven bowls came and spoke with me, saying, Come here, I shall show you the judgment of the great harlot who sits on many waters" [Rev. 17:1]. She is described as "great" because she is great in her corruption because fornication is symbolic of corruption. She is the fount of the great corruption in the world. He continues describing her as "sitting upon many waters," in other words, peoples, nations, and languages. As to his Word: "with whom the kings of the earth committed acts of immorality, and those who dwell on the earth were made drunk with the wine of her immorality" [Rev. 17:2]. This is another proof that this [harlot] is the UN and the Security Council in 1990 and after [that date the harlot] that turned the Security Council into the world government with armies punishing peoples, countries, kings, and rulers.[10] This was after the proclamation of the new world order and international law. Thus all of

10. B. 'Abdallah notes how the Antichrist has never let any Muslims onto the Security Council: "There is no community on the face of the planet so subject to enmity as is the Islamic community. Catholic Christianity is represented on the Security Council by France, Orthodox Christianity by Russia, Protestant Christianity by America and Great Britain, while Buddhism is represented by China. Judaism controls all of these and is above them all" (1994, 429).

the rulers or most of them have committed acts of immorality with her; in other words, betrayed their Creator and their peoples, and submitted to her decrees at the expense of their peoples.

His Word: "And he carried me away in the Spirit into a wilderness" [Rev. 17:3]. This is another proof that he was taken to North America, to the place where New York is today, because during the time of the vision it was nothing but a barren wilderness. (B. 'Abdallah 1994, 421–22)

Bashir 'Abdallah then expands upon the position of the "woman in scarlet" (Rev. 17:4) as the United Nations, while the beast upon which she rides is Zionism, led by the Antichrist. His interpretation of Revelation 18 is entirely devoted to the destruction of New York, for which he gives the following reasons:

1. The seven-headed beast must be the five members of the UN Security Council with the addition of Germany and Japan.

2. The multiethnic nature of the city of New York proves it to be the harlot mentioned in Revelation 17:15.

3. The territory in which the harlot will dwell was barren at the time of the apostle John's vision of Revelation; therefore, it must have been in North America.

4. The robe of the harlot is scarlet, which appears on the flag of the United States (the red stripes).

5. The riches and power ascribed to the harlot are only present in the United States.

6. The harlot is drunk with the blood of the saints (Rev. 17:6), who are the Muslims; therefore, she must be the United States, which murders Muslims and fights Islam.

7. She reigns over the entire earth (Rev. 17:18).

8. She says: "I sit as a queen and I am not a widow, and will never see mourning" (Rev. 18:7). "This is exactly how America and its people—government and people—speak. [President] Bush [Sr.] said: 'The twenty-first century will be the century of the United States of America,' and [President] Bill Clinton said: 'The United States of America is the greatest military power on earth.' "

9. The harlot sells the bodies and souls of people, which is true of the United States.

10. The sounds of music described in the vision are those of the United States (such as jazz, which 'Abdallah says is specified in Rev. 18:22).

"The strongest proof is that 'because its merchants are the greatest on earth' [Rev. 18:23], and the great ones of this world are those who have become so arrogant—they are the Jews in their final corruption, and they are the greatest merchants in America generally and in New York specifically" (B. 'Abdallah 1994, 446–49).

One can easily see how indebted Bashir 'Abdallah is to Revelation and to Christian writers in general in this portrayal of the judgment of the United States. He has taken the prophecies of Revelation, attached to them anti-Semitic-based hatred of both New York and the world institutions located there, and placed their judgment within an Islamic context.

In short, Bashir 'Abdallah presents a powerful and coherent vision of the future. 'Abdallah is at home with biblical material; much of his scenario is related to the West and is dependent upon evangelical apocalyptic interpretations. It is a reactive scenario, a judgment upon the evil of the West, which ultimately is based on the West's own critiques of its culture and society. These are adopted and then amplified by the Muslim apocalyptist and made only the more powerful by their obvious origins. While some Muslim material is used, it clearly plays a mere supporting role, present simply to deflect critics who would rightly say that this is an Islamized Christian apocalypse with the anti-Semitic conspiracy theory as a unifying factor and in order to provide it with the necessary connection to the state of Israel. 'Abdallah, insofar as the United States is concerned, does not express a very positive outlook. Unlike other Muslim apocalyptists who foresee the conversion of the United States to Islam (to which he alludes, but upon which he does not expand), 'Abdallah chooses to concentrate on God's judgment of the sinful nation and its ultimate removal from the world scene. Others, however, take a different path in their apocalyptic predictions.

In Muhammad 'Isa Da'ud's scenario (see chapter 6 of the present book), the Mahdi never conquers the United States, but other writers have explored this possibility. 'Abd al-Hamid, for example, finds mention of America in the traditions about the mysterious city of al-Qati', which in the classical apocalyptic sources is described as a city one thousand miles by five hundred miles located beyond Rome on the Atlantic Ocean (Cook 2002c, 171–72, 369). Although this is a large city, it still does not cover the present-day territory of the United States. Therefore, 'Abd al-Hamid postulates that after the Earthquake of the Hour (described in so much detail by both him and Bashir 'Abdallah), which will strike the United States in judgment for its sins, it is possible that the country will simply be split into three or more sections, one of which would be the size indicated by the tradition about the city of al-Qati' (H. 'Abd al-Hamid 1997a, 146–56, 190–200).

In several different books 'Abd al-Hamid develops the theme of the future conquest of America. He uses a great deal of Muhammad 'Isa Da'ud's scenario, but he does not detail an initial conquest of Europe by the Muslims. Instead, he believes that Europe will, in the near future, come to see the United States as its greatest enemy and will willingly make a treaty with the caliphal Muslim state, which will rule all Asia and Africa, to attack America jointly:

> America is the greatest enemy of the Muslims and will become during the next years the greatest enemy of the European countries as well. . . . In accordance with what we have explained in this book,[11] the European Community will strike first by bombarding America with bombs and missiles (there is a possibility that they will be nuclear bombs), and then will invade it together with the Muslims during the time of this truce and the signed agreement between the two of them.[12] Most of the countries of the world will support them, and some of these countries will participate with token forces. This will be after God strikes America with the Great Earthquake [Qur'an 22:1], which will cause the country to be divided into three parts or countries, and this will be in addition to other disasters that God will rain down upon it [the United States] such as birds of prey, killing plagues, and famines. (H. 'Abd al-Hamid 1998, 106–7)

But eventually, Europe will betray the Muslims and lift up their crosses in the Muslims' faces—in other words, manifest their Christianity in an offensive

---

11. 'Abd al-Hamid is referring to his previous book, *Halak wa-damar Amrika al-muntazar.*

12. It is curious that he would use the word *ghazw* for this invasion, since this is a word usually used of Muslims alone when they are attacking territory in jihad (whereas here the Europeans are clearly leading the invasion and the Muslims are in a supporting role).

manner—just as the alliance is pillaging the United States. This insolence will necessitate the invasion of Europe by the Muslim armies together with Europe's destruction and total conversion to Islam.

> After the mutual invasion of America by the Muslims and the Byzantines [i.e., the European Community] and their victory over it, one of the [soldiers of the] European Community's armies will lift up the cross and proclaim among the forces of the joint alliance of the Byzantines and the Muslims that without the cross there would have been no victory over America. One of the [soldiers of the] Muslim armies will be angered by this statement and proclaim among the joint forces that "No! Without Allah we would not have been victorious!" and these statements will go back and forth between them a number of times. In the end one of the [soldiers of the] Muslim armies will come to the cross they lifted up and proclaimed as a sign of victory over the land of the battle, and break it and destroy it. Then one of [the soldiers of the] Byzantines will kill that Muslim soldier, and the Muslim armies will begin fighting with the armies of the European Community. God has ordained victory for those Muslim armies. The affair will reach the general headquarters of both the [European and Muslim] sides, and the commander of the European Community will make the decision to break the agreement between them and the Muslims, and betray them. (H. 'Abd al-Hamid 1998, 108–9)

As in Muhammad 'Isa Da'ud's scenario, this course of events leads directly to the battle of Armageddon; however, because 'Abd al-Hamid has already killed all of the Jews, this battle is only between the Muslims and the Christians. After the Muslims' victory in the battle of Armageddon, they conquer all of Europe, destroy the Vatican, and convert all of the European countries to Islam (H. 'Abd al-Hamid 1998, 118–19, 163–64).

Conclusions about the Second 'Ad

One cannot doubt the profound hostility entertained by Muslim apocalyptic writers toward the United States, nor can one discount their intense desire to humiliate it and see it destroyed or converted to Islam (Cantwell Smith 1957, 76–79). Qur'anic exegesis has proved a fertile field for Muslim apocalyptists with regard to the United States, and it is clear that they have made every effort to maximize the possibilities of the text. This exists in sharp contradistinction to classical trends in which the Qur'an was rarely quoted and was never used as a source for apocalypses.[13] The interpretation of 'Ad as a type of the United States stands as one example of the contemporary trend of trying to anchor important apocalyptic beliefs about present-day peoples in the Qur'an. This is most likely a reaction to the heavy use of biblical passages that is more common in Muslim apocalyptic writings. Many conservative opponents of apocalyptists condemn these exegetes for using the biblical passages; in using the 'Ad interpretation, writers such as Bashir 'Abdallah and 'Abd al-Hamid show they are knowledgeable about the Qur'an and capable of producing an entirely new line of commentary on it.

Taking this chapter together with the previous one, the level of fantasy reveals the writers' perception of the outer world. For example, the appearance of the Mahdi gives us insight into the perception of how the world would be conquered for Islam. It shows no realistic approach, however; indeed, the principal battles are won not because of preparation, intelligence, or strategy, but because of God's active support of the Muslim armies. The attack on the United States is facilitated by the incredible strategic blunders made by the American forces (which are not out of the question, of course). Muhammad 'Isa Da'ud's blatant desire for Muslim power and domination over the world is remarkable in its ignorance of how like the Westerners he himself sounds in his pronouncements. There is absolutely nothing in what the Mahdi says, either in rationalization or in justification of his actions, that has not been used by Western leaders many times over, mainly in their aggressive and imperialist ventures. Da'ud's Mahdi sounds exactly like many who have been prominent on the world scene, claiming to bring peace and being aggrieved when their "peaceful" overtures are rejected.

The most striking element of this new Muslim discourse lies in the fact that the writers have simply allowed their Western opponents to dominate the discourse of their scenarios. Both Bashir 'Abdallah and Muhammad 'Isa

13. This tendency was already noted by Muslims in classical times, where we find casual comments such as, "People everywhere follow after the hadith and have left the Qur'an entirely" (Ibn 'Asakir 1995–99, 27:309).

Da'ud are especially guilty of this—they clearly want to be Westerners. All Muslim apocalyptists, of course, wish for the West to become Muslim, and many predict this will occur in the near future. However, some of these apocalyptic writers seem to want to transfer the entirety of Western civilization to the Muslim world. One must ask in the final analysis whether Muhammad 'Isa Da'ud's portrayal of the Mahdi is a Muslim one. Or is Bashir 'Abdallah's presentation of the divine judgment upon the United States really mandated by the Qur'an? In the Qur'an, while judgments are inflicted upon nations (or alleged nations, such as 'Ad), there is always the warning of a prophet and frequently divine signs previous to the absolute judgment. Where have these occurred vis-à-vis the United States? 'Abdallah never answers this question.

One must also ask the question whether this type of apocalyptic discourse actually provides the Muslims with the hope they need to overcome the negative present-day circumstances. Here hope is provided through the humiliation of one's opponents and their forced acceptance of Islam. Muhammad 'Isa Da'ud makes every effort to point out that there "is no compulsion in religion" (Qur'an 2:256), but where is the freedom to choose when nations are forced to take the oath of allegiance? It is clear that he wants to have it both ways. Some apocalyptists seek to emphasize hope for a brighter Islamic future in a different manner:

> The community of Muhammad is like the rain that grows good [things] in the earth and causes the earth to live after its death, and so too people live in Islam after they were dead in infidelity. The [Prophet] said: "My community is like the rain, it is not known whether the first part is best or the last part." This has been difficult for some people, what he says, "it is not known whether the first part is best or the last part"—this tradition shows that the generation of the end times will be close [in merit] to that of the companions. (al-Faqir 1995, 13)

At least one can say for Muhammad 'Isa Da'ud's Mahdi that he does make a concerted attempt to rebuild the world after the destruction he has provoked, and thus, despite its negative overall tone, it ends on a constructive note.

Bashir 'Abdallah mentioned "the war on terrorism" while writing in 1993–94. He apparently anticipated that this would become an all-out war, as it did in the wake of the September 11, 2001, attacks by radical Muslims on New York and Washington, D.C. These developments have led to an entirely new twist in the above scenario.

EIGHT

APOCALYPTIC PREDICTIONS CONCERNING AFGHANISTAN AND THE TALIBAN

The Messianic Kingdom of the Taliban

From 1996 until the end of 2001 the Taliban movement in Afghanistan established what could be called a contemporary radical Muslim messianic kingdom (more precisely, in Islamic terms, an amirate). In this chapter we will examine the expectations regarding the Taliban, the *amir al-mu'minin* Mullah 'Umar Muhammad Mujahid, and the symbiotic relationship between the Taliban and the foreign radical Muslim groups led by Usama bin Ladin (al-Qa'ida).

The apocalyptic writer Muhammad 'Isa Da'ud produced a messianic scenario (recounted in chapter 6) centered upon Mecca and Medina that was followed by a number of Egyptian apocalyptic writers. Another, more widespread messianic scenario current in classical Muslim apocalyptic literature centers upon the region of Central Asia, known in the classical sources as Khurasan.[1] This region was the focus of the propaganda effort of the 'Abbasid family, which ruled as caliphs in Baghdad (for the most part) during the period 747–1258. The 'Abbasids sought to present their movement as the fulfillment of messianic expectations, and so they produced a great quantity of materials given in the form of hadith traditions to indicate that the Mahdi would come from this region.

The identifying marks for the Mahdi's followers in these traditions naturally were those of the 'Abbasid armies: black banners, long hair, and so on (Cook 2002c, chap. 3). These armies will proceed from the region of Khurasan to Iraq and defeat those who oppose them (historically in 747–49). Many of these traditions did not enter the canonical books of tradition (Bukhari, Muslim, etc.), but were assimilated into apocalyptic literature that has flourished alongside the more respectable collections. One tradition cited by the canonical collection of Ibn Maja is rather coy: "Then the black banners will rise from the east, and they will kill a number of you the like of which has never been seen previously[2]. . . . When you see him [coming] swear allegiance to him, even if you have to crawl on the snow, for he is the caliph of God, the Mahdi" (Ibn Maja n.d., 2:1367 no. 4084).[3]

Other traditions are much more direct and specify black banners coming from Khurasan and advancing through the area of Iran in the direction of Syria with the ultimate goal of establishing the messianic capital in Jerusalem (Ibn Hammad 1993, 115–22). This strategy was first revived in contemporary times by the Palestinian Muslim radical 'Abdallah 'Azzam, who emigrated from Jordan (from where he had been fighting Israel periodically through the 1970s) to Afghanistan after the Soviet Union invaded in 1979. 'Azzam's work in popularizing jihad was significant in formulating the contemporary radical theories of how warfare should be waged, but he also popularized the position of Afghanistan as the messianic precursor to the future

---

1. The region of Khurasan in its broadest sense covers the eastern part of present-day Iran and most of the countries of Afghanistan, Turkmenistan, and parts of Uzbekistan.

2. In the 1980s some groups attached the tradition of the "black banners advancing from the east" to the Islamic revolution in Iran; see al-Judhami (1992, 25).

3. This is a reference to the leader of the 'Abbasids.

liberation of Palestine from Israel. In his book *Min Kabul ila al-Quds* (From Kabul to Jerusalem), he established that the liberation of Kabul was a necessary precursor to the liberation of Jerusalem ('Azzam 1989; 1991; n.d.; and see azzamjihad.com).

Although 'Azzam was assassinated in 1989 and did not live to see the liberation of Afghanistan from Communist rule in 1992, his ideas were very influential among globalist radical Muslims such as Usama bin Ladin (who had been one of 'Azzam's pupils). A Muslim state in Afghanistan seemed to be the answer that these radicals were looking for. The Afghan population had been radicalized by war—moreover, war that was religious in nature and demonstrated success against a superpower (the USSR). Afghanistan was far from the centers of either Muslim power (such as Egypt or Saudi Arabia) or Western attention so that a bona fide Muslim state (according to the radical interpretation) had a chance of germinating and eventually growing. According to their conception, therefore, the Muslim state of Afghanistan would be the destination of *hijra* (emigration) for those radicals who were looking for a truly Muslim state. In such a place these emigrants could plan a purification of the corrupt regimes currently ruling the core Muslim lands (both the Arabic— and the Urdu-speaking regions), and form the heart of a revived caliphate that would eventually encompass the entire Muslim world.

This bold vision did not become a reality during the first years after the liberation of Afghanistan. Usama bin Ladin tried, and failed, to bring about some type of unity with this global objective in mind during 1990–92.[4] After this he returned to Saudi Arabia and then migrated to the Sudan, which was just then proclaiming a jihad under the radical Muslim regime of Gen. 'Umar Bashir against the Christian rebels in the southern part of the country. In Afghanistan, the "government" established in the wake of liberation from the

---

4. Materials concerning Bin Ladin's personal apocalyptic thought are weak, to date. To the extent that one can speak of his apocalyptic beliefs, they are closely associated with the waging of militant jihad, especially drawing on traditions indicating that jihad will be fought until the Hour of Judgment (e.g., "The World Front Declaration Against Jews and Crusaders," *al-Quds al-'Arabi*, Feb. 23, 1998); in a proclamation of contested authenticity (Oct. 27, 2002) Bin Ladin spoke of the "eternally victorious" group in Islam that will continue to wage war until the Hour (alneda.com).

Communists did not achieve any unity, and each warlord represented in the government spent his time fighting the others and raping the country. In 1994 the Taliban, a radical Muslim movement under the leadership of Mullah Muhammad 'Umar, appeared and over the next two years captured much of Afghanistan, culminating in the conquest of Kabul in 1996. Fortuitously for Usama bin Ladin, therefore, he had a place to go after he was expelled from the Sudan that same year.

That same year, Mullah 'Umar proclaimed himself to be *amir al-mu'minin,* a claim that was treated as a joke by most of the Muslim world. However, for globalist radical Muslims, who have egalitarian tendencies, the qualifications of 'Umar (who was uneducated and not an Arab) were more than enough.[5] Relations between the Taliban and their foreign Muslim supporters (largely grouped together under al-Qa'ida) were far from harmonious at times; there were factions within the former that did not approve of the global apocalyptic vision of Usama bin Ladin.[6] Nevertheless, the relationship between the two groups was cemented by the common threat posed by the United States, which made periodic attacks in 1998 and 2001). Key for the establishment of the messianic kingdom in Afghanistan was the decision in early 2001 to destroy the Buddhas of Bamiyan, huge and ancient statues of Buddha carved into sandstone cliffs in the Bamiyan valley. For radical Muslims worldwide this act demonstrated the complete fidelity of the Taliban regime to the literal implementation of the *shari'a* in its totality, something unknown in any other "Muslim" state (according to their interpretation).[7] The willingness of

5. See some of these more messianic attitudes in Muhibb Allah al-Qandahari's document praising Mullah 'Umar, "Rabih al-bay', ya Amir al-Mu'minin!" at alneda.com (accessed 5/10/2002).

6. See the bbc.co.uk report concerning the attempt by Wakil Ahmad Mutawakkil, the Taliban's foreign minister, to warn the United States about the September 11, 2001, attacks (reported Sept. 7, 2002); see also msnbc.com, "Computer in Kabul Holds Chilling Memos" (Dec. 31, 2001).

7. See, for example, the numerous fatwas of the radical Saudi circle of Hamud b. 'Uqla al-Shu'aybi (available at aloqla.com); the materials written by Abd al-Rahman al-Barak, 'Abdallah b. Jibrin, 'Abdallah al-Ghunayman, and Sulayman al-'Alwan and collected by azzam.com; and materials written by Salah al-Sawi, 'Abd al-'Aziz al-Jalil, Nasir al-Fahd, Nasir b. Sulayman al-'Umar, Bishr b. al-Fahd al-Bishr, and numerous others, posted by alneda.com. See also 'Abd

the Taliban to buck world opinion—even Muslim opinion—in favor of the destruction of "idols" was for them the sign that Afghanistan was truly the messianic Muslim kingdom.[8] By the late 1990s radical Muslim groups were fighting in Central Asia and even in western China with some success, and there was a creeping "Talibanization" in large parts of Pakistan, especially the Northwest Frontier Province and the areas adjacent to the Kashmir. All of these successes apparently signaled to globalist radical Muslims that it was time to attack the world's remaining superpower, the United States, which they did on September 11, 2001.

Apocalyptic Interpretations of the "War on Terror"

In the wake of the terrorist attacks of September 11, 2001, the United States accused the Taliban government of supporting and protecting radical Muslim groups led by Usama bin Ladin, and facilitating their training for the purpose of attacking targets in the West. When the Taliban rejected the American demand to hand over Usama bin Ladin and to close the training camps, the United States together with the Afghan opposition (the so-called Northern Alliance) was able to defeat the Taliban and remove them from power. For many radical Muslims this scenario was one that demanded an apocalyptic interpretation.

This interpretation was available from the classical Muslim apocalyptic sources, where we find the following tradition (dating approximately from the eighth century):[9]

---

al-Mun'im Mustafa Halima (better known as Abu Basir), "Barqiyyat Shukr wa-ta'yyid li-l-Taliban" at aloswa.org/akhbar/tayedtalb.html (dated Apr. 3, 2001).

8. See, for example, Hamud b. 'Uqla al-Shu'aybi's influential fatwa "Nusrat al-Taliban li-hadmihim al-awthan," at aloqla.com/mag/sections (dated Sept. 15, 2001); 'Abd al-Ghaffar Hashimi, "Kamm min sanam hawa 'indama suqita Buddha," at alemarh.com (the author was a high-ranking cleric in Kandahar). See also Abu Abdallah Shibli Zaman, "The Buddhas of Bamiyan: Refuting Those Who Call for the Preservation of Idols in the Name of Islam," at alribat.com/Jihaad2.htm. Abu 'Abdallah al-Zulaytani's messianic poem "Allahu akbar: Huddamat al-asnam" can be found at alemarh.com/writing_cooperating_alemarh/muqatila_shaar.htm.

9. The interpretations given below are taken from khurasaan.com, "Afghanistan and Iran in Light of the Prophecies," and "The Current Situation and Prophecies of the Holy Prophet"; and the following articles are posted on asifal3sim.org/_private/Khilafa12.htm: "Al-Khulafa'

You [Muslims] will make a peace with them [the Byzantines] for ten years, and during this peace *(sulh)* a woman will cross the pass in safety, and you, together with the Byzantines, will raid beyond Constantinople against an enemy of theirs and be victorious over them. When you have finished . . . then you together with them will raid Kufa and flatten it like leather, and then you together with the Byzantines will also raid some of the people of the East, and you [pl.] will be constant over them, and take progeny and women prisoners, and take possessions.[10] Then while you are camped returning, you will begin to divide the spoils. The Byzantines will say: "Give us our portion of the progeny and the women," and the Muslims will say: "This is not possible for us in our religion; but take from the rest of the things." The Byzantines will say: "We will only take from the sum total." The Muslims will say: "You will never get it." The Byzantines will say: "You were only victorious because of us and our cross," and the Muslims will say: "Nay, because God aided his religion [Islam]." While they are doing this, wrangling back and forth, they will lift up the cross and the Muslims will be enraged and a man will leap upon it and break it. Some of the group will move away; and there will be a short fight between them. (Ibn Hammad 1993, 280–81)

According to contemporary interpretations, this prophecy was fulfilled when the Muslims fought against the USSR in Afghanistan with the aid of the United States (1979–91), which is referred to as the Byzantines in the tradition (as is often seen).[11] The real issue in the tradition is the question of to whom the victory should be ascribed. Obviously the Christians (the United States) saw the victory over the "people of the East" as a result of the influence of the cross (demonstrating the power of Christianity), while Muslims saw the victory as an affirmation of the truth of Islam. Therefore, when the inevitable

---

al-Ithna' 'ashara," "Mafhum al-khilafa 'ala minhaj al-nubuwwa," 'Audat al-khilafa 'ala minhaj al-nubuwwa," "Khurasan," and "Inhisar al-Furat 'an jabal min dhahab."

10. "Kufa" is in present-day Iraq.

11. The interpretations described here have frequently been dismissed by mainstream Muslims, who note that the traditions are "weak" (according to the classification of their chains of transmission). See, for example, "Irrelevant use of Ahadeeth regarding Taliban," at www.alja-maat.org/articles/1.htm. The Jordanian radical Abu Muhammad al-Maqdisi refuted some of those doubts in a fatwa dated summer 2002 at tawhed.ws (section on *fatawa*).

fighting breaks out between these two unnatural allies, it concerns this essential religious question.

The war does not initially progress well for the Muslims:

The fight between the Byzantines and the Muslims will rage—victory will be denied and weapons will dominate each other—nothing struck will be unaffected. The caliph of the Muslims will be killed then among seventy commanders on one day, and the people will swear allegiance to a man of Quraysh. There will not be a single peasant or nomad but will join the Byzantines, and tribes in their entirety with their flags will join the Byzantines. The Muslims will be constant—until one part will join with infidelity *(kufr)*, another will be killed, and a third will flee, [but a fourth] will be victorious. . . . The Arabs will fight from [their] side, and God will grant the victory—the king of the Byzantines will perish then, and the Byzantines will be defeated.

Men will rise from their saddles on the backs of their horses and cry out with loud voices: "O Muslims! God will never grant a victory like this again if we turn from it," and so the Muslims will catch them [the Byzantines] and kill them in every plain and hill. Not a single buried treasure nor city will stop them until they camp in front of Constantinople. The Muslims will find a community of the people of Moses [Jews?] there to join the victory with them. The Muslims will shout: *"Allahu akbar!"* (God is great!) from one side, and the wall will be split. The people will rise and enter Constantinople, and while they are guarding their possessions and captives, fire will fall from the heavens on a side of the city, and it will blaze up. The Muslims will leave with what they gathered and camp in al-Qarqaduna (Chalcedon). While they are dividing up the spoils God has granted them, they hear that the Antichrist has appeared in the midst of their families, and they will leave and find the news false. They will go to Jerusalem, and it will be their refuge at the Antichrist's appearance. (Ibn Hammad 1993, 280–81; cf. Josh. 6–7)

Again, we see that the Muslims are defeated initially, and the caliph (Mullah Muhammad 'Umar) is actually killed in the fighting. Although this has not occurred as yet (in reality), it is clear that citation of the tradition has prepared Muslims for this eventuality. The tradition also predicts a great slaughter among the commanders of the Muslim army after the invasion of the Byzantines (the United States), but eventually the remaining Muslims will swear allegiance to "a man of Quraysh." It is difficult to know whether Usama bin Ladin could or would fill this position. To date bin Ladin has demonstrated no interest in becoming a messianic figure, although he occasionally uses messianic and apocalyptic imagery to convey his message to the Muslim world.[12]

Of even greater significance is the reaction of the Muslim side to the invasion by the Christians—the United States—leading the "war on terror." According to the tradition, not only is unity lacking in the Muslim camp in the wake of the invasion, but a preponderant number of Muslims either betray the overall goal of Islam (victory over the infidels) and join the other side or abandon the battle altogether. With this betrayal highlighted in the classical tradition it is easy to see why radical Muslims have chosen it as their interpretation for their defeat in Afghanistan (October-December 2001). From their point of view the entire conflict was clearly a religious one, of truth versus falsehood, Islam versus Christianity (or the "West"). Muslims worldwide should have rallied to their cause, after overthrowing their corrupt, compromised apostate Muslim governments. The fact that few Muslims joined the radicals in Afghanistan demonstrated to the latter their betrayal of the ideals of Islam.

However, of course, the tradition does not end at this low point. As a matter of fact, the betrayal of the majority of Muslims is actually necessary for God's power to be revealed. The radicals have now purged their ranks of the mediocre and nominal Muslims. Let them join the enemy ranks, since the Muslims are better off without them (the test of Gideon, see Judg. 7:1–8). This apocalyptic interpretation has yet to be fulfilled, but all the indications— including the discussions about proclamations of large, even preponderant,

---

12. However, one should note that the propagandist Louis 'Atiyatallah, in his hagiographical rendition of the Sept. 11, 2001 attacks, "Lahazat qabla al-irtikam, bi-sm Rabb al-Tisa' 'ashara" (at jehad.net [accessed 1/22/2003]), refers to Usama bin Ladin as the *mujaddid* (the renewer that God will send to the Muslim community every one hundred years); see also the selection of poems in praise of bin Ladin at almaqdese.com, which frequently use messianic themes; and Husayn bin Mahmud's article of Jan. 27, 2003, "al-Mahdi al-muntazar" (at jehad.net), which describes the Mahdi and states that any one of the top leadership of al-Qa'ida could fit his description.

numbers of Muslims apostate because of their unwillingness to fight—are that this may very well come about.[13]

The Final Battle

The Egyptian apocalyptic writer Amin Jamal al-Din also wrote a book in the wake of the American attack upon Afghanistan, calling the attack the precursor of the battle of Armageddon. He identifies the Taliban with the black flags supporting the Mahdi (Jamal al-Din 2001, 28–31), and uses the traditions cited above to prove that Western powers, after they have finished with Afghanistan, will attack Egypt. Just as Muhammad 'Isa Da'ud did to bolster his Mahdi scenarios, Jamal al-Din cites "new manuscripts" with apocalyptic material in them, but does not identify them, stretching the reader's credulity to the maximum. For example, the apocalypse he cites (dating from the eleventh century, according to him) names a number of the Egyptian leaders of the twentieth century by name: Gamal 'Abd al-Nasser is said to be "Nasir"; and Anwar al-Sadat is said to be "a black man who is a lord [the meaning of Sadat], whose name is Anwar, and who will make peace with the thieves of the al-Aqsa Mosque in the sorrowful land" (Jamal al-Din 2001, 39). It is difficult to take this exaggerated detail seriously.

Jamal al-Din subscribes to the Mahdi scenario of Da'ud in its entirety; therefore, there is no need to repeat most of his description. After the United States attacks Egypt, the Muslim world will be united under the leadership of the Mahdi, who will fight and destroy the Western armies at Armageddon. After this victory, the Mahdi will go on to (re)conquer Constantinople, and then Rome, which will be purified by the complete destruction of the Vatican (Jamal al-Din 2001, 77–79). In general, Jamal al-Din is simply connecting current events to the above scenarios, and his version of events has been severely criticized (like most of Jamal al-Din's previous works).[14]

---

13. Note the legal discussions by Abu Sa'id al-'Amili, "Wujub nusrat al-harakat al-jihadiyya wa-munaqashat fatwa Jawaz qatl dhurriyyat al-murtaddin" at aloswa.or/adab/nosra.html on the question of whether it is permissible to kill the families of 'apostate' Muslims (by which the author means any Muslims who do not support the *jihad*).

14. See Hamid al-'Ali, "Tanbih al-maftun bi-kitab Harmageddon" at www.h-alali.net.

The Palestinian radical Salah al-Din Abu ʿArafa also penned an apocalyptic interpretation of the end of the United States and the swallowing up of the American army, using the Qur'anic stories of Moses and Pharaoh as a basis.[15] As ʿArafa sees it, Pharaoh is the United States, while Usama bin Ladin is Moses. Since Abu ʿArafa sees a cyclical view of history (resting upon Qur'an 35:43), he does not feel that there is any difficulty with saying that what happened during biblical times will happen again (Abu ʿArafa 2001, 2–3). From this starting point Abu ʿArafa finds a great many similarities between the United States and Pharaoh: both are arrogant and completely opposed to God. For example, he says that the White House has declared its own godhood (Abu ʿArafa 2001, 4). That both Pharaoh and the United States oppress the believers is self-evident for him. In response to this oppression Moses (Usama bin Ladin) came to liberate the believers from this oppressive anti-god system (which in the Qur'anic version includes the figures of Haman, who Abu ʿArafa identifies with the United Kingdom, and Korah, who is identified with Saudi Arabia). Pharaoh and the United States have legions of helpers: in Pharaoh's case, the magicians who attempt to duplicate the miracles of Moses in order to confuse people, while the United States uses the international media, which tries to frighten and confuse the people (Abu ʿArafa 2001, 7–8).

Both Pharaoh and the United States have a profound contempt for the small number of believers that oppose them. God will demonstrate to the world, therefore, in a dramatic and incontrovertible manner, that these believers are truly his followers and chosen ones by swallowing up the armies of the unbelievers (in the case of Pharaoh in the Red Sea, and in the case of the United States by destroying the White House and the evil military, political, and economic power of the United States). Abu ʿArafa even makes a prediction that this will happen before the end of President George W. Bush's term in office (2004; Abu ʿArafa 2001, 14). This apocalyptic scenario does not seem to rely upon any of the classical tradition, and it is odd that Abu ʿArafa does not cite any of the traditions that would bolster his case.

Some presentations are not so much apocalyptic as they are set in the ide-

---

15. The popularity of this tract was the subject of Khaled Abu Toameh's "Booklet Predicting the end of the US is PA bestseller," *Jerusalem Post Internet Edition* (Sept. 10, 2002).

alized future. For example, on jehad.net, a primary outlet for al-Qaʻida propaganda, a short play has been published called, "It Has Reached Us That over the Seas There Was a Great God Called America." This play is set in Kandahar (referred to as the capital of the Islamic Amirate of Afghanistan) in the *hijri* year 1634 (approximately 2200 C.E.), and employs the rhetoric of Edward Bellamy's *Looking Backward* in order to explain to young Muslim students what America was and how it was destroyed. The shaykh teaching the students explains that America was a heathen god that the entire world worshiped centuries before, and that God sent Usama bin Ladin to save the Muslims from being oppressed by it. Bin Ladin destroyed the symbols of the idol's power (the World Trade Center and the Pentagon), and incurred the wrath of "America." In this Bin Ladin was following the example of Abraham, who destroyed his people's idols and concerning whom was said: "You have had a good example in Abraham" (Qur'an 60:4). The shaykh and the students then proceed to praise Usama bin Ladin as a messianic figure (Musharraf n.d.).

One of the most common traditions used to describe the conflict between radical Islam and the United States is what is known as "the tradition of Thawban." It reads:

> The Messenger of God said: The nations are about to flock against you [the Muslims] from every horizon, just as hungry people flock to a kettle. We said: O Messenger of God, will we be few on that day? He said: No, you will be many as far as your number goes, but you will be scum, like the scum of the flash flood, since fear will be removed from the hearts of your enemies, and weakness *(wahn)* will be placed in your hearts. We said: O Messenger of God, what does the word *wahn* mean? He said: Love of this world and fear of death. (al-Silfi 2001, 7)[16]

This tradition epitomizes what radical Muslims dislike about the status of

---

16. Full sources for "the tradition of Thawban" in the hadith literature are listed in al-Silfi (2001, 8–10). Other sources citing this tradition include "Fatawa al-Shaykh al-Fazazi" at alneda.com (accessed 3/1/2002), which also has comments on it; and "Urgent Appeal to Defend Afghanistan," at azzam.com (when the United States attacked the regime of the Taliban in October 2001).

present-day Islam and is the core of their critique. As they see things, contemporary Muslims have abandoned fighting the jihad and because of this are in a humiliating position in the world. In 2001, apparently just before the September 11 attacks, the Morocccan writer al-Silfi wrote concerning thirteen benefits that the contemporary Muslim world can extract from this tradition.

Al-Silfi starts out by stating that the only unity the non-Muslim world has is its collective hatred for Islam. It is self-evident, therefore, that Muslims must unite against this hatred. For al-Silfi, like so many other apocalyptic and radical writers, Muslim unity is the key to any success. He notes that the outside world is given to spying upon the Muslims and promoting conspiracy theories to keep them disunited.[17] Because Muslims in the tradition above are compared to a kettle, they are said to be the source of all goodness in the world. Al-Silfi repeats the ideas that the Muslims' riches have been stolen by the infidels and that the infidels have turned the Muslim countries into miniscule, defenseless states. As the tradition indicates, the opinions of the Muslim community are given no weight as far as the world goes (he specifies the Untied Nations, for example; al-Silfi 2001, 19–20). But, as indicated by the tradition, numbers and technological preparations are not going to be the Muslims' defense against their enemies. Their true defense will come from reviving the aggressive jihad and overcoming their fear of death. So, in the end, al-Silfi takes comfort from the fact that the rest of the world is terrified of the Muslims and will never be able to "completely uproot" the Muslims (i.e., kill them), which must mean that Islam will be victorious in the end. The future is for Islam.

Clearly, these recent events have both modified and to some extent enlarged the focus of apocalyptic interpretations of Islam. The tradition has proven to be quite malleable, having the ability to deal with new situations as they have appeared, and to reinterpret the classical material in a convincing and powerful manner.

17. For example, Silfi states, "The enemies of the Islamic community use economic delegations and send mobs of tourists to spy upon the Muslims, to reveal news about them and to seek out their sensitive places. This continues even today!" (2001, 16n. 3)

NINE

THE FIGURE OF THE ANTICHRIST

The Antichrist's Lineage and Location

Consumed as they are by conspiracies, it is hardly surprising that many modern Muslim apocalyptic writers have focused on the figure of the Antichrist.[1] This figure did not receive as much attention in classical Muslim sources—where one rarely finds a book dedicated to him, in sharp contrast to the Mahdi, who was of major interest to Muslims during this earlier period. However, because of the influence of the anti-Semitic conspiracy theory, which has come to dominate the discourse almost to the exclusion of all other components in the stories about the Antichrist—and because of his Jewishness (even in the classical sources)—he is central to any thesis of the radical school.[2] As

1. For what is probably the best summary of the contemporary material on the Dajjal, see Tottoli (2002).

2. Note the citation of Hal Lindsey, *Late Great Planet Earth* on the jacket of Sharfi's book, *Dajjal Is Coming* (1985): "This person [the Antichrist], who is called the second beast, is going to be a Jew."

184

a result, the conservatives and neoconservatives are forced to deal with him as well. In the classical sources it is difficult to picture the attraction of the Antichrist. While he is said to be the worst of all temptations humanity will experience and the most dangerous of all the end-time tribulations to the Muslim, a slightly ridiculous air surrounds him. He does not look or act in a way that would give anybody reason to characterize him as a temptation, even those who are not well-versed in Islamic writings. Some Muslim apocalyptists (at least modern ones) have commented on this: as if people would be tempted to follow a monstrous and hideously ugly man, blind in one eye, with the word "infidel" written on his head! (Tawila 1999, 132; Shakir 1993, 26; M. Da'ud 1992, 136–40; 'Abdallah 1994, 115–16). One thinks in direct contrast to this of the contemporary evangelical Christian portrayal of the Antichrist as the suave, urbane politician or the telegenic, corrupt religious leader, whose outer good looks and personal magnetism conceal his inner satanic malevolence. With the Muslim Antichrist it is difficult to speak of a deception in this area, because his outer looks accurately reflect his true personality.

However, in the interest of finding an absolute evil for the apocalyptist to focus on, writers of the radical school have removed references to the Antichrist's ridiculous appearance. This is more problematic than it may sound, because in dealing with the Antichrist, one is constantly encountering the difficulty of defining what exactly the Muslim apocalyptist means by this word (in Arabic, *dajjal*).

There are several major categories of possibilities:

1. The Antichrist is a literal, physical being with a life span similar to that of other human beings. According to this interpretation, the Antichrist has been born into the world during the recent past and right now is gradually working his way to prominence in some country's leadership (probably that of the United States, but possibly that of the European Union). It is very probable that, like the Mahdi, even he does not know his true function in the world and sees his rise merely as natural success in the world of politics.

2. The Antichrist is a physical being, but one who has an unnatural life span. Explaining when the Antichrist was born, for example, Muhammad 'Isa Da'ud says:

He was born during the seventeenth century, Christian era, with an extended lifetime—elderly in age, but a youth in strength. When he appears, it will seem that he is about fifty or sixty years old. . . . The Antichrist is from the Yemen, and no wonder, since they are the cleverest of the Jews, and they are superior, despite what is said about them, to the Jews of Europe and the United States. . . . The parents of the Antichrist will die without knowing that their child is the expected king of the Jews, the master of the latter-day tribulation, and the mover of the strings of conspiracies. . . . More than one person among the Jews will adopt him, and they will find within him a blood lust and an unnatural attraction to evil. . . . A Jewish personality from England will adopt him and take him from the lands of the Arabs to the West to grow up there and study the latest sciences, to possess minds and build a fortress for himself. (M. Da'ud 1992b, 20–24)[3]

The reason why there are differing views about this subject is the strength of the traditions that indicate that the Antichrist was physically present during the Prophet's lifetime (see chapter 10 of the present book).

3. The Antichrist is not human at all. This view is expressed by 'Arif in the following passage:

The Antichrist is without a doubt a cursed sorcerer, and not only that, but I believe that he is a demon incarnate and not, as some have claimed, that he is a knowledgeable person who has arrived at the level of development, advancement, and frightening technology that prepares him to accomplish these miracles. He has lived all of his life chained, a prisoner in darkness, all alone and in ignorance of the knowledge God teaches, and as a tribulation to humanity from God to teach the people [humanity] that the Jews are an impending evil and that their king, whom they are preparing the world to receive, is this evil demon who claims divinity. ('Arif 1997, 37–38; al-Sharbati 1994, 91)

3. M. Da'ud writes, "He loves America and loves its people, and most of his followers are in it, and he has a frightening, terrifying castle in it, whose exact location I do not know, but with Islamic intuition I will say: it is in Florida" (1992b, 112).

4. The Antichrist is a malevolent but unseen force. Within this interpretation, the antichrist is often conceived of as being embodied in a country, usually identified either as Israel (see, for example, Ayyub 1987, 231–32) or the United States, but by older writers sometimes identified as Great Britain. Sometimes the Antichrist is seen simply as the West[4] or "world Zionism." There are those who try to understand his presence in terms of all of these tendencies, reasoning that since the Antichrist is apparently more than human, he must have some force that he projects over the world.

5. One final view of the Antichrist is that put forward by Muhammad 'Isa Da'ud, who contends that the Antichrist is a Samaritan Jew. He connects the Antichrist's appearance with that of the mysterious al-Samiri (the Samaritan) who appeared during the time of Moses (Qur'an 20:85–95). According to Da'ud, it was the Antichrist's appearance in this form that corrupted the original Israelites, drawing them away from the true revelation brought by Moses toward the Antichrist creed of Judaism. This idea at least explains why the Antichrist, although a Jew, does not seem to do anything beneficial for his own people (M. Da'ud 1994a, 52–59).

> Didn't I say to you: he is a Jew, and his morals are those of Jews. But he is a Jew of a special type: he is a Samaritan Jew—those who only recognize of the Torah the five books of Moses, and whatever other than that is idle talk. These are Jews who despise the Jews. The race of Samaritan Jews is a superior race in his opinion, and so most of his close associates are Jews, but they will never be lords of the world, as they have fancied for so long. Destruction is waiting in ambush for them. (M. Da'ud 1997, 169)

Da'ud then explains that the Antichrist had visited quite a number of countries and peoples during the distant past, apparently before he was chained up in the Bermuda Triangle. These countries included India, China, and Japan, in each of which he was responsible for the populace's adopting a false religion (M. Da'ud 1994a, 59–70).

---

4. See al-Bar (1998, 126); and see the article by al-Khayl bin Yousouf, "Dajjal the Deceiver," at www.ilaam.net/Articles/Dajjal.html.

However, while there obviously is some doubt as to the reality of the Antichrist in the minds of some of the apocalyptic writers, there can be no doubt as to the identity of his followers. These, as one might expect after reading about the anti-Semitic conspiracy, are the Jews. In the words of 'Abdallah:

> The Antichrist is Jewish in aim and intention in that they [Jews] are the greatest corruptors upon the earth, and he is the greatest antichrist of all the ages. His appearance and theirs is one. . . . The Jews are also antichrists with respect to the aim and the means; that is to say the arrogance upon the earth is the aim, the corruption is the means. The traditions prove that there is a unity of origin and purpose between the Antichrist and the Jews. He is their king and their god who will lead them in the second corruption and will complete for them their great arrogance upon the earth. ('Abdallah 1994, 124–25; and see 'Abd al-Hakim 1998a, 52)

Not only the Jews, however, but also their hidden followers from all the non-Muslim faiths participate in his armies. As has been noted, Muslims took from Protestant apocalyptic scenarios the idea that the Roman Catholic Church is one of the expressions of the Antichrist; both 'Arif and Da'ud emphasize that there is a continuous link between the Antichrist's headquarters in the Bermuda Triangle and the Vatican (for example, 'Arif 1997, 16). His communication with his followers is accomplished in the following manner:

> The invalid present-day Jahili [Arab and Islamic] governments would like very much not to mention the Antichrist from the wood of the pulpits, as if he were a fable, or a hint toward evil powers in the future opposing values and morals. The truth is that the Antichrist is a power chained on a remote island, sending his orders through demons subordinated to him, and working before him as servants. They inspire Jews, and their slaves the Masons, with decrees, plans, aspirations, and futuristic conspiracies until such time as his appearance and release [when he will arrive] like a rabid dog to ravage corruption upon the earth. ('Arif 1997, 44–45)

His other servants—the Masons, the Rotary and Lions clubs, and the United States, together with the Illuminati—have already been described.[5] But all of these lists of followers beg the question of how the Antichrist manifests himself and how he seduces the people of the world.

The Antichrist's Domination of the World

Muslim apocalyptists usually focus upon the Antichrist's covert domination of the world. His open, physical appearance is of less importance, especially in light of the ambiguity of the above description. There is a close connection between the domination of the Antichrist and the Zionist world government. As in so many other cases, Ayyub gives the clearest formulation of these ideas:

> The Antichrist is the goal of all of the camps of unbelief that have allowed the realm of thought to cease, and did not listen or pay attention to the set-path God has placed as a fortification for all who believe. The Jews have gained mastery over the path to the Antichrist, after they carried a strainer with all the parasites, blemishes, and suppurations of the whole of humanity, and they loosed it [i.e., all the evil they had strained out] when they did not support and believe in the final message [Islam]. God foretold that they would cause corruption in the world and that they would make haste in that corruption with any intelligence and any ability, and they would go with that corruption into the future. (Ayyub 1987, 22)

Essentially, the extensive time spent by apocalyptic writers in explaining the Antichrist's domination of the world is to answer the question unanswered by the classical texts: how does the Antichrist gain followers so fast when he is allotted such a short amount of time (oftentimes just forty days in classical sources) in which to achieve his aims? The theory of a Jewish world government conspiracy led by the Antichrist allows them to say that his work

5. Zarzur, Rabi', and al-Ansari (1996, 61–63) wrote an exposure of these groups (including the activities of the Jehovah's Witnesses and the Bna'i Brith, both of which are said to be fronts for the Masons); and Hamada produced a large (624 pages) study of the Masons (1994); see also Mansur (1998).

is already essentially being accomplished and his followers are eagerly awaiting his imminent revelation ('Abdallah 1994, 118). Ayyub, for his part, has to go deep into an anti-Semitic rendition of Jewish history to explain this part of the conspiracy, and he also explains how the Antichrist psychologically prepares society for accepting him:

> It is well known that God created humanity and made it to bear many great dispositions. God said, "By the soul and him who fashioned it well, inspiring it to profligacy and piety. Prosperous shall be he who purifies it, and ruined he who corrupts it" [Qur'an 91:7–10]. He made clear to the soul what was good and what was evil. The one who purifies his soul prospers in obedience to God and cleanses it of the lower morals. He decreed that chains of the soul be placed upon the soul that needed perishable things causing immorality to grow, and the man would be confused and fall, and turn his dispositions toward the things around him. The chains of the soul are always together with gods that the natural corrupt disposition, of a corruptly educated level, makes up. Every time that human conduct departs from this natural state, he is closer to the Antichrist, the ruler of the Jews . . . and after that the chains of thought and the chains of the soul are counted as idols above the earth and under the skin, then comes the societal chains.
>
> The societal chains are those that overshadow whole societies, since the society is a container bearing filthy things and protects all of its idols, and because the Antichrist is a worldwide leader, and because the Jews work to ensure that the scattered societies here and there have the same content, even if their flags are different, so the societal chains impose themselves in content after the chains of thought and soul on any society. . . . The laws of the rebellious, corrupt natural disposition that guard the idols and passions are themselves the laws of the Antichrist, because he works to preserve them as a worldwide law that does not serve anybody other than perverts of all sorts. (Ayyub 1987, 116–17)

Thus the Antichrist is trying to establish a type of godless order through his Jewish minions. His corruptions, according to Ayyub, start at the personal level of one's habits (the chains of the soul), and work their way up to thought patterns, and eventually become part of the society at large, which is then controlled by the Antichrist himself: "The goals of the tribulation during our present-day time are the establishment of circumstances far distant from the way of God in order to make people polytheists and the religion to be for [the sake of] something other than God. It was because of these very goals that the Jews have decreed the chains to be placed" (Ayyub 1987, 120).

As far as the apocalyptist is concerned, the world is already prepared for the coming of the Antichrist. The Jews and their hidden allies have for two thousand years been preparing for this appearance; their master's influence therefore now stretches into every society, every country, and every religion (with the exception of true Islam, whatever that is). Most rulers are his Jewish minions (either openly or by being "hidden Jews"); most educational systems teach people to worship him; and the financial systems of the world are his in their entirety. Moreover, military and technological equipment and personnel are at his beck and call. In view of this scenario, one might reasonably ask: with a conspiracy this complete, this powerful, deep and prepared, what is he waiting for? And why would anyone want to resist him when he does appear? After all, no one resists the Mahdi's overwhelming force after he has won his battles; why should they view the Antichrist any differently?

The Antichrist's Open Appearance and Ultimate Defeat

The Antichrist's open appearance and physical domination of the world by contrast are of less concern to the Muslim apocalyptist. This is at least partially due to the more imaginatively restricted aspect of this portion of the Antichrist's career—because of the more detailed nature of the classical traditions, which gives the apocalyptist much less freedom to improvise. For those who tie his appearance closely to the end of the state of Israel, this latter event will be the sign for the Antichrist to appear. In other words, the conquest of Israel (and the subjection of the West as a whole) by the Mahdi will be the sign that the conspiracy has to go public because extreme measures are needed to ensure its success:

> The state of Israel in relation to the corrupting arrogance of the Banu Isra'il is nothing but a fruit plucked in sin after the Zionist snake—or according to the interpretation of John [in Rev. 12], the dragon—as encompassed all the inhabited areas [of the world]. In other words, the existence of Israel will not

be ended until after their [the Jews'] great arrogance is ended, and not the opposite as some have imagined. Then when God has defeated the Israeli army, and the "men of great might" [Qur'an 17:7] have entered in upon them for the last time, as they entered in the first time, that will not mean the end of the corruption and the great arrogance in the world, because the cutting off of the prominent branch from the evil tree does not mean the end of the latter, because its outstretched roots quickly appear in other places in the world. Ending it will not happen until there is a complete uprooting of all of the roots, and for this a jihad is necessary during the time until it [Israel] is finished. ('Abdallah 1994, 127)

Therefore, 'Abdallah's understanding of the war against the West and its Antichrist leader is that of a defensive war. There cannot be peace until the root problem (the Jews and their great arrogance) is uprooted and finished off in its entirety. He lists the stages of the Antichrist's career (they are not all compatible with those of the Mahdi scenario detailed in chapter 6, since there is not much overlap between the writers on the Antichrist and those who write on the Mahdi):

1. The Muslims under the leadership of a nonmessianic figure (called by 'Abdallah either al-Sakhri, the Assyrian [taken from Biblical prophecies] or al-Sufyani) will enter into Jerusalem and kill half of the Jews in Israel, fulfilling the prophecy in Qur'an 17:4–8.[6]

2. The true messiah (the Mahdi) will come from Afghanistan bearing the black banners of his rule, and he will enter Palestine and kill the rest of the Jews, and establish the caliphate with its capital in Jerusalem.[7]

3. The Antichrist will gather together the European Community [now European Union] to fight the Mahdi. God will enable the Mahdi to defeat the

6. Many speculated that this figure was Saddam Husayn, and even though he hardly qualifies as a messianic figure, even to the most hardened and callous of the apocalyptic writers, some believe that he still has a role to play in the visions of the end. See B. 'Abdallah (1994, 155, 237–56); F. Salim (1998c, 137); 'Abd al-Hakim (1998a, 28–31); M. Da'ud (1997, 129–32). However, Salim (1998a, 137) predicted that the (projected) murder of Saddam in 1999 would be the trigger for the apocalyptic wars to begin.

7. Note the apocalyptic speech delivered by al-Khumayni in 1400/1978–79, reproduced by Bayumi (1995c, 52–54); see also Ayyub (1987, 165, 171); and al-Judhami (1992, 25).

Europeans and conquer all of Europe, finishing off with the idolatrous European Catholic Church and the Vatican.

4. The Antichrist, enraged at this turn of events, will begin to activate his vast circle of agents and pseudo-Muslims throughout the Mahdi's empire. He will attack the true Muslims in Jerusalem.

5. Jesus will descend and lead the believers, who will be besieged in Jerusalem ('Abdallah 1994, 128–29). This will lead immediately to the fulfillment of the "rocks and the trees" tradition:

> This battle will finish with the final and complete purification of the earth from the Jews when the stones and the trees will speak, and everything behind which a Jew is hiding will speak, and say, "O 'Abdallah [Servant of God], there is a Jew behind me, come and kill him." The killing of the Antichrist and his Jewish and non-Jewish followers in their totality and their uprooting from the earth will be counted as the uprooting for the great corruption [of the Jews], and the judgment upon the great corruptive arrogance of Banu Isra'il [Israelites] in the third and final stage, and there will be no further Jews upon the face of the earth until the Hour. ('Abdallah 1994, 129)[8]

'Abdallah also says flatly: "This means that the end of the Antichrist will be the end of the Jews, and the end of the Jews is together with the end of the Antichrist. This is the completion of a total uprooting for them because of their corruption on the earth" ('Abdallah 1994, 126). One should note that this end for the Jews is considerably different from that predicted by Muhammad 'Isa Da'ud, in which they are killed by the Mahdi.

While Jews will obviously form the core of the Antichrist's following, many other peoples will join him as well. Conservatives do not speculate on this subject much, but the radicals and neoconservatives enjoy listing all the different peoples and faiths that will see the Antichrist as their messiah and fol-

---

8. Note that F. Salim (1998a, 93) emphasizes that it will be Jesus who will "wipe them out of existence," which is appropriate, because they rejected his ministry. Tawila (1999, 222) says that the world will be purified of Jews entirely.

low him to attack the Muslims.[9] One realizes upon reading the classical sources that in addition to these followers outside of the Muslim community, there are a great many Muslim followers as well. This last point is not brought out much by modern apocalyptists, who prefer to believe that virtually all Muslims—at least those who are not Jews pretending to be Muslims, a dominant community in the upper echelons of most governments of Muslim countries—will resist the Antichrist. For example, 'Abdallah says concerning this matter:

> Is it possible for the devil or the Antichrist and his armies to force even one of the people [Muslims] to infidelity or to follow him? Of course not, because of God's word to the devil: "Over My servants you have no authority" [Qur'an 15:42], and because of the divine tradition *(hadith qudsi):* "I have created My servants pure *(hunafa'),* all of them," [10] so how can anybody imagine that an evil thing like the Antichrist, no matter what tricks and slogans of deceit, temptation, and deceptions he brings upon the people, can appear and people or most of them worship him between morning and evening? Is this in accordance with God's law concerning his creation? No, of course not. God says that there will never be a way for the infidels and their satanic leaders— both the jinn satanic version and the human satanic version—to [have power] over the believers. "And Allah will not give the unbelievers the upper hand over the believers" [Qur'an 4:141]. ('Abdallah 1994, 116)[11]

The only question not answered by this statement is who the true Muslims or believers are. The apocalyptist regularly states that the vast majority of

9. Often his followers are convinced by his miracles: see H. 'Abd al-Hamid (1996, 29–31, 192–97). For Muslims who join him in classical sources, see, for example, al-Tabarani (1996, 4:115 no. 2872).

10. Ibn Hanbal n.d., 4:162.

11. See also Ayyub (1987, 129–31, 248–49); and al-Bar (1998, 123–27). Ayyub says, "How is it possible that the Antichrist could proclaim his divinity in a land ruled by the Qur'an?" (1987, 129). However, one could answer this question by pointing out that numerous Muslims have proclaimed themselves to be prophets or to be divine (al-Hakim of Fatimid Egypt, Akbar of Mogul India, etc., and very probably Shah Isma'il of Safavid Persia as well).

Muslims are not true believers, so this question remains unanswered. Whoever they are, the Antichrist, making use of these dupes, begins his career.

Some of his followers are identified in the classical sources:

> Did the Messenger of God not inform us that most of the followers of the Antichrist will be children of illicit sexual relations? Is it possible (therefore) that he could appear previous to the spread of immorality, when illicit sexual relations became permitted in Western culture, such that children of fornication constitute more than 40 percent of all births? For this reason we affirm that the tribulation of the Antichrist starts previous to his final appearance, long before the day in which he proclaims himself openly. ('Abdallah 1994, 118)

According to this argument, the era of the Antichrist has already begun, his arrival heralded by current social trends that are creating the preconditions for his rule.

The Antichrist's career is one of movement. He does not establish any one center of rule; he himself is the government of the world. It is clear that eventually he would like to seat himself in Jerusalem and establish it as his capital, but this is not the fate in store for him. In fact, although he also attacks the two other holy cities of Islam, Mecca and Medina—which are protected by God from his aggression—his primary focus is upon Jerusalem. According to classical sources the truly believing Muslims will be located there, under siege and about to fall to the forces of the Antichrist. It is very unclear where the other Muslims are, since the only other places given in the apocalyptic texts as refuges from him are the mountains of Lebanon and the cities of Mecca and Medina. Considering the fact that there are well over a billion Muslims in the world, one has to wonder what percentage of them could fit into these areas.

> The Final Battle when the stones speak. When the Antichrist comes from Khurasan [eastern Iran] to Kirman and to the straits of Hormuz to occupy Mecca and Medina, disaster will strike him.[12] He then will leave Kirman at

---

12. The fact that the Antichrist is coming through Iran has allowed certain Sunni apocalyptists who hate the Islamic Republic to develop a subplot at this point. Iranian Jews support the

the head of the Jews of Isfahan for the Shatt al-'Iraq [the border between 'Iraq and Iran] . . . and devastate the area of Syria until the Jordan River. . . . Israel will join him. . . . The Muslims will flee to the mountains of Syria, to Jabal al-Dukhan, and he will come upon them and besiege them, and they will suffer terribly. (Ayyub 1987, 281; punctuation breaks are his)[13]

Ayyub goes on to say that after the Muslims swear allegiance to a leader to fight the Jews,

they [the Muslims] know that God most high demanded from them to prepare to fight their enemies as long as they can. Then the Jews cut them off from their support. . . . Then they [the Muslims] advance upon their enemy. The Antichrist and his supporters are placed in a press, like the press into which the pride of the men of Armageddon disappeared during the great apocalyptic war. . . . Then the last battle will occur, when the results of age-long deceit will fall into oblivion. I mean by this the problem of the heritage of Israel . . . this problem from which the belief in the godhood of the messiah of Israel stems, and all of the economic and political ideologies that cause the world to be always at war. Because of this [problem], chains and fetters have been placed upon the Islamic world for such a long time [283–84]. . . . Jesus will return to earth in the midst of the Muslims during the siege, while the Christians help the Jews cut the Muslims off, together with the false messiah, may God curse him! (Ayyub 1987, 285)

As Jesus and the victorious Muslims advance upon Jerusalem to slaughter their enemies, Ayyub continues,

Rejoice, O daughter of Jerusalem![14] The Jew in the courtyard will be like a broken man, prepared for death in any form. The Christian on the crossroads

---

Antichrist (as in classical sources), but Iranian Shi'ites are his followers as well. They would love to destroy the Muslim holy places (according to this interpretation), and are in league with the Jews in Israel in any case. See F. Salim (1998a, 12–13, 39–41); this is fully developed in his 1999 book.

13. The location of Jabal al-Dukhan has never been identified, but one would assume that it is somewhere in the mountains of Lebanon or northern Syria.

14. A parody of Zech. 2:10, 9:9.

will find that his "messiah" [the Antichrist] has collapsed. . . . Then the Prince of Peace [the Antichrist] will die.[15] Jerusalem was never made for the Jews. Weep, O daughter of Jerusalem behind whatever wall you please. The dictator [the Antichrist] will die. And your destiny will be in the hands of fate. He who came through Kirman and the Straits of Hormuz and Shatt al-ʿIraq, and made his legions of darkness advance upon Syria. He who caused the blood of Muslims to flow. . . . As the Prophet said: His—the Antichrist's—followers will retreat, and on that day there will be nothing that will conceal them, so that the stone will say: "O Believer, here is an infidel." And the Jew will conceal himself behind stone and trees, and the stones and the trees will say: "O Muslim, O servant of God, here is a Jew behind me—come and kill him." Do not remove your hands from the stones! The game has ended; the dog race has ended. Jerusalem is behind you, and not in front of you. So, where do you go now? Everything in the way of corruption has ended, and justice is in the future. . . . If only you [the Jews] would not lie, nothing would happen to you! But the crimes of years sometimes are judged in a very short time! This is harvest time!

All of the books will be burnt at the end of the road. Those who sucked at deceit, spying, and hypocrisy will be burnt beneath the feet of the prophet of God, Jesus, and the army of Islam—the agents, the followers, the collaborators, the thinkers, the observers, the supporters, the fans, the mob, the dogs, the wolves, the monkeys, and the pigs [i.e., Jews and Christians]. They will be trampled under after the dawn. . . . [There will be] a sound like the sound of a groan, but it will not avail, because his [the Antichrist's] followers believed in him even before they saw him. (Ayyub 1987, 286–88; compare Tawila 1999, 80)

The end of the road for the Antichrist and his followers is the appearance of Jesus, who comes down from heaven to save the Muslims. There is something of a single combat between the two of them, as they are essentially a

---

15. Both Ayyub and ʿArif frequently call the Antichrist the "Prince of Peace." See, e.g., M. ʿArif (1997, 9), who says: "The signs that are previous to the appearance of this Antichrist are the calls for peace, peace conferences, peace agreements, peace cities, and peace palaces [all of these images taken from the negotiations with Israel], at the same time as humanity groans under the horrors of the war, overflowing with hatred in brutal tyranny and international control, in the shadow of the Islamic revival" (29–30).

negative and a positive personality (Christ versus Antichrist), and some of the quirkiness of the Antichrist's personality is probably dictated by the fact that he has to be Jesus' direct opposite in everything. 'Abdallah, as he does so well, takes the final allegorical scene in its entirety from Revelation 12:

> In the twelfth chapter of the book of Revelation there is mention of the struggle between the Zionist-Crusader beast, which rules the earth in its entirety, on one side, and the Islamic community, which is bringing forth in suffering with the birth pains [on the other]. Those [Zionist-Crusaders] wish to stop the birth or kill the expected child after its birth before it can grow and strengthen. The expected child is the Islamic revival or the Mahdi, and with him the Islamic youth foundation, and the Afghan fighting army, because they together are the tool and basis for the establishment of the rightly guided Islamic caliphate a second time.[16] Then, "a woman clothed with the sun and the moon under her feet and a crown of twelve stars on her head. She was pregnant and cried out in pain as she was about to give birth" [Rev. 12:1–2]. This woman is the Islamic community at the beginning of the fifteenth century [*hijri*] and the end of the twentieth century [Christian], when the Islamic revival and the renewal movements appeared from before while it was in pain, and the sun is light and Islam is light, whereas all the other opposing faiths are ignorance and darkness. The moon is also a hint at the Islamic community, since it is the only community in the world that relies upon the crescent [moon] for its exactitude in time for the fasting and the Hajj, and the sign of the community is the crescent. As for the crown with twelve stars on her head, they are the twelve rightly guided caliphs whom the Prophet foretold would rule during the history of the community.
>
> And then John says, "Another sign appeared in heaven: an enormous red dragon with seven heads and ten crowns and seven crowns on his heads." This enormous dragon is Zionism, which is deeply embedded in the white race or the blond Byzantine [Christian] peoples or yellow [haired] peoples. This Jewish dragon that has dominated over them completely and in their entirety after the corruption, indefatigably throughout twenty centuries, since the time beginning with the alterations of Paul the Jew to the Gospels

16. Although the caliphate was abolished in 1924, 'Abdallah is probably referring to the "rightly guided caliphate" of the first four caliphs (632–61).

and the monotheistic creed which the Messiah [Jesus] brought,[17] and before him the prophets of Banu Isra'il, and Moses. This ended with the propagation of the humanistic atheistic schools and the enticement of the Western world to the lowest nadir in the materialistic and atheistic schools, and with the spread of fornication and sexual dissolution among the people, and other means of corruption, and also to the domination of the Jews through the present-day Zionist movement, and through the other secret apparati such as the Masons and the Rotary, upon the organizations ruling in most of the countries of the world today and especially in the great nations. (Abdallah 1994, 410–11; cf. M. Mustafa 1998, 67)[18]

"The dragon stood in front of the woman who was about to give birth, so that he might devour her child the moment it was born" [Rev. 12:4]. . . . This is what has happened in the Islamic world now as a result of the prevention of the fighting Muslims from attaining power, as happened in Algeria [1992] and other places that have fabricated elections. . . . This is what has happened now to the fighting Muslims and missionaries in the attempt to finish them off entirely in imprisonment, arrest, torture, and murder. Likewise it is expected for the arrival of the Mahdi and his appearance, in order to try to finish him off in his capacity as the head that the body [Islam] expects. The body is the Islamic revival that seeks a leader to gather its various parts. "She gave birth to a son, a male child, who will rule all the nations with an iron scepter" [Rev. 12:5]. This is the Mahdi, who for over thirty years has been a focus of interest for the Western world, with all the apparati of the dragon and the beast seeking to finish him off. But God is dominant over his rule. ('Abdallah 1994, 414–15; cf. 'Abd al-Hakim 1998b, 201; 'Ali 1996, 109)

However, 'Abdallah's interpretation breaks down after this point because he cannot explain why Michael the Archangel (in v. 7) is fighting against the dragon, which he has said represents world Zionism, as in Islamic lore Michael

17. Of course, not only Paul but all of the other writers of the New Testament as well (with the exception of Luke) were Jewish. See M. Qutb (1991, 75–77).

18. For a description of the actual end of the world, see al-Harithi (1998), who, to the best of my knowledge, is the only Arab scholar to have actually done research on apocalyptic literature as it exists in the contemporary Arab world.

is said to be the patron angel of the Jews. He is forced to say that from this point on, the text must be corrupt, as it is not Islamically accurate.

At the end two great battles will take place. The Antichrist's Jewish and Christian supporters ('Abdallah believes that the ten crowns of the beast in Revelation 13:2 are the European Community) will fight the Muslims in Jerusalem, where the former will all be slaughtered (B. 'Abdallah 1994, 132–33, 160; taken from Isa. 34:1–8, Zeph. 1:14–18). After this, the victorious Muslims will conquer Europe and destroy the "idolatrous church in the Vatican" (B. 'Abdallah 1994, 131). This will lead to the brief reign of the Mahdi, which will be ended by the physical appearance of the Antichrist himself (ruling for only 429 days), who will gather another huge army to fight the battle of Armageddon (160–67). As the material in this chapter illustrates, the modern Antichrist scenario, as in the earliest period of Islam, has become completely dependent upon Christian ideas and sources.

TEN

PROBLEMS WITH THE TEXTS AND HOW THEY ARE OVERCOME

In constructing their predictions of the coming end, modern Muslim apocalyptists have been hampered by various inconsistencies, either between current world events and the religious texts and traditions on which their apocalyptic scenarios are based or between those religious texts and traditions and modern received knowledge, particularly in the sciences. Criticisms arising from these inconsistencies have prompted ingenious attempts at resolution by the apocolyptists, often presented in the form of question-and-answer exchanges. Many of these exchanges have been discussed earlier, but others, ranging from the 1997 birth in Israel of the "red cow" and its place in Muslim schemes to other methodological questions of a more general nature (Jamal al-din 1996, n. 1; 1998, 47–50; and F. Da'ud 1999, 31) will be outlined here.[1]

1. The fact that this "red cow" became unfit for the religious purpose for which it was intended during 1998 has not been assimilated thus far. See, on this issue, M. Kh. (1997); and Bayumi (1997).

Another problem that has been raised is that of the sun rising from the West, which is one of the major signs. Apparently certain groups have questioned the possibility of this happening in light of what is known about the earth's orbit around the sun. 'Ashur (a neoconservative) is less than successful in his explanation—he simply says that "the astronomers and atheists deny this, but they themselves will shortly see that it [the sun] will rise from the west . . . when God shows them that the sun is in his power" ('Ashur 1987, 91–92; cf. Salim 1998a, 49).

Several difficulties are worth probing in depth. Two of them concern geography, or more precisely reconciling the apparent difficulties of present-day knowledge of the world's geography with the understanding presented in either the Qur'an or the hadith. The third issue is somewhat subjective, and concerns the question of the violence and terrorism found in the apocalyptic literature.

Tamim al-Dari and the Bermuda Triangle

The first difficulty concerns an odd variation on the story of the Antichrist. Usually, texts or traditions concerning the Antichrist focus on his appearance in an apocalyptic future rather than on any appearance in the past. However, two versions do concern confrontations in the Prophet's own lifetime between the prophet Muhammad or his close companions and an Antichrist-like figure. The first, the story of Ibn Sayyad, does not present modern-day apocalyptists with very much difficulty and will not be dealt with here. However, the second version, that of Tamim al-Dari, does create inconsistencies for modern apocalyptists.[2]

This second story relates how Tamim and his clan, some thirty strong, were shipwrecked on an island described indistinctly as out west. Once ashore, they met a Polyphemus-like figure chained on the island, who asked them several mysterious questions and then told them that he was the Antichrist and was about to be loosed upon the world. The account is unclear as to how the tribesmen got off the island, but in the end Tamim was welcomed by the

---

2. On Tamim, see D. Cook (1998); and especially al-Zankuri's in-depth article (1994) about the literary nature of the story.

Prophet in Medina, who attested to the veracity of the tale by telling it himself. Classical commentators make much of this last point; this was one of the
few occasions on which the prophet Muhammad was actually the transmitter
of a hadith rather than its source—a very significant detail when considering
the relative value of this tale.

During classical times there were few problems with this story. The world
was large and the fluent tongues of sailors and adventurers frequently brought
back tales of the Antichrist's island. It is possible to identify it in at least a
dozen different accounts recorded faithfully by Muslim geographers. However, during our own time such tales have been far more difficult to come by.
The world is now fully explored, and since the Antichrist has clearly not appeared yet, according to the story his island must be out there somewhere,
with him still on it, chained to his cave, waiting for his time to come. The only
other alternative would be that the prophet Muhammad himself related a
story that is a tall tale (see Veliankode 1995, 290 for rationalization). This last
is not an option for a Muslim religious writer. The neoconservative writer
Muhammad al-Bayumi tells the following story of what happened when he related this tradition to a class with a curious student (presumably young) in it:

> A student listening to the lesson said to me: "Could we take a trip and go to
> this island and see the Antichrist?" I said to him: "Why would you want to see
> him? There are many antichrists, and when you have been fortified with the
> truth, you will be saved from them, and from the greatest of their number
> when he appears." He [the student] said: "Hasn't anybody visited this island
> since Tamim al-Dari?" I preferred to remain silent and diverted the student
> from the subject with dexterity. (al-Bayumi 1995a, 40)

But even al-Bayumi recognized that diverting this boy did not really answer the question—or banish it. In his book he polemicizes with the modernist writer Muhammad al-Ghazali, who had stated that this island is
nowhere to be found. Bayumi notes that al-Ghazali is unwilling to deny the
existence of the "barrier" containing Gog and Magog (see below), which unlike the story of Tamim al-Dari is mentioned in the Qur'an specifically, despite
the fact that it too has not been discovered (al-Bayumi 1995a, 39–41). Thus,
the charge is refuted because of al-Ghazali's timidity, and not on the basis of

the evidence. Other neoconservatives such as Tawila are forced to say that God has hidden the island from men's eyes (and he even hints at the Bermuda Triangle explanation described below; Tawila 1999, 120–21; Shakir 1993, 20).

Several radical apocalyptic writers have dealt with the problems of this text; Ayyub does not address the question of location (1987, 219–26). 'Abdallah, for example, has an allegorical interpretation to offer. The Antichrist in the Tamim al-Dari story says that he is about to appear (during the time of the Prophet, fourteen centuries ago) and go throughout the earth. Yes, that is true, argues 'Abdallah, and this appearance means that his corruption and the evil effects of his loose morals and love of killing were loosed upon the earth at that time. All of these evils have been around ever since then, enabling the Antichrist—when he physically appears at the end of time—to have a pool of followers waiting to greet him. Therefore, the physical appearance of the Antichrist on the mysterious island in the west is not a problem, because most of the corruption in the world flows from the west (the United States and Europe) anyway ('Abdallah 1994, 118–20).

'Abd al-Hamid explores the question of how far the boat carrying Tamim and his companions could have gone, and comes to the conclusion that during thirty days (the period of time they sailed, according to the tradition) they could have sailed approximately seventy-two hundred miles. This distance would place them somewhere out in the Atlantic Ocean (since, obviously, 'Abd al-Hamid is trying to send them to the Bermuda Triangle); however, it would have been remarkable for these tribesmen to have made this journey without being able to stop anywhere along the way, or to pass through the Straits of Gibraltar without even knowing it, or stopping there at all, or for the storm to have accompanied them all the way, as the story indicates ('Abd al-Hamid, 1996, 37–41). According to this scenario the Bermuda Triangle, together with the Formosa Triangle in the east, are the two locations from which the Antichrist's power emanates ('Abd al-Hamid 1996, 42–61; also Sulayman 2000b, 67; al-'Irbawi 2000; Abu al-Ru'us 1999). Although it is not clear from 'Abd al-Hamid's story upon which island the Antichrist is chained, since according to the story the tribesmen do land somewhere, this explanation at least places the entire tradition inside the framework of the Bermuda Triangle, which causes questions to be raised in Western societies as well.

Thus, the burden of proof and of solving the entire issue is removed from the Muslim apocalyptist and placed upon any who would dare to solve the question of the Bermuda Triangle. It remains to be seen whether this approach, which is considerably different from those previous to it, will be accepted. In a real way these explanations do not answer the boy's curiosity, but they may answer his questions when he grows older.

Gog and Magog

The conservative school has also suffered difficulties with the literal existence of the barrier restraining Gog and Magog (mentioned in Qur'an 18:94–95, 21:96), and the whereabouts of these peoples. In essence the same problems occur as with the Tamim al-Dari story, but they are magnified because the references in question are not taken from the hadith (which in the end can be disavowed), but from the very word of God. There can be no question that the latter must be right, no matter what the physical evidence says. Apocalyptic scholars—those who are honest at least, and most from the radical school have dealt with this problem—have had to answer to this. 'Abd al-'Azim al-Khilfi says:

> There is a problem that has presented itself to some people, and that is that during this time the geography of the world is known, but despite this advance, this "barrier" [Qur'an 18:94] is not to be heard of. . . . The answer is that not everything in existence can be seen. Human intelligence cannot be seen, despite its existence, jinn exist though we cannot see them, and angels as well. (al-Khilfi 1996, 58)

Among other apocalyptic writers, Layla Mabruk, for example, realizes there is a problem, but she simply says that God has concealed Gog and Magog from human eyes (Mabruk 1986, 67, 103–4).[3] Sha'rawi is also con-

---

3. See also Bayumi (1995a, 65) and al-Tayr (1986); Al-Tayr believes that the barrier holding them (see Qur'an 18:94, 21:96), the exact location of which is the focal point of the controversy, has disappeared, and that the Mongol invasions were in fact those of Gog and Magog (al-Tayr 1986, 1676).

cerned with the problem of the location of the barrier; his answer is that it is located in Georgia (in the Caucasus, the former Soviet Union).[4] However, he does not answer the more fascinating question of the identity of Gog and Magog (if we accept this identification). 'Ashur, another conservative, pours a good deal of analysis into the problem; in the end he decides to accept the modern Christian interpretation that Gog and Magog are actually code names for Russia and China.[5] Some conservatives, such as Hasan Fulayfal (1991) and Hamza al-Faqir (1994), have managed to write entire pamphlets without addressing the question of location.

So much for the conservatives and neoconservatives. Radicals have not been much more successful. In short, their explanations are either derived from the evangelical Christian understanding of the Gog and Magog verses in the Bible (usually attaching them to Communist Russia or China), or else they have fallen back on their old friend, the anti-Semitic conspiracy theory. The Jews are truly infinite in their possibilities, it seems. Salim has written an entire book on the idea that Gog and Magog are actually the Jews themselves. This he accomplishes by several sleights of hand. Working primarily with the Qur'anic passages (and then viewing the biblical material through their lens) and with the idea that most modern Jews are descended from the Khazar tribes of the area north of the Caspian Sea, he fleshes out his thesis. The Qur'anic passages speak of barriers that hold back the fearsome tribes from consuming the world. The heart of the geographical question is the location of those barriers, since they must still be in existence (otherwise we would know who Gog and Magog actually are because they would be destroying the world). Salim is honest enough to admit that the features described in the Qur'an are nowhere to be found. He lists off six "truths" in his interpretation of the Qur'anic material, such as: Alexander the Great never built a barrier; the barriers described in the Qur'an are nonexistent; they do not exist between two mountains: and they will never be discovered.

4. Sha'rawi 1990, 70. See also Jamal al-Din (1996, 108–12), who avoids the hard questions; as does 'Abd al-Haqq (1993, 49–58); and Veliankode (1998, 386–403).

5. See 'Ashur, who quotes Ezek. 38–39, Josephus, and St. Jerome (1987, 71–72). S. Ahmad (1996, 47–49) identifies Gog and Magog with the nomadic invasions from Central Asia, and counts seven appearances in the past, one in the present and one in the future.

His "truths" do not stop there, however. He first notes that Gog and Magog in the classical texts are headed for Jerusalem (they are emigrating there, as the Jews did). Then, he suddenly comes up with an explanation for the missing barriers: although during the present time the Jews are not apparently held back by such barriers, they were kept in ghettos for the duration of the Middle Ages. The interpretation of this historical fact is that God was holding them back from the world, protecting the world from them by placing them within these ghettos surrounded by walls (barriers). What happened when they were let out? The world was practically destroyed through their conspiracies and control over the United Nations and the United States! (F. Salim 1998b, 99–100; also 'Abd al-Hakim 1998a, 16–17). The seventh truth, therefore, is that the Jews are descended from the Khazar tribes and are actually Gog and Magog (there are several other truths following upon this; among them, Salim notes that the Jews are draining the Sea of Galilee dry, which is what Gog and Magog are supposed to do in the classical sources). That this scenario is not entirely successful is apparent when one compares the classical texts (and especially the Qur'anic texts) with the selective reading offered by Salim. For example, he must deny that the Jews had any connection with the Banu Isra'il [the Israelites] mentioned in the Qur'an (see this book, chapter 5), and yet he also seems to believe that the state of Israel is prophesied in Qur'an 17:4–8, which speaks about "Banu Isra'il" being allowed a second corruption in the land of Israel (the modern state). Purely by sleight of hand he attempts to influence us to ignore the fact that the prophet Muhammad was intimately acquainted with Jews (according to the Qur'an) and yet never gave any indication that they were Gog and Magog in any of the numerous traditions about them from his mouth.

Others have tried to solve this problem as well. Hisham Kamal 'Abd al-Hamid also wrote on the subject, largely plagiarizing from Salim (as he had done previously from 'Abdallah and Da'ud in earlier books). He delves into the historical material to prove that Gog and Magog cannot be Russia, an idea he took from Protestant evangelicals and then abandoned after the collapse of Communism. Following the same lines as Salim above, he comes to the conclusion that the Jews are Gog and Magog and that the sign of their imminent invasion of the Muslim world is the immigration of Russian Jews to Israel (1989–92 and continuing into the present; H. 'Abd al-Hamid 1997b,

127–51). He does not take the idea any further; for example, he does not mention when their invasion of the world will occur.

Fundamentally, the problem of Gog and Magog probably cannot be resolved at this time. The Qur'anic text, backed up by the classical exegetical tradition, apparently points to a very specific geographic location that cannot be located in the contemporary world. This unfortunately is a geographically unprovable sequence in Muslim apocalyptic beliefs and continues to remain a festering sore point among apocalyptic writers. One foresees in the near future a number of additional books and further ingenious attempts to solve this difficulty.

Apocalyptic Violence

One of the most intriguing issues in Muslim apocalyptic is that of the nature of the violence described in the apocalyptic texts. There can be no question that Muslim apocalyptic writers resent the idea that they are frequently described as terrorists.[6] Therefore, it is legitimate to ask whether this resentment has actually brought about a change in the actions they foresee for their own future as portrayed in the apocalyptic literature. In apocalyptic books a great deal of time is spent refuting the "terrorist" charge, and turning it on the West to say *tu quoque* (you are equally guilty, usually of terrorist-like military adventures, such as various invasions of Iraq or support for Israel). However, these charges based on readings of history are difficult to substantiate in an absolute sense, especially as Muslim historians have never been able to develop a self-critical tradition (al-Shihabi 1997, 16–75; Zarzur, Rabi' and al-Ansari 1996, 29–41). (Nor, one might add, have they ever shown any appreciation for the self-critical traditions of others; for this reason we find extensive citations of biblical verses criticizing the Jews, and comments from the anti-establishment or countercultural press in the Western world in Muslim apocalyptic literature). Therefore, what is bad or existentially evil in the con-

---

6. See, for example, Ayyub (1987, 144–45; 161), who says that the Mahdi will immediately be labeled a "terrorist" upon his appearance (322). See also F. Salim (1998c, 38); B. 'Abdallah (1994, 138, 159–61); M. Da'ud (1997, 167; 1999, 349–59, 366–70); Zarzur, Rabi' and al-Ansari (1996, 73–74); and M. Mustafa (1998, 18–19, 90).

text of the West (the Crusades, the colonial period, present-day economic and cultural imperialism) is good and positive when an analogous event occurs in the context of the Muslim history or apocalyptic future. An apocalyptic historian is quite capable of denouncing the evils of colonialism and calling the Crusades a "hellish conspiracy" and then, on the same page, moving on to laud the capture of Constantinople and the other aggressive Muslim conquests, not noticing the irony.[7] Similarly, those expecting the Mahdi do not appear to notice how closely he resembles a contemporary Western imperialist in both his actions and his public statements.

For centuries Muslim Arabs were imperialists and colonialists in almost exactly the same fashion as the West, and even today suffer the hatred and resentment of a wide range of colonized or formerly colonized peoples (Persians, Berbers, black Africans, Indians, etc.).[8] Moreover, in general these writers have failed to notice that many of their own attacks on Western behavior are in fact taken literally from Western historians or eyewitnesses and thrown back, not realizing the self-critical nature of the historical analysis on the part of the writers cited.[9] One should note that in the Mahdi messianic-age scenarios detailed in chapter 6, the world presented is not qualitatively different from the one presently "ruled" (or dominated) by the West. The only noticeable difference is that in the messianic age, the Muslims rule it. They do

7. Both Salim (1998a, 9–12, 21–23) and M. Da'ud (1999, 407) do notice the irony. When 'Arif discusses the fact that Jews are prohibited from converting out of their faith, he says: "Oh! What pictures, which must be counted as the pinnacle of arrogance, and if this proves something, it proves the feeling of error and contemptibleness of the Jewish soul, and the attempt to rob even the lowest pit of putridity, when it has stayed long and become very putrid, until it has become a microbe which has no antidote other than the fire of annihilation" (1996, 93).

8. Justifications for this historical reality also sound strikingly Communistic (or smack of the "white man's burden"). Al-Marta'i states: "The conquests of Islam were only for the propagation of light and truth, and to free the nations from unjust systems, and to inform the people of the call of their Lord, and to liberate their minds and consciences from the subjection to those [deities] other than God. The goal of the conquests was, first, to guide the people to truth, and then, second, to establish a proof for God against all who denied Him, and, third, the realization of benefit for the nations whose lands were conquered" (1992, 71).

9. One example is the extensive use of biblical citations designed to portray the Jews in a negative light that are actually taken from the self-critical tradition of the biblical writers.

not act any differently than the West did toward the outside world. Ayyub says in defense of this attitude:

> As for the camp of belief, in it will be the power of Islam in the consciences of its individuals and in their feelings. War for them is not just for the sake of war, because the sword of Islam is not raised other than at the order of God, the One, the Unique, "He did not beget and is not begotten, and none is his equal" [Qur'an 112:3–4]. The sword of Islam strikes in order to prevent aggression and does not strike in order to fulfill every means that is brought to it to receive its due. (Ayyub 1987, 161)

> The scholars of *ahl al-kitab* [Jews and Christians] say concerning the camp of belief [the Muslims], the camp of the Faithful, the True [cf. Rev. 19:11, here equated with the Mahdi] that we [the Muslims] will confront first the Western coalition and then the Eastern coalition.[10] This is our fate! This is our fate that we face off with the heavily armed. We will break his [the Antichrist's] nose in the great apocalyptic war, the Day of God, who is able to do everything. This is our fate, we will face the heavily armed Antichrist and he will shed most of our blood, and then we will drown him in it. This is our fate from the Day of Badr [624] to the Day of the Antichrist. It is our fate that we would have battle chants upon the Yarmuk [636] from the first, and that we would have battle chants in Rome at the end of time. It was our fate that we would hear the Crusaders singing and finish them off twice.[11] This is because the Muslims are troops in the service of God, utensils in a community calling to the right and enjoining the good, and forbidding the evil. A

10. This is, of course, an inaccurate statement. What he meant was that *Christian* scholars (Jews had no part in the formulation of the evangelical Christian apocalyptic scenario), who interpreted all of these events as pertaining to Christians, said this, and Ayyub took all of the references to Christians in their books and applied them to the Muslims instead. But the evangelical scenario does not involve any fighting on the part of Christians themselves; only Jesus (Rev. 19:11) fights in reality. It is only after combining the Muslim and the Christian texts together that Ayyub can legitimately state what he does.

11. Ayyub is referring to the Crusaders of the historical period of the Crusades (1097–1291) and to the modern-day West, which is usually called "Crusader" by apocalyptists and radicals alike.

community living simply in the understanding of right and wrong. (Ayyub 1987, 241)

In other words, Ayyub sees the Muslim community as one whose existence has been determined by warfare—either the aggressive warfare of the first centuries, or the defensive warfare of the end times. At all times, however, this warfare is essentially defensive, since the hostility of the outer world to Islam is sufficiently apparent to justify even obviously aggressive moves against it. Apparently by definition those on the Muslim side cannot be terrorists or be aggressive. However, this defensive attitude does not actually go so far as to enter into the apocalyptic discourse and change the Muslims' actions from violent ones to nonviolent ones. While the charge of terrorism is continually refuted on paper, the Muslims' own actions are not modified as a result of their own criticism of their opponents' activities.

While addressing the question of religious tolerance, Muslim apocalyptists will frequently cite verses from the Qur'an to "prove" that Islam has tolerance (for example, the usual citation of Qur'an 2:256, "There is no compulsion in religion"; M. Da'ud 1997, 168; 'Abd al-Hakim 1998b, 87), as if the mere citation of this verse absolves Muslims from ever having contradicting it at any time in their past history or at any time in the future. One writer, Muhammad Mustafa, innocently says (after telling us that the United States or Israel was really responsible for the massacre of the Western tourists at Luxor, Egypt, on November 17, 1997):

Islam is entirely free and pure of any extremism, acts of violence and terrorism, and forbids the killing of an innocent soul. Everyone should know that God said, "Whoever kills a soul, not in retaliation for a soul or corruption in the land, is like one who has killed the whole of mankind" [Qur'an 5:32].[12]
. . . Everyone who participates in acts of terror or conceals it does not belong

12. There is no question as to what any radical would say to the citation of this verse as part of an attempt to stop terrorism. After all, the verse clearly allows for violence in cases of revenge and a need to stop "corruption in the land."

to Islam at all, even if he is Muslim. This proves that whoever did this criminal act or aided in the planning of it was not Muslim. (M. Mustafa 1998, 90)

Unfortunately this proof is not clear to an outside observer, since no apparent action has been taken to declare Muslims who commit violence against
civilians to be non-Muslims. For example, legal action is regularly taken by the
courts in Egypt to declare liberals apostate (Nasr Abu Zayd [Bälz 1997] and
others); there have been no similar attempts to declare suicide bombers or
other terrorists who attack civilians (which are both patently against the laws
of jihad in the classical sources) to be non-Muslims (Cook 2002d; and forthcoming). Thus, one must suspect this "defense," if it is indeed such, to be
rather thin—when Muslim apocalyptists make such remarks, it does not in-
spire much confidence in their other pronouncements. The above statement
following the massacre of the tourists at Luxor could be duplicated numerous
times—since it is rare in the recent past that Muslims have admitted that violent actions were accomplished by Muslims without blaming Israel or the
United States in some way.

Apocalyptic violence is an excellent example of this attitude of extreme to
disingenuous innocence. Islam is peace, says one apocalyptist, therefore Muslims are not violent and cannot commit violence (M. Da'ud 1997, 179–80).
One then asks, if this is true, what *is* the Mahdi's violence? How can that be rec-
onciled with these protestations? Discussing the fighting to achieve the Mahdi's
empire, Da'ud says—and one must read his comments in light of the fact that
his Mahdi practices indiscriminate nuclear warfare and exterminates the Jews:

This does not mean those who boast, destroy, kill, and terrify children,
women and the elderly, and societies. Islam does not mean terrorism. True
jihad is on the battlefield and not against the unarmed. . . . Those who harm
the ones given the *aman* [safe conduct] are the furthest of people from the
understanding of Islam, and they have no connection with it, either near or
far. Islam is mercy, and the Mahdi is in his time, either near or far [off], mercy.
(M. Da'ud 1997, 18, and 26–27, where he speaks again in the same vein)[13]

13. M. Da'ud cites descriptions that Westerners will use of the Mahdi: "He is crazy with a
psychological disease, wanting to kill Jews, a tyrant, a dictator" (1997, 26–27).

Thus, apparently, these questions are already answered for the apocalyptist. But, as we have cited from Da'ud previously, there is no religious requirement for the Muslim to practice restraint toward infidels, as the Mahdi said in his opening statement to the Muslim world.

Ayyub and many others likewise do not hesitate to revel in violence, as we have seen:

> Let the Christian know that he who lives by throwing bombs and with the policy of guns will meet tomorrow a Muslim whose patience has limits when his rights are taken. With blood! and with guns! and at that time it will not be appropriate for the world to promote tolerance proper for the nature of wolves. That is because the Qur'an is read in the brave society with complete understanding [of its contents], which is not proper for the natural disposition, and is not proper for the wolves, the monkeys, and the pigs [Jews and Christians] tomorrow. Then the land will be flowing with rainwater, but it will be red rainwater, sorry to say. Soon the world will see a man flying in the air, coming toward it, able to speak and move, who will not know patience, with a rod of iron in his hand to strike with, to strike with, to strike with, so that the thieves will flee and it will be possible for every oppressed person to build his home, and the winds will not be feared.[14] On that day there will be a camp of belief, with no hypocrisy in it, and in it Abu 'Abdallah, the expected Mahdi, will sit. . . . There will be a camp of infidelity and a camp of belief without a third [one]. (Ayyub 1987, 159–60; 1991, 161, 195–96)

Unfortunately, the possibility of self-criticism and perspective that the question of apocalyptic violence and its place in the ushering in of the Muslim messianic future should have raised in these writers is already stillborn. Clearly the violence done to the Muslims (as perceived by them and usually augmented numerous times through conspiratorial fantasies) absolves them from all guilt and does not require them to seek a different standard while hoping for the future.

---

14. The "man flying in the air" is Jesus, taken from the vision in Rev. 19:11–16.

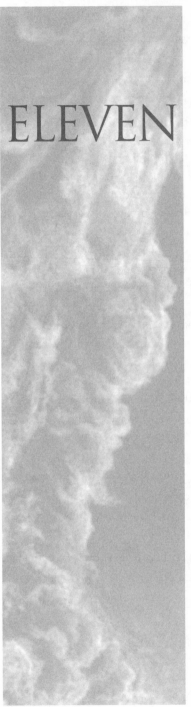

ELEVEN

CONCLUSIONS

The modern Muslim apocalyptic scenario that has gradually been taking shape during the past fifteen to twenty years is a development built upon several sources. It is a unique construct, unrivaled in its vision and power since Muslim apocalyptic literature was surrendered into the hands of the hadith specialists some thirteen centuries ago. Since that time it has sat dead and cold, repeated and commented on by the hadith commentators who have carefully denuded it of all real life and pushed its relevance far into the distant future. That future, however, is today; it is now. The bill they refused to pay is now due, and thanks to their procrastination, others have gladly taken over the payment of it. Ayyub and the radical school represent an incredible explosion of dissatisfaction with the attitude that one cannot build anything new with this apocalyptic material, cannot ever touch it or bring it to life. They desire intensely to bring it back into the mainstream and to connect it—or perhaps one should say reconnect it—with reality, and to bring in the messianic age. Unlike those cautious hadith trans-

214

mitters, they would embrace that messianic age, for they have finally come to the point where they do not have anything to lose. Looking around the world and not seeing any hope in it for them, they realize that they are far from the position Muslims should rightfully find themselves in: the dominant place in the world.

In some ways conservatives have responded to this excitement and desire. It is they, for example, who are overwhelmingly responsible for the publication of the vast classical Muslim apocalyptic heritage, during the same time that the radical school was gathering itself together (e.g., the work of Muhammad 'Abd al-Qadir 'Ata' and Suhayl Zakkar, along with many others). It is difficult to analyze why exactly they undertook such a project; it is very probable that some hoped that the publication of authoritative and easily accessible texts would induce the radical school to check some of their more preposterous predictions.[1] Others were probably interested in the texts only as hadith books and may have hoped that the difficulties of working with the huge mass of material would deter the radicals. This has not occurred, if such was their intention, as the radicals regularly embrace challenges that have stumped generations of conservative scholars, who in the past have simply given their stock answer of *Allahu a'lam* (God knows) to many complex problems. This answer for the radicals is no longer sufficient. Instead, the net result of this publication effort has been the flowering of study where there was none previously. Anyone can now open Nu'aym ibn Hammad, al-Dani, or al-Sulami and find a number of messianic prophecies and create his own scenario. To this the conservatives have no answer. Their authority, in the final analysis, was the result of their control over the sacred knowledge (the *'ilm*), and their status as the keepers and interpreters of the tradition. Now that this status has been challenged in such a powerful way by the radicals, it is difficult to see any way they can regain it. Nor is their close kinship with the neoconservative group one that can give them much solace, for the methodology of this group is equally problematic for the conservatives—although sometimes their con-

---

1. Sukayl Zakkar in his introduction to Ibn Hammad's *Kitab al-fitan* (the earliest classical apocalyptic book) says that he published it (in 1993) as something of a refutation of the huge number of apocalyptic traditions floating around at the time of the Gulf War. It has turned out to have quite the opposite effect.

clusions are a bit more satisfactory. While the neoconservatives can at least refute some of the more blatant and bizarre ideas that Ayyub and his followers
produce, they, in the end, are a stopgap solution from the perspective of the
conservatives, and are gradually in certain ways being dragged toward the positions of the radical school. It is their school, for example, that has spear-
headed so much of the dating and calculations of the end, which even Ayyub
avoided and relegated to a footnote.

No one can take away, however, from Ayyub and his initial followers the
credit for the intellectual and exegetical richness created by the assimilation of
biblical material into the Muslim apocalyptic scenario. In some ways, the two
are like long-lost cousins who have been reunited. They speak the same language, only with different accents. As shown in *Studies in Muslim Apocalyptic*
(Cook 2002c, introd.), classical Muslim apocalyptic was developed under the
influence of and in polemical contact with Christian and Jewish sources. The
apparent kinship is therefore not just coincidence. The reopening of this treasure chest has enabled the Muslim apocalyptist to see so many more possibilities than those previously available from his own tradition. However, at the
same time, it must be noted that this use of two other faiths' apocalyptic heritage has not brought any real level of understanding to the Muslim side.
Coming to it as they do with a great deal of Muslim intellectual baggage, reading the Bible in the Arabic—which has been an Islamic language for fourteen
centuries—inevitably gives it an Islamic hue, and further needing to justify
themselves before a hostile audience of conservatives, they have not made any
attempt to bridge the gap between Islam and Christianity. In fact, it is very
probable that they are widening it.

A good example of this attitude is the question of Jesus, who is the single
major overlapping figure between Christianity and Islam. Christian missionaries have exploited this fact for polemical purposes throughout the centuries,
starting already in Byzantine times, and now Muslims use him to speak to the
Christians in their turn. However, there can be no comparison between the
two usages, since while Jesus is a revered figure in Islam and a prominent character in the end-times scenario, he is by no means the crucially central personality that he is in Christianity. Christians immediately lose their Christianity
upon accepting the Muslim view of Jesus; the reverse for the Muslim is not
true; as a matter of fact, he enriches his Islam by incorporating new visions of

Jesus (so long as they are not blasphemous in the Christian manner).[2] So, while Jesus is used liberally by both Christians and Muslims in their apocalyptic writings, the considerable difference between the interpretations of his function in the apocalyptic literature does not serve to bring the two faiths together.

This willingness to attach Muslim apocalyptic interpretations to non-Muslim scriptures is probably the result of the fact that the Qur'an is not an apocalyptic book (with the exception of the sequence of Qur'an 17:4–8 discussed in chapter 5),[3] and therefore any Muslim who wants to build an apocalyptic scenario must of necessity look elsewhere, since many of the radicals are also suspicious if not hostile toward the tradition literature of Islam. There may also be the feeling that Muslims need traditions or revelations that speak to an apparently defeated and disillusioned group (Daniel, Ezekiel, and Revelation all have this in common). Additionally, this usage of biblical material shows the modern Muslim apocalyptist's overwhelming consciousness of the Christian world culture (from the Muslim's point of view)—just imagine a popular evangelical Christian apocalyptist such as Hal Lindsey using the Qur'an! Of course, at least part of the usage here does not indicate any respect. It is merely the traditional polemic approach of using one's opponents' material to prove the truth of one's own beliefs. For example, Ayyub says:

> In this study I have set forth the proofs that are agreed upon by the books of the three faiths: Judaism, Christianity, and Islam. When I set forth a text that is agreed upon by the three faiths, then I put the interpretation of the *ahl al-kitab* [Jews and Christians], and only then do I put forward the Islamic interpretation. Many times I do not have any commentary whatsoever, and I simply rely upon the interpretation of *ahl al-kitab*. But other times I discuss with them the open problems and those that are hidden to them, and all of the sources that have been transmitted that are read by *ahl al-kitab* today. (Ayyub 1987, 11)

2. M. Da'ud (1997, 246), for example, cannot understand how Christians allow Jewish attacks on Jesus to occur or why. He cites the example of Prof. Geza Vermes, who he says defamed Jesus publicly on television and must be punished for it. See also Mustafa (1998, 91–92), who equally cannot comprehend defamation of Jesus.

3. By monumental effort, certain apocalyptists manage to find references to the Antichrist and the Mahdi in the Qur'an. See 'Ali (1996, 110–14); and Veliankode (1998, 324–27).

Christians reading this are not convinced to change their core beliefs, especially when they already have a well-developed exegetical tradition that sends them in entirely different directions while reading the Bible. Ayyub's message to the leaders of the West is that Islam is the superior religion and that they should convert. If they do not take this step, then at least they should abandon thoughts of world domination and aggression caused by their infidelity. He asks that they consider the West's best interests in the Middle East, and that they no longer protect Israel. They should also stay away from Muslim countries and stop stealing their resources, according to his perception (Ayyub 1987, 320–22). Such is Ayyub's plea to the world.

Arabic-language Muslim apocalyptists feel an intense loneliness and anger at their ignored status, as well as a profound lack of self-esteem. In this book we have explored some of the ramifications of the apocalyptists' attitudes toward the outside world. It should be reemphasized here that they, above all, want to communicate with the outside world, using the biblical material, and to speak to the Christian audience; it is doubtful whether any of them consciously believe that they could communicate with the Jews, if only because of the power of the anti-Semitic conspiracy theory.[4] This desire leads to a reading of the scriptures and a feeling of wanting to be included, of trying to find their issues and hopes addressed in this text, since they know that Christians rarely, if ever, open the Qur'an or care what it has to say.[5] The fact that they do find so many issues and prophecies of relevance to them is more indicative of their need, for although the Bible is almost infinitely malleable (as is the Qur'an or any holy text), one can come to the conclusions only by first immersing oneself in Islamic culture and tradition and then by reading the text in Arabic. This fact does not seem to be understood by them—and indeed, if they really believe that they are finding truth in the biblical text, it cannot be—and so one finds them lashing out in anger at the Christians for not seeing or refusing to believe what is supposedly right before their very eyes.

---

4. Uniquely, Ayyub (1987, 322–26) has a message for the Jews. He says that he is not anti-Jewish; all he really wants to do is to stop the Jewish conspiracies against Islam.

5. This attitude of speaking to the Christian (and the Jewish) audience is common in the Qur'an as well, substantial portions of which are directed toward these faiths in an attempt to find common ground. See, for example, Qur'an 3:64.

This attitude creates a block between Muslims and Christians. It is also doubtful that the frequent proclamations of Islamic superiority in the apocalyptic texts or the graphic descriptions of the slaughter of Christians will aid them in this endeavor. At the end of the battle of Armageddon, when the Christians finally realize too late that they were on the wrong side and get massacred, Ayyub has the following to say:

> What a tragedy! The Jews began it and the Christians fell into their nets—those [people] who had never used their brains even once during the stretch of their long history. They were seduced by the civilization, and they [the Jews] said to their followers and their servants that it was Christian civilization. They never thought that when you use your mind, God opens all sorts of discoveries to it. The Japanese modernization does not go back to Buddha, but to the mind created by God. (Ayyub 1987, 182)

One should note, if it is indeed their desire to persuade others, that historically, significant numbers of Christians have become Muslims only when a Muslim government is ruling over the land in which they dwell (and is thus in control of the public discourse and the educational system), or through the tolerant, interconfessional attitude of Sufism, which creates a common language.[6] Apocalyptic polemic is not creating a common language, if such is the intent.

There is a strong attempt here to speak to certain groups and to win them over to the positions promoted by Muslim apocalyptists. Many of the apocalyptists insist that they are speaking to both Muslims and Christians, and I believe—although one could argue the opposite on the basis of the numerous pejorative and vituperatively hateful comments they write about Christianity—that they are sincere in this. It would seem that they would like to break Christians away from the apocalyptic philo-Judaism so prevalent among Protestant evangelicals, and at the very least bring them to see Islam in a positive light, if not convert them outright ('Arif 1996, 5 [written by 'Abd al-Sattar al-Satuhi]; Ayyub 1987, 320–22). However, the methods chosen to

6. One exception to this rule is the Black Muslim movement; on its apocalyptic beliefs, see Ansari (1981); Walker (1994; 1998); Berg (1998); and Gardell (1995).

accomplish this aim are so insulting that occasionally one wonders whether they can be serious in this endeavor. 'Arif, for example, has this to say after listing off the supposed attacks and insults to Christianity in the Talmud:

> Thus the Jewish slap on the faces of the Christians continues, who apparently enjoy and allow this sort of humiliation and attack, and give them their other cheek [Matt. 5:39] so that the Jew can continue to slap the Christians—just as we see—ruling them in Europe through the Masons who dig the grave of Western civilization through corruption and promiscuity. The Crusader West continues like a whore who is screwed sadistically, and does not derive any pleasure from the act until after she is struck and humiliated, even by her pimps—who are the Jews in Christian Europe—and it will not be long before they will be under the rubble as a result of the Jewish conspiracy. ('Arif 1996, 85)[7]

Selections of this type show how incomprehensible both Judaism and Christianity are to the Muslim apocalyptist. Buried so deep in their conspiratorial vision of past history and present reality, and never having actually tried to understand why exactly Christians believe what they do, they apparently believe that Christians will want to be freed from their supposed servitude to the Jews ('Arif 1996, 83–85). Ayyub tries to grapple with the reasons for the Jews' and Christians' unbelief:

> They say about themselves that they are not infidels, and indeed accuse those other than themselves of infidelity, and that is for a simple reason: they are not feeling, and they are not feeling because they do not entrust themselves with the trouble of thinking. Their intellects have become hardened after [reading] the last line found in the [Church] Fathers or rabbis. The Jews have lived in dreams of awakening ever since the Babylonian captivity, and a land that would rain clothes of wool *(suf)* and rain gold in bulk like cows' kidneys (?), filling their homes. Dreams of a prisoner! Is there [intellectual] effort in

---

7. Compare with Abu Zayd (1999, 60); and Mustafa (1998, 92–95), who tell the story of how the Virgin Mary was drawn by a Jewish group with the head of a cow; and 'Amaluhu (1992, 170–71).

dreams? They persist in a world without feeling until one day they will come to an end with the stone, and the stone will say, "O Muslim, there is a Jew behind me, kill him." Then they will leave the domain of no feelings into the domain of the senses during the critical moment [the Day of Resurrection]. There will not be any weight [given] there to supplication or to weeping.

And likewise the Christians. Their intellects have hardened in accordance with the philosophy that says, "Since the sun is in the middle of the sky during the hottest part of the day, we must be in the middle of the day!" They also dream of the day when they will be caught up and taken to the heavens to meet the Messiah [Jesus] in the clouds. Where is the [intellectual] effort in that? (Ayyub 1987, 141)

Although perhaps 'Arif and Ayyub can win some points using mocking techniques of this sort from Muslims who do not know anything about Judaism or Christianity, they will win no converts to their cause from these faiths speaking in this manner. No one will pay any attention to them.

However, it is by no means clear what the Muslims have to offer to the freed Christians—were they to take this path—other than conversion to Islam.[8] Muslim apocalyptists regularly show a paranoid view of what Christians and Jews would like to do to them:

The *ahl al-kitab* would like nothing so much as to cause this community [Muslims] to fall into error from its belief. This belief is the rock of salvation and the line of defense. The *ahl al-kitab* both then and now know that and spare no effort to change this community from its belief—everything in their ability, every stratagem and trick, and likewise [the use of] power, when they are unable to fight it themselves. They gather troops of hypocrites and pretend Muslims or those who claim to be Muslims and troop them together to burrow them into the body of this belief [Islam] from inside the house, to cause people to deviate from it [the belief], and they paint for them other

8. Indeed, Ayyub (1987, 320–22), in his message to the leaders of the West, says just that; see also Mustafa (1998, 99–103); and note that 'Abd al-Hamid (1997a, 202–17) says that America has willfully rejected the message of Muhammad and has denied his mission, so that God is right to destroy it.

paths that are not its paths. Whenever one of the *ahl al-kitab* finds one of the Muslims . . . they employ all of this in an effort to lead him astray. They [Jews and Christians] lead them [Muslims], and will lead the entire community behind them, to infidelity and error. (Ayyub 1987, 127–28, cited from Qutb 1996, 1:438)

Reading this apocalyptic material is interesting not only because of what it says but also because of what it reveals about the people writing it and how they perceive their culture and the larger world around them. Arabic-language Muslim apocalyptists have a large inferiority complex that they apparently seek to overcome by the aggressiveness and brutality described above. They feel that their culture is being denigrated and ignored, that they have been left on the "ash heap of history." One constantly comes across references to three phrases that seem to exclude them, and toward which they are extremely resentful. Those three are the "new world order,"[9] "the end of history,"[10] and the "clash of civilizations." These three phrases (stated by George Bush Sr., Francis Fukayama, and Samuel Huntington, respectively) were stated in the context of the end of the cold war and the general disappearance of the ideological conflict that has plagued Western civilization since the French Revolution (1789). In the context of the "clash of civilizations," in which an entire thesis is built upon the perception that Islam is the next enemy of the West, Muslims are specifically targeted as the likely successors to the Communist threat of the past.[11] However, the ascription of a level of malevolence is in fact fallacious, especially since the last two phrases are merely de-

9. For nonapocalyptic critiques and discussions from an Arab perspective, see Sadiki (1995); Isma'il (1992); al-Himsawi (1992); al-Sayyid (1991); al-Zayn (1992); and Azzam (1993).

10. Salim (1998a, 11) interprets "the end of history" as a plan to wipe Muslims off the face of the earth in 1999; note that for earlier students of Israel, the "end of history" was seen as symbolic of the messianic nature of Zionism: see al-Musayri (1973); and for Arab and Muslim critiques of Fukayama, see Mula'b (1998); Bakr (1993); Virailio (1998); and A. 'Ali (1996, 182–86).

11. F. Salim 1998c, 19–21; however, one should notice that several years before Huntington put out this thesis, Ayyub had already talked about the "clash of civilizations," using those words and coming to much the same conclusion (1987, 110). For Arab and Muslim critiques of

scriptive and not prescriptive, and, although both Fukayama and Huntington are influential, neither one actually wields any policy-making power. In the case of the "new world order," at the very least, these Muslim writers are vilifying a policy that has actually saved Muslim lives in Bosnia, Kosovo, and Somalia, among other places. (Muslims contributed nothing to the fighting of these wars).[12] However, because of the paranoia of the apocalyptic conspiracy theories detailed in this book, all of these three phrases are read as essential threats to the existence of Islam, which is absurd in any case.

Another and far larger barrier to communication with the outside world is the anti-Semitic conspiracy theory. As repeatedly and graphically illustrated throughout this book, this element of the apocalyptic landscape is not a feature to be dismissed lightly. On the contrary, it is both fundamental to the scenario and exciting (and terrifying as well), and a draw to the Muslim audience. It provides, according to the perception of the Muslim writer and audience, the most cogent explanation for the state of the world. This material, while owing its intellectual and religious origins in its entirety to Christian literature and to later racist European anti-Semitic writings, is not going to bridge the gap between Muslims and the outside world. While there can be no doubt that there are many in the West who subscribe to certain elements of it, there is also no doubt that after the Holocaust it is not socially acceptable to advocate genocide.[13] This is what writer after writer from both the radical and the

---

the thesis (only a selection), see al-Sharif (1996); al-Asad (1997); al-Bayyuti (1997); Dahir (1996); B. Abdallah (1998); and further Mahmud (1993, 85–96); 'Ali (1996, 187–207). According to Abu Zayd (1999, 122–32), the world is witnessing the final collapse of Western civilization at the present time; and for further discussion, see 'Abd al-'Aziz (1993a, 1993b); 'Atiyya (1993); Abu 'Amud (1993); 'Alawani (1997); and al-Dabbagh (1997).

12. Note that 'Abdallah says that the Somalian people were actually fighting the Antichrist; speaking of those countries that resist the Antichrist—Iraq, Sudan and Afghanistan—he notes, "One should add to them the Somalian people who fight this very day [1993] against the forces of the Antichrist which they call the forces of the UN" (1994, 164).

13. M. Da'ud (1997, 32–33) says that his book is a response to several articles on the Mahdi published in the *New York Times* on January 19, 1992 (a search of the paper at this date revealed no such articles) that say that the Mahdi stories are ones that Muslims use to overcome and exterminate the Jews and reconquer Jerusalem. This enraged Da'ud, who says that the whole approach

neoconservative schools do, and they will inevitably repulse most of those in the West who come into contact with their writings.

Many Westerners are shocked when they hear the depth of Arab or Muslim feeling concerning the subject of the anti-Semitic conspiracy theory; for example, the story comes to mind of King Faysal of Saudi Arabia trying to persuade both Richard Nixon and Henry Kissinger of the truth of *The Protocols of the Elders of Zion*.[14] In the aftermath of such disappointment, unless the Muslim conspiracy-theorist is capable of self-criticism, for which few of the above writers have demonstrated a capacity, he will be forced by the internal logic of the conspiracy theory to place those people (the Christians or secularists in the West), who he would like to gain as allies, on the other side by default. If they are not going to join the Muslim side, then they must be part of the Jewish world conspiracy. Mustafa raises this point in disbelief:

> If the Christian West felt the same as Islam [does about the Jews], then the matter would be understandable. Islam recognizes the prophethood of Jesus and believes in him, and says about him [that he is] the Word of God [Qur'an 3:45], that he is a Spirit from God [4:171], and that his mother was true, virgin and pure, and that she is the best of the women of the world. But instead the opposite has happened. The Christian West has joined with the Zionists, because the dominating force was passion, interest, and desires, and not religion. They [Christians] have no religion and no faith in anything, and they only want to use the other to get what they want, and that is to strike at Islam. (Mustafa 1998, 92)[15]

---

is not reasonable discussion between people but incitement of blind hatred. 'Abd al-Jabbar (1993) writes that the scenario of the battle of Armageddon is used by Western Christians to destroy Islam (citing Hal Lindsey and Jerry Falwell [295–98]); she seems unaware that Muslims use this theme as well to destroy Jews and Christians.

14. Pipes 1996, 123–24; see also Hasan (1996–97) for the use of *The Protocols*; and Ahmad (1973–74).

15. Other writers, such as al-Tawil (1995), explore further the theme of Crusaders making an alliance with Israel. They ignore the fact that the original Crusaders were hardly known for their philo-Judaism, although the original Crusader persecution of the Jews is sometimes denied; see Qasim (1997).

This statement, wholly within the spirit of Muslim apologetics, epitomizes the problem of trying to understand another faith from the context of one's own. It would be clear to any Christian that a shared feeling for Jesus (however strong) is not the basis for an interfaith relationship, any more than the shared heritage of the Jewish Bible necessarily means that Jews and Christians have a bridge between each other. The considerable differences in interpretation of the commonalities (Jesus between Christians and Muslims, the Jewish biblical prophecies between Jews and Christians) actually oftentimes tend to drive a wedge further between these groups.[16]

The conspiracy theory, therefore, is a closed circle. It has created its own world and successfully locked out the Jews, denying their messianic aspirations, plagiarizing from their scriptures, dehumanizing them, and placing the world under their supposedly demonic control. Not only have the conspiracy theorists locked out the Jews, but they have locked out other Muslims as well. The result is clear: no one is going to want a dialogue with a group that advocates genocide and world conquest (or at least domination) for what appear to outside observers to be paranoid and inexplicable reasons. Acceptance of this conspiracy theory will destroy for the apocalyptic writer any chance of finding a sympathetic audience.

The question that most obviously presents itself now is: what is next for the Muslim apocalyptic writer? Given the realities as he perceives them, what does he propose to do? With the world totally controlled by this conspiracy, is there any practical action to be taken? In this area, unfortunately, the apocalyptist is particularly weak—or perhaps it is better for the world that he is. Sa'id Ayyub says:

> What is the part of the believer in the victory that will be gained in the final end? The part of the believer is that he takes his place in the camp of faith and that he places himself in the path defined by being well-trodden [i.e., the shari'a], and that he lives his life in accordance with that definition. There is

16. Even detailed volumes such as those of 'Ajak (1998) amount largely to a polemic rather than genuine dialogue; other "descriptions" of Christianity are less even-handed: see Shahin (1992); al-Hajj (1992); overall, see Haddad (1996).

nothing for him, until the rule *(amr)* of God appears. (Ayyub 1987, 18; cf. Jamal al-Din 1996, 126–31; Mustafa 1998, 96–97; F. Da'ud 1999, last pages, unnumbered)

In other words, the Muslim apocalyptist knows how to frighten his audience, but he does not know what to do with them once they are really and fully frightened. He does not seem to have any practical vision to provide, and in this regard the radical school is as unprepared for its popular success as were the conservatives trying to refute them.

There is one exception to this total lack of a plan, and that is the proposal to renew the caliphate, with the Mahdi as the candidate for the position, who would then go about unifying the fragmented Muslim world and establishing a type of millennial rule (to the extent to which such a term can be used in Islam). This is a fundamental and powerful plank in the apocalyptists' arsenal, and one that resonates with most radicals and even with the conservative school.

All these flags, the black, the red, and the white,[17] which gather spurious slogans, are nothing but a collection of colors, symbols and names, most of them submissive to humanism, which divides between religion and the state, and reinforces the principle of absolute freedom, which causes corruption to spread, and the person is chained in shackles of servitude and slavery, so that he can be a slave to the republic and to socialism and to the Ba'th [parties of Syria and Iraq]. These are all synonymous words of the Jahiliyya, and in their ridiculous essence are Masonic and Jewish. It is impossible that a group that claims to be Muslim, [yet] has permitted what God has forbidden, renounced the constitution of the heavens [i.e., the Qur'an], and fought the people of faith [Muslims], will be victorious. The Arabs and the Muslims, if they returned to God in truth and pure belief, would become in truth the servants of God, victorious over the Jews, because God promised: "As for those who disbelieve, disaster will not cease to afflict them because of what they did, or will settle near their homes until Allah's promise is fulfilled"

17. Flags are the symbols of the differing religious and political parties in early Islam, who used these colors. Black is the 'Abbasid color (and Sunnis overall); red came to be used for the Syrian-based parties; and white (or green) for the Shi'ites; see 'Athamina (1989).

[Qur'an 13:31], and "If you go back, We shall come back" [Qur'an 17:8]. The return to God is the path of victory, and of overcoming and of victory. ('Arif 1996, 175)

There is an intense desire to be rid of the politically fragmented Muslim present—and a tendency to blame this condition upon the West, which bears at most only partial responsibility—and regain the mythical Islamic unity of classical time in preparation for the end of the world (e.g., Mowla 1998). Unity is the goal for the apocalyptist, and he desires to rid Islam of the weight of its history:

Has not the wind *(rih)* of the Arabs and the Muslims gone during these days? Have they not fallen under the Jewish world domination and the powers influenced and dependent upon it? The Arabs and the Muslims have torment imposed upon them, and are enduring the subjection and humiliation of their enemies, who fight the Arabs and the Muslims and kill them in their own homes, steal their possessions, and make them into slaves. This we have witnessed with our own eyes, and we have witnessed the slaughter of our children, the violation of our honor and our holy places, and the rape of our homelands, while we are not able to protect ourselves. Even more than that, when we begin to beg our enemies to stop and leave off their trampling upon us, we do not find anything other than derision and contempt, in addition to the humiliation [of begging]. For what? Because we are divided in our faith. Hasn't the time come that the Muslims would understand that all of their schools, and their sects—the Shi'a, the Sunna, and the Sufis—hasn't the time come that they would understand that they are all Muslims and rally under the banner of Islam, and its name alone?. . . . We must simply define our identity by one word: either "Muslim" or "non-Muslim." (al-Shihabi 1997, 132–33; cf. H. 'Abd al-Hamid 1998, 164–65)

Traditions such as "Whoever dies without having sworn the oath of allegiance [to a caliph], dies the death of the Jahiliyya" (Muslim al-Qushayri 6:21; Ibn Hanbal 3:446, 4:96) or "Whoever dies while he is not under obedience [to a caliph] dies the death of the Jahiliyya, and if he turns against it after he has sworn [lit. after it is around his neck], then he has no excuse before God [at the final judgment]" (al-Hindi 6:26 no. 14857) continue to resonate, especially since several generations have now passed without movement to reestablish the caliphate (abolished in 1924).

The principal obstacle to the selection of a caliph is practicality. While everyone—with the exception of the ruling leadership of Muslim countries and some of the more hidebound *'ulama'*—desires a caliph, theoretically at least,[18] there is no method by which one can be chosen, nor is there a method through which some forty-five independent Muslim states would surrender power to such a person, once chosen, other than by forcible conquest (Mowla 1998, 340). In addition to these practical problems, there is also the question of what the Western countries would do to stop a caliph from being chosen. Some, such as 'Abdallah, see the West as the principal obstacle to the selection of a caliph (1994, 139). All previous caliphs in the history of Islam have first attained power, and only afterward was their authority legitimized in retrospect. At this time—according to the hypothetical theory—authority would first have to be bestowed and only then would power and sovereignty be handed over. This seemingly impossible step is made all the more frustrating as the Muslims watch the European Community accomplish precisely this action before their very eyes—admittedly bumbling in the process and with many reservations on the part of a number of different countries (see, for example, Nafi'a 1993).

To this, the apocalyptist has an answer. The candidate will be chosen by God, and he will be proclaimed with divine signs so that all will *want* to hand over their power to him—although note that even Da'ud does not seriously believe that this will persuade the Muslim governments to take this step; at every point in his scenario force was required to persuade them. While this might not seem to the outside observer to be the most ideal solution to the paradox, it both postpones the solution to the problem until the indefinite future, and places the time, the selection of the candidate, and the burden of proof upon God. It is not certain what practical benefits are derived from this procrastination, but the psychological benefits are enormous, and it very probably contributes to a more stable society as well.

There is a further benefit that the apocalyptist should bring out but which

---

18. These 'ulama' are attacked by M. Da'ud (1997, 17); and see al-Badri (1966) and Khalidi (1997).

is not given much consideration in the literature as it now stands. Since the original abolition of the caliphate resulted from a Zionist conspiracy (according to the interpretation of the apocalyptic writers) and the present-day realities of the conspiracy are, in the apocalyptist's mind, so strong and well-documented by his own work, what chance does the movement to reestablish the caliphate actually have? Assuming that a caliph was actually chosen, though, and assuming the vast conspiracy that apocalyptic writers have painted for us (which of course is a fantasy), then the very fact of his proclamation in the face of such an overwhelming perceived opposition would probably be tantamount to divine confirmation. Because the apocalyptist has built up this vast straw man, he has actually lessened the difficulties of confirmation, although he might not be aware of this fact.

What does the outside observer gain by gazing in at Muslim apocalyptic literature? We see how the Muslims view the modern technological world and their place in it. We also see, sadly, some very disturbing characteristics: the lack of self-criticism (Reid 1987; al-Zaydi 1996); the defensive attitude toward anything that comes from the outside world;[19] the self-imposed prison walls of the conspiracy theory; the hatred and envy of the West, with its attendant desires to either humiliate or destroy it—or at least dispossess it; and the view of technology as a number of toys with which to play, rather than a result of knowledge that must be cultivated and constantly expanded through free inquiry. What criticism of Muslim society there is in the apocalyptic literature is unfortunately directed against precisely those persons who are finally, gradually, turning their backs on these negative attitudes. One could, therefore say that while there are many positive qualities in contemporary Muslim society, in reading the apocalyptic literature, we are able to see the depth of the opposition to those same qualities.

Do Muslim apocalyptists really believe what they write? The visions are so fantastic, and many of the predictions and the dates given are so specific, that

---

19. See, for example, the huge body of literature critical of Orientalism: Zaqzuq (1983); al-Da'mi (1986); al-Sharqawi (1989, 1993); al-Fayyumi (1993); Salim (1994); Matbaqani (1995); Mu'aliqi (1996); Zarzur, Rabi' and al-Ansari (1996, 107–46); Fawzi (1998); al-Namla (1998); al-'Allani (1998); and al-Julaynid (1999).

reading the material begs the question of the personal veracity of the authors. Can a Muslim actually believe the scenarios detailed above? In all honesty, no one knows to what extent this modern Muslim apocalyptic scenario has been accepted at a popular level. There have been few empirical studies of Muslim beliefs at the popular level, and none about apocalyptic are known to me.[20] As to the authors' motives, unfortunately speculation is also the only answer to the question of whether they believe what they write. In reading the material there are certain authors who stand out as sober and believable, such as Bashir Muhammad 'Abdallah, 'Abd al-Wahhab Tawila, and Amin Jamal al-Din. This is not because they are any less anti-Semitic or vituperative, but their tone is still more measured and their statements less extreme. By contrast Sa'id Ayyub, Muhammad 'Isa Da'ud, and Hisham Kamal 'Abd al-Hamid write in an unbalanced tone. In any case it is difficult to take seriously a writer who uses UFOs as the backbone of his theory, and Da'ud especially shows signs of being a megalomaniac. But whatever their writing style, all of these writers have described in depth a scenario which they must know to some degree or another is a fantasy. It is remarkable how many of the authors are well read: Ayyub, for example, cites many of the greats of the Western humanist tradition (Will Durant, Bertrand Russell, Plato, Jean-Paul Sartre), and 'Abdallah does as well. But they have written compositions indicating that their primary source of understanding about the contemporary world is not this humanist tradition but the ambiguous words of prophecies and the oftentimes fabricated tales of UFO crackpots. It is tempting to believe that the more hysterical of the authors are writing for the money, and that the more sober ones are writing because they believe what they say. But truthfully, there is no proof one way or another. 'Abd al-Hamid writes in conclusion to one of his books:

> Finally, I would say that it is incumbent upon us to utilize these prophecies
> that the prophets have told us about the events and the wars of the end of

20. See, however, the article of Elise Ackerman, "Muslim, Christian Doomsday Visions Converge," posted for Knight-Ridder newspapers (May 2, 2003). Ackerman interviewed Amin Jamal al-Din and cites his figure of more than a million copies of his books sold. This does not seem credible, but probably several thousand at least have sold.

time when plans and special policies concerning our dealings with the countries of the world are made. The prophets did not tell us of them [the prophe-
cies] for our amusement,[21] but for us to utilize them, just as we have shown
previously. However, this does not mean that we should take these prophecies as a reason for creating enmity between us and the countries with which
there will be wars in the future, as the Jews, the West, and the Americans have
done. If we did that, then we would be going astray in our understanding of
these prophecies, just as the Jews and Christians did. We should simply take
warning and be cautious, making peace with those who make peace with us,
and warring upon those who war with us, and, as we prepare for every future
event, we should know that the appointed time is close because of the
prophecies of the prophets. . . . We should not just trust entirely in fate and
leave the events to happen. This would be an incorrect understanding of the
prophecies of the prophets. God does not change what is in a people until
they change themselves, because God does not bring the daily sustenance he
foreordained for his creatures when they are [just] sitting at home. But he
brings them daily sustenance, in accordance with his predestination for them,
when they themselves strive for that sustenance by work and effort. ('Abd
al-Hamid 1998, 164)

Is the apocalyptic literature a venue for learning, as some (notably
Richard Landes of the Center for Millennial Studies at Boston University)
have pointed out? Material is definitely communicated in the literature. One
learns incidentally a huge amount about Western civilization, and usually at
least snippets about scientific discoveries and truths—although frequently
they are refuted on the basis of Qur'anic material and blackened with the
hated name of Darwin. In their accounts of the Antichrist's flying saucers,
Da'ud and 'Abd al-Hamid have extensive scientific discussions, although they
are not of a sort that is likely to produce any true knowledge. Biblical material
is often cited verbatim, and this is probably good for the Muslim audience to
hear (seeing the Christian faith as it presents itself, rather than through the
lens of Muslim prejudice). One should notice that frequently the history of
the Jews is given accurately enough, although nasty comments can appear on

21. Compare 'Arif (1996, 152), who also denies a fatalistic point of view.

the side. On the other hand, the hostility toward Jews is greatly magnified beyond what the classical apocalyptic sources would allow, where Jews appear only incidentally. This magnification is based on Western anti-Semitic sources, which are accepted uncritically by the overwhelming majority of these authors. This is the principal difference between the radical school and the neoconservatives. The former are perfectly willing to use (and abuse) the texts of other faiths to prove their point, and make use of a grand Jewish conspiracy *(The Protocols of the Elders of Zion)* throughout history to show the truth of their scenario. They have reworked the classical Muslim texts into harmony with this scenario; and, while the basic dialogue remains Muslim, the overarching concept is foreign to Islam.

One also cannot help but notice that the centrality of the establishment of the state of Israel is one of the things that Muslim and Christian apocalyptists have in common, although its meaning is diametrically opposed in the traditions. It is quite amazing to note the extent to which Islamist apocalyptists are willing to go in the effort to find a scenario acceptable to them, even digging into their opponent's apocalyptic and messianic expectations in order to corrupt these. One can fairly say, for example, that the identification of the Jews' expected messiah with the Antichrist is so firmly rooted in Muslim apocalyptic that it even appears in certain conservative works, as well as appearing in all radical ones. This identification enables them to see the Arab-Israeli conflict in its entirety as an apocalyptic event and one in which the Arabs are destined to be victorious, despite the present gloomy situation. Of course, for many of these authors, the Arab-Israeli conflict is simply part of a greater conflict between Islam and the West, which must also be resolved in favor of the former before the end of the world.

The emphasis in the apocalyptic literature is much more on the horrifying events scheduled to occur before the end rather than on the messianic age: to terrify the audience, rather than raise the expectations for the Messiah. In classical apocalyptic literature there is no single work that is devoted entirely to the Antichrist or to Gog and Magog, while a surprising number of them are dedicated strictly to the traditions about the Mahdi or about the messianic age. The situation during our own time is almost exactly the opposite. There is comparatively little material on the Mahdi—much of it from the conservative school; notice that Ayyub almost entirely ignored the Mahdi, although the radicals are starting to catch up in this area—most of the literature concerns the Antichrist, Gog and Magog, or the other disastrous events of the end. Also, unlike classical apocalyptic sources, in modern apocalyptic there is no break between the events of this world and the next. Most of the apocalyptic books and tracts go right from events in this world into the Day of Resurrection, something that classical authors almost never do. Obviously, an equally important theme is that of the moral apocalypse. Essentially this sort of material is well known in classical sources, but it is used here with new urgency to combat the influence of Western culture. All of the writers surveyed believe that they are living in the last days, and in order to prove their point to an already sympathetic audience, the material about corruption, fornication, and so forth at the end of time is rehashed.

Modern Muslim apocalyptic literature, therefore, combines reinterpretations of classical sources and biblical apocalyptic materials with expositions of a Western and Jewish "conspiracy." A radical change in the direction of this writing took place in the 1980s and early 1990s. Rejecting the traditional, conservative approach to the sources, the Muslim apocalyptist increasingly emphasized the coming apocalypse in order to give the texts life. Does this new scenario work for the audience? In the short term, until field research can be conducted, one must answer yes to this question. The short time needed for incubation, the quick and general spread of the ideas, the frequent citation of the thesis by those outside the apocalyptist's immediate circle, all contribute to success, allowing the Muslim apocalyptist to explain away (at least to himself) the frustrating and enraging events of the modern world, which he sees as attacking his values and those of his fellow believers at every juncture. There is a limited tendency to promise a glorious future; the more prominent necessity is to explain the dismal present. However, because of the negative effects of the apocalyptic scenario, it is very likely that it will result in self-fulfillment and prolong that dismal present beyond what would be strictly necessary.

WORKS CITED
INDEX

WORKS CITED

Note: As many of the radical Islamic websites have been suppressed since 2001, some of the sources cited here may now be inaccessible. The author will provide full details on request.

'Abdallah, Bashir Muhammad. 1994. *Zilzal al-ard al-'azim*. Cairo: n.p.

'Abdallah, Taufik. 1998. " 'The Crash of Civilizations': A Prognosis for the Future or the Lure of the Past?" *Studia Islamika* 5:77–96.

'Abd al-'Aziz, Zaynab. 1993a. "Mawqif al-gharb min al-Islam fi sira'ihi al-hadari." *Mustaqbal al-'Alam al-Islami* 3, no. 9: 63–76.

———. 1993b. "Naqd mawqif al-gharb min al-'Arab wa-l-Muslimin." *Al-Fikr al-'Arabi* 14, no. 2: 86–94.

'Abd al-Bar, Muhammad. 1987. *Al-Masih al-muntazar wa-ta'alim al-Talmud*. Jidda: Dar al-Sa'udiyya.

'Abd al-Bari, Farag Allah. 1991. "Al-Yawm al-akhir fi al-Yahudiyya, al-Nasraniyya wa-l-Islam." *Majallat al-Azhar* 63:894–99, 1232–37, 1350–57.

'Abd al-Hakim, Mansur. 1998a. *Al-Harb al-'alamiyya al-thalitha qadima wa-taduqq 'ala al-abwab*. Cairo: Maktaba al-Tawfiqiyya.

———. 1998b. *Al-Mahdi al-muntazar*. Cairo: Maktaba al-Tawfiqiyya.

———. 1998c. *Nihayat dawlat Isra'il 2022*. Cairo: Maktaba al-Tawfiqiyya.

———. 1999. *Nihayat wa-damar Amrika wa-Isra'il*. Cairo: Maktaba al-Tawfiqiyya.

'Abd al-Hamid, Hisham Kamal. 1996. *Iqtaraba khuruj al-masih al-Dajjal*. Cairo: Dar al-Bashir.

———. 1997a. *Halak wa-damar Amrika al-muntazar*. Cairo: Dar al-Bashir.

———. 1997b. *Yajuj wa-Majuj qadimuna*. Cairo: Dar al-Bashir.

———. 1998. *Isharat al-Islam wa-l-kutub al-samawiyya ila al-harb al-'alamiyya al-qadima fi al-sharq al-awsat*. Cairo: n.p.

———. 2000. *'Asr al-masih al-Dajjal: Al-Haqa'iq wa-l-watha'iq*. Cairo: Markaz al-Hadara al-'Arabiyya.

Abd al-Hamid, Muhyi'd-din. 1996. *Yajuj and Majuj,* translated by Aisha Bewley. London: Dar al-Taqwa.

'Abd al-Haqq, Salah Sayf al-Din. 1993. *Fitnat al-masih al-Dajjal wa-'aja'ib Yajuj wa-Majuj.* Cairo: Dar al-Rawda.

'Abd al-Jabbar, Salima. 1993. "Al-Masihiyya al-gharbiyya wa-nazariyyat Harmageddon fi muwajahat al-Islam." *Majallat Kulliyyat al-Da'wa al-Islamiyya* 10:284–307.

'Abd al-Mun'im, Shakir Mahmud. 1994. "Hiwar al-mufassirin wa-l-mu'arrikhin fi qissat Iram dhat al-'Imad." *Al-Mu'arrikh al-'Arabi* 19, no. 47: 149–56.

'Abduh, Muhammad (d. 1905). N.d. *Tafsir al-manar.* Cairo: Al-Manar.

'Abd al-Wahid, Khalid. 2001. *Nihayat Isra'il wa-l-Wilayat al-Muttahida al-Amrikiya.* Cairo: n.p.

Abu 'Amud, Muhammad Sa'd. 1993. "Al-Istijaba al-'Arabiyya al-Islamiyya al-matluba li-l-tahaddi al-hadari al-gharbi." *Mustaqbal al-'Alam al-Islami* 3, no. 9: 121–50.

Abu 'Arafa, Salah al-Din. 2001. *Al-Qur'an al-'azim yunabbi bi-damar al-Wilayat al-Muttahida wa-gharq al-jaysh al-Amriki.* Jerusalem: n.p.

Abu Da'ud al-Sijistani (d. 888). 1998. *Sunan.* Beirut: Mu'assasat al-Riyan.

Abu Ghazala, Mahmud. 1994. *Islamiyyat Bayt al-Maqdis: Fada'il wa-thawabit.* Jerusalem: Jami'at al-Masjid.

Abu al-Ru'us, Ayman. 1999. *Lughz al-alghaz muthallath al-tinnin.* Cairo: Maktabat Ibn Sina'.

Abu Sahiliyya, Sami 'Iwad. 1992. "Dururat taghyir al-Umam al-Muttahida aw tarkuha." *Al-'Irfan* 76, no. 5: 16–21.

Abu Zayd, Ahmad. 1997. "Hayat Isra'il 76 sara na-nihayatuha fi 2022" (The [extent of the] life of Israel is 76 years and its end is in 2022). *Al-Rabita* 392 (Oct.-Nov.):18–19.

———. 1999. *Al-Sartan al-Yahudi wa-nufudhuhu al-a'lami wa-nazariyyat al-muwajaha.* 'Amman: Dar 'Ammar.

Addams, C. C. 1944. "A *Fatwa* on the Ascension of Jesus." *Muslim World* 34:214–17.

Ahmad, Mirza Bashir al-Din Mahmud, Khalifat al-Masih (d. 1965). 1986. *Tafsir-i kavir.* N.p.

Ahmad, Muhammad Naji. 1973–74. "Al-Yahudiyya wa-l-Sihyawniyya min qadim ila al-yawm wara' ma'si al-bashariyya wa-jarahiha." *Majallat Kulliyyat al-Lugha al-'Arabiyya wa-l-Dirasat al-Islamiyya* 1:15–62.

Ahmad, Rifa'at Sa'id. 1988. *Rasa'il Juhayman al-'Utaybi.* Cairo: Matba'at al-Madbuli.

———, ed. 1997. *Rihlat al-damm la-ladhi hazama al-sayf: Al-A'mal al-kamila li-shahid al-duktur Fahti Shiqaqi.* Cairo: Markaz Yafa li-Dirasat wa-Abhath.

Ahmad, al-Shafiʿ al-Mahi. 1996. *Yajuj wa-Majuj: Fitnat al-madi wa-l-hadir wa-l-mustaqbal.* Beirut: Dar Ibn Hazm.

ʿAjak, Bassam. 1998. *Al-Hiwar al-Islami al-Masihi.* N.p.: Dar Qutayba.

Akhbari, Suzanne Conklin. 1997. "The Rhetoric of Antichrist in Western Lives of Muhammad." *Islam and Christian-Muslim Relations* 8:297–307.

Akram, Muhammad. 1995. "Al-Quds: A Historical Perspective." *Journal of the Pakistan Historical Society* 43:239–44.

ʿAlam, Jalal. 1977. *Qadat al-gharb yaqulun: Dammiru al-Islam, ubidu ahlahu.* Cairo: Mukhtar al-Islami.

ʿAlami, Ahmad. 1992. *Al-Hufriyyat al-Israʾiliyya hawala al-Haram al-Sharif.* Jerusalem: Matbaʿa al-ʿArabiyya al-Haditha.

ʿAlawani, Abd al-Wahid. 1997. "Muwajahat aw hiwar? Al-Islam wa-l-gharb al-masharif qarn jadid." *Al-Kalimah* 16:131–37.

ʿAli, ʿAbdallah. 1996. *Aqwa wa-akhir umma fi al-taʾrikh.* Beirut: Dar al-Safwa.

ʿAli, Mawlana Murad. N.d. *Tafsir-i kavir.* Tehran: Mashhad-i Sharif.

ʿAli, Sayyid Amr. N.d. *Mavahib-i Rahman aw Jamiʿ al-bayan.* Lahore: Qurʾan-i Makpati.

al-ʿAllani, Muhammad al-Sahabi. 1998. *Al-Istishraq al-Faransi wa-l-adab al-ʿArabi al-qadim.* Tunis: Al-Alfa.

ʿAmaluhu, Muhammad. 1992. *Mawduʿiyyat al-Islam fi muwajahat al-Sihyawniyya.* Tripoli: Manshurat Kulliyat al-Daʿwa al-Islamiyya.

Amir-Moezzi, Mohammed. 1994. *The Divine Guide.* Translated by David Straight. Albany: State University of New York Press.

ʿAmr, Yusuf Muhammad. 1997. *Min ashrat al-saʿa al-kubra: Khuruj dabba min al-ard al-mujawira.* Cairo: Dar al-Dhahabiyya.

Ansari, ʿAbdallah. 1928–29. *Tafsir-i adabi va-ʿirfani: Kashf al-asrar.* Tehran: Shirket-Nasibi-yi Iqbal.

Ansari, Z. I. 1981. "Aspects of Black Muslim Theology." *Studia Islamica* 53:137–76.

ʿArif, Jamil. 1999. *Al-Muʾamarat al-Sihyawniyya ʿala Misr.* Cairo: Maktab al-Misri al-Hadith.

ʿArif, Muhammad ʿIzzat. 1990. *Nihayat Saddam.* Cairo: Dar al-Iʿtisam.

———. 1995. *Al-Mahdi and the End of Time.* Translated by Aisha Bewley. London: Dar al-Taqwa.

———. 1996. *Nihayat al-Yahud.* Cairo: Dar al-Iʿtisam.

———. 1997. *Hal al-Dajjal yahkum al-ʿalam al-an?* Cairo: Dar al-Iʿtisam.

al-ʿArusi, ʿAbd ʿAli b. Jumʿa al-Huwayzi (d. 1600s). N.d. *Tafsir nur al-thaqalayn.* Qumm: Maktabat al-Hikma.

al-Asad, Nasir al-Din al-Asad. 1997. "Al-Islam wa-l-tafa'ul al-hadari." *Afaq al-Islam* 5, no. 18: 30–39.

'Ashur, 'Abd al-Latif. 1987. *Thalatha yantazaruhum al-'alam*. Cairo: Maktabat al-Qur'an.

'Ata', Muhammad 'Abd al-Qadir. 1999. *Al-Masih al-Dajjal*. Cairo: Dar al-Fajr li-l-Turath.

al-Atat, Faysal. 1992. *Al-Harb al-'alamiyya al-thalitha wa-l-akhira*. Beirut: Al-Irshad.

'Athamina, Khalil. 1989. "The Black Banners and the Socio-political Significance of Flags and Slogans in Early Islam." *Arabica* 36:307–26.

'Atiyya, Ahmad 'Abd al-Halim. 1993. "Al-Islam wa-l-gharb." *Mustaqbal al-'Alam al-Islami* 3, no. 9: 97–120.

al-'Awadi, al-Sayyid Mahdi. 2000. *Al-Mahdi wa-akhir al-zaman*. Sidon: Dar al-Janub li-l-Tiba'a.

Ayyub, Sa'id. 1987. *Al-Masih al-Dajjal*. Cairo: Fath li-l-A'lam al-'Arabi.

———. 1991. *'Aqidat al-masih al-Dajjal fi al-adyan*. Cairo: Dar al-Hadi.

———. 1999. *Ibtila'at al-umam*. Cairo: Dar al-Hadi.

———. 1998a. *Al-Tariq ila al-Mahdi al-muntazar*. Beirut: Al-Ghadir.

———. 1998b. *Wa-ja'a al-haqq*. Beirut: Al-Ghadir.

Azad, Mohamed, and Amina, Bibi. 2001. *Islam Will Conquer All Other Religions and American Power Will Diminish: Read How Allah's (God's) Prediction Will Soon Come to Pass*. Brooklyn, N.Y.: Bell Six Publishing.

al-'Azizi, Muhammad Ramiz 'Abd al-Fattah. 2001. *Al-Masjid al-Aqsa fi al-Islam wa-shurut zawal dawlat Isra'il al-mazu'ma kama warada fi al-Qur'an al-karim*. Amman: n.p.

'Azzam, 'Abdallah. 1989. *Basha'ir al-nasr*. Peshawar: Markaz al-Shahid 'Azzam al-I'lami.

———. 1991. *Min Kabul ila al-Quds*. A posthumous collection of articles. Peshawar: Markaz al-Shahid 'Azzam al-I'lami.

———. N.d. *Al-Islam wa-l-mustaqbal al-bashariyya*. Peshawar: Markaz al-Shahid 'Azzam al-I'lami.

'Azzam, Maha. 1993. "Islamist Attitudes to the Current World Order." *Islam and Christian-Muslim Relations* 4:247–56.

al-Badri, 'Abd al-'Aziz. 1966. *Al-Islam bayna al-'ulama' wa-l-hukkam*. Medina: Maktaba al-'Ilmiyya.

al-Baghdadi, al-Khazin (d. 1325). 1995. *Tafsir al-Khazin*. Beirut: Dar al-Kutub al-'Ilmiyya.

Bahlul, Raja. 1993. "The Liberal Concept of Freedom in Modern Arabic Political

Thought." *International Journal of Islamic and Arabic Studies* 10:27–66 (Arabic).

al-Bahrani, Hashim al-Musawi (d. ca. 1696). 1996. *Al-Burhan fi tafsir al-Qur'an.* Qumm: Mu'assasat al-Bi'tha.

Bakr, Hasan. 1993. "Mutariha naqdiyya li-nazariyyat Fukayama: *Nihayat al-ta'rikh* um ideologiyyat al-rajul al-akhir?" *Mustaqbal al-'Alam al-Islami* 3, no. 9: 263–76.

al-Balanisi, Muhammad bin 'Ali (d. 1380). 1991. *Tafsir mubhimat al-Qur'an.* Beirut: Dar al-Gharb al-Islami.

Bälz, Killian. 1997. "Submitting Faith to Judicial Scrutiny Through the Family Trial: The 'Abu Zayd Case.' " *Die Welt des Islams* 37:135–55.

al-Bar, Muhammad 'Ali. 1992. *Al-Masih al-muntazar wa-ta'alim al-Talmud.* Jiddah.

———. 1998. *Tahrif al-Tawrah wa-siyasat Isra'il al-tawassu'iyya.* Damascus: Dar al-Qalam.

al-Barak, Mubarak. 1999. *Al-Da'if wa-l-mawdu' min ashrat al-sa'a.* Cairo: Maktabat Jazirat al-Ward.

Barth, Donna Lee. 1997. "Abortion, Islam and the 1994 Cairo Population Conference." *International Journal of Middle Eastern Studies* 29:161–84.

Bashear, Suliman. 1991. "Early Muslim Apocalyptic Materials." *Journal of the Royal Asiatic Society,* 173–207.

———. 1993. "Muslim Apocalypses." *Israel Oriental Studies* 13:75–99.

al-Basri, al-Hasan (d. 728). 1997. *Tafsir.* Cairo: Dar al-Hadith.

al-Bawwab, Sulayman Salim. 1996. *Al-Atfal: Wala'im damawiyya 'ala ma'idat al-Yahud.* Beirut: Al-Manara.

Baydun, 'Isa Mahmud. 1993. *Dalil li-masjid al-Aqsa al-mubarak.* Kafr Kanna: Markaz li-Takhtit wa-Dirasat.

Bayumi, Muhammad. 1995a. *'Alamat yawm al-qiyama al-kubra.* Cairo: Maktabat al-Iman.

———. 1995b. *'Alamat yawm al-qiyama al-sughra.* Cairo: Maktabat al-Iman.

———. 1995c. *Al-Mahdi al-muntazar.* Cairo: Maktabat al-Iman.

———. 1997. *Al-Yahud wa-usturat al-baqara al-hamra'.* Cairo: Maktabat Jazirat al-Ward.

al-Bayyuti, Sabri Mustafa. 1997. "Scenario sira' al-hadarat." *Dirasat 'Arabiyya* 33, nos. 7–8: 47–58.

Berg, Herbert. 1998. "Elijah Muhammad: An African-American *Mufassir?*" *Arabica* 45:320–46.

al-Brusawi, Isma'il Haqqi (d. 1724). 1984. *Tanwir al-adhhan tafsir ruh al-bayan.* Damascus: Dar al-'Ilm.

Busse, Heribert. 1996. "The Destruction of the Temple and Its Reconstruction in the Light of Muslim Exegesis of *Sura* 17:2–8." *Jerusalem Studies in Arabic and Islam* 20:1–17.

al-Buti, Muhammad Sa'id. 1997. *Al-Jihad fi al-Islam: Kayfa nafhimuhu wa-kayfa numarisuhu?* Damascus: Dar al-Fikr.

Carr, William Guy. 1950. *Pawns in the Game,* translated into Arabic by Sa'id Jaza'irli. 1984. *Ahjar 'ala ruqa'at shantraj.* Beirut: Dar al-Nafa'is.

Cherep-Spiridovich, Count. [1926] 1983. *Al-Hukuma al-'alamiyya al-khafiyya* (The secret world government). Translated into Arabic by Sa'id Jaza'irli. Beirut: Dar al-Nafa'is.

Collins, John. 1979. "Morphology of a Genre." *Semeia* 14:1–20.

Cook, David. 1996. "Muslim Apocalyptic and *Jihad*." *Jerusalem Studies in Arabic and Islam* 20:66–104.

———. 1997. "Moral Apocalyptic in Islam." *Studia Islamica* 86:37–69.

———. 1998. "Tamim al-Dari." *Bulletin of the School of Oriental and African Studies* 61:20–28.

———. 1999. "Muslim Sources on Comets and Meteorites." *Journal for the History of Astronomy* 30:131–60.

———. 2000. "Muhammad, Labid al-Yahudi and the Commentaries to *Sura* 113." *Journal of Semitic Studies* 45:323–45.

———. 2002a. "An Early Muslim Daniel Apocalypse." *Arabica* 22:55–96.

———. 2002b. "*Hadith,* Authority and the End of the World: Traditions in Modern Muslim Apocalyptic Literature," *Oriente Moderno* 21 n.s.: 31–53.

———. 2002c. *Studies in Muslim Apocalyptic.* Princeton, N.J.: Darwin Press.

———. 2002d. "Suicide Attacks or 'Martyrdom Operations' in Contemporary *Jihad* Literature." *Nova Religio* 6:7–44.

———. 2004. "Implications of Martyrdom Operations for Contemporary Islam." *Journal for Religious Ethics* 32:129–51.

Cook, Michael. 1992a. "Eschatology, History and the Dating of Traditions." *Princeton Papers in Near Eastern Studies* 1:23–48.

———. 1992b. "The Heraculean Dynasty in Muslim Apocalyptic." *Al-Qantara* 13:3–24.

———. 1993. "A Muslim Apocalyptic Chronicle." *Journal of Near Eastern Studies* 52:25–29.

al-Dabbagh, Riyadh. 1997. "Afaq al-mustaqbal wa-da'm al-hiwar bayna al-Muslimin wa-l-gharb." *Majallat al-Majma' al-'Ilmi al-'Iraqi* 44, no. 3: 33–45.

Dahir, Mas'ud. 1996. "Saddam al-hadarat." *Al-'Arabi* 39, no. 452: 26–30.

al-Da'mi, Muhammad 'Abd al-Husayn. 1986. *Al-Mutaghayyir al-gharbi.* Baghdad: Dar al-Shu'un al-Thaqafiyya al-'Amma.

al-Dani, Abu 'Amr 'Uthman (d. 1052). 1995. *Al-Sunan al-warida fi al-fitan wa-l-malahim.* Riyadh: Dar al-'Asima.

al-Dasuqi, Faruq. 1998a. *Al-Bayan al-nabawi bi-damar Isra'il al-washik wa-tahrir al-Aqsa wa-amarat al-sa'a.* Cairo: n.p.

———. 1998b. *Al-Qiyama al-sughra 'ala al-abwab (al-juz al-thalith).* Cairo: n.p.

Da'ud, Fa'iq Muhammad. 1999a. *Taraqqibu zuhur al-masih al-Dajjal wa-l-mahdi.* Amman: Dar al-Isra'.

———. 1999b. *Al-Umur al-'izam qabla zuhur al-Mahdi 'alayhi al-salam.* N.p.

Da'ud, Muhammad 'Isa. 1992a. *Hiwar sahafi ma' jinni Muslim.* Cairo: n.p.

———. 1992b. *Ihdharu: Al-masih al-Dajjal yaghzu al-'alam min muthallath Bermuda.* Cairo: Mukhtar al-Islami.

———. 1994a. *Al-Khuyut al-khafiyya bayna al-masih al-Dajjal wa-asrar muthallath Bermuda wa-l-atbaq al-ta'ira.* Cairo: Dar al-Bashir.

———. 1994b. *Al-Ladhina sakanu al-ard qablana.* Cairo: Dar Randa Amun.

———. 1997. *Al-Mahdi al-muntazar 'ala al-abwab.* Cairo: Dar Randa Amun.

———. 1998. *Saddam al-nubuwat: Al-Ashuri, al-Sufyani umm al-Shaysabani?* Cairo: Mu'assasat Tahir.

———. 1999. *Ma qabla al-damar.* Cairo: Dar al-Bashir.

Dibaja, Jamil. 1999. *'Aja'ib al-'adad wa-l-ma'dud fi al-Qur'an al-karim.* Beirut: Dar al-Mahajja al-Bayda'.

al-Dimashqi, 'Umar b. 'Adil al-Hanbali. 1998. *Al-Lubab fi 'ulum al-Qur'an.* Beirut: Dar al-Kutub al-'Ilmiyya.

Donner, Fred M. 1998. *Narratives of Islamic Beginnings.* Princeton, N.J.: Darwin Press.

Encyclopedia of Islam. 2d ed. 1960–2002. Edited by B. Lewis, C. E. Bosworth, et al. Leiden: E. J. Brill.

Fadlallah, al-Husayn. 1986. *Min wahy al-Qur'an.* Beirut: Dar al-Zahra.

Fa'iz, Ahmad. 1983. *Al-Yawm al-akhir fi zilal al-Qur'an.* Reprint. Beirut: Mu'assasat al-Risala.

Fakhry, Majid. 1997. *The Qur'an: A Modern English Version.* London: Garnet.

al-Faqir, Hamza. 1994. *Yajuj wa-Majuj.* Amman: Dar al-Isra'.

———. 1995. *Thalatha yantazaruhum al-'alam*. Amman: Dar al-Isra'.

Faraj, 'Ali Musa'd. 1993. *Isra'il ila ayyina?* Beirut: 'Ayn li-l-Dirasat wa-l-Buhuth al-Insaniyya wa-l-Ijtima'iyya.

al-Faramawi, 'Abd al-Hayy. 1992. *Al-Sirbiyyun khanazir Urubba*. Cairo: Dar al-I'tisam.

Farouki, Suha Taji. 1995. "A Case-Study in Contemporary Political Islam and the Palestine Question: The Perspective of Hizb al-Tahrir al-Islami." In *Medieval and Modern Perspectives in Muslim-Jewish Relations*, edited by Ronald Nettler, 35–58. Oxford: Harwood Academic Publications.

Fatawa Islamiyya: Islamic Verdicts. 2002. Riyadh: Darussalam.

Fawzi, Faruq 'Umar. 1998. *Al-Istishraq wa-ta'rikh al-Islam*. Beirut: Al-Ahaliyya.

al-Fayyumi, Muhammad Ibrahim. 1993. *Al-Istishraq risalat isti'mar*. Cairo: Dar al-Fikr al-'Arabi.

al-Fazazi, Muhammad. 1983. *Hukm Allah al-'adil fi zawal dawlat Isra'il*. Casablanca: Dar al-Tiba'a al-Haditha.

Ferooz, Muhammad Rashid. 1979. "The Abolition of the Caliphate: A Zionist Conspiracy Against the Muslim World." *Majllat kulliyyat al-lugha al-'Arabiyya* 9:3–12 (English language section).

Frankel, Jonathan. 1996. *The Damascus Affair*. Cambridge: Cambridge University Press.

Frayha, Anis. 1950. "Al-Harakat al-la Samiyya fi al-ta'rikh." *Al-Abhath* 3:463–82.

Fulayfil, Hasan Zakariya. 1991. *Haqiqa aghrab min al-khayal: Yajuj wa-Majuj*. Cairo: Maktabat Ibn Sina.

Gabr, Rokaya. 1991. "Les signes de l'heure d'après le Coran et la Sunna." *Majallat al-Azhar* 63:1308–16, 1449–56 (French language section).

Gardell, Mattias. 1995. *Countdown to Armageddon: Minister Farrakhan and the Nation of Islam in the Latter Days*. Stockholm: n.p.

Gorenberg, Gershom. 2000. *The End of Days: Fundamentalism and the Struggle for the Temple Mount*. New York: Free Press.

Guest, A. R. 1900. "End of the World." *Journal of the Royal Asiatic Society*, 794–96.

Haddad, Yvonne. 1996. "Islamist Depictions of Christianity in the Twentieth Century." *Islam and Christian-Muslim Relations* 7:75–94.

al-Hajj, Muhammad Abu al-Qasim. 1990. *Al-Bahth 'an haqiqa fi afkar wa-mu'taqidat al-Yahud*. Tripoli, Libya: Jami'at al-Da'wa al-Islamiyya al-'Alamiyya.

al-Hajj, Muhammad Ahmad. 1992. *Al-Nasraniyya min al-tawhid ila al-tathlith*. Damascus: Dar al-Qalam.

Hamada, Husayn 'Umar. 1994. *Al-Adabiyyat al-Masuniyya*. Riyadh: Wizarat al-A'lam.

Hamidullah, Muhammad. 1982. "The Jewish Background of the Battles of Jamal and Siffin." *Journal of the Pakistan Historical Society* 30:235–51.

Hamis, 'Adab Mahmud. 2001. *Al-Mahdi al-muntazar fi riwayat ahl al-sunna wa-l-shi'a al-imamiyya: Dirasa hadithiyya naqdiyya*. Amman: Matba'at al-Sharq.

Hancock, Graham. 1995. *Fingerprints of the Gods*. London: Heinemann.

Haras, Muhammad Khalil. 1993. *Nuzul 'Isa wa-qatluhi al-Dajjal*. Reprint. Cairo: Maktabat al-Sana.

al-Harbi, Abu Muhammad. 1998. *Al-Sayf al-batar 'ala muhandis al-Azhar*. Cairo: Madbuli al-Saghir.

al-Harithi, Dawka b. Zayd b. 'Ali. 1998. "Min mashahid Yawm al-Qiyama." *Majallat al-Buhuth al-Islamiyya* 54:135–221.

Hasan, Hamdna Allah Mustafa. 1996–97. "*Brotokolat hukama' Sihaywn*: Qira'a jadida." *Hawliyyat Kulliyyat al-Adab, Jami'at 'Ayn Shams* 25, no. 2: 1–41.

Hashim, Ahmad 'Umar. N.d. *Mihnat al-khalij*. Cairo: Maktabat al-Turath al-Islami.

Hashimi, Maulana Abdul Quddus. 1981. "The Holy Qur'an and the Figure 19." *Islamic Studies* 20: 271–74.

al-Hawali, Safar Ibn 'Abd al-Rahman. 1992. *Wa'd Kissinjir wa-l-ahdaf al-Amrikiyya fi al-khalij*. Dallas, Tex.: Mu'assasat al-Kitab al-Islami.

———. 2001. *Yawm al-ghadab: Hal bada' bi-Intifadat Rajab?* Cairo: n.p. Also available online in translation as *The Day of Wrath: Is the Intifadha of Rajab Only the Beginning?* translated into English by Safar al-Hawali, at http://www.islaam.com/books/intifadha.htm.

Hawwa, Sa'id. 1985. *Al-Asas fi al-tafsir*. Amman: Dar al-Salam.

al-Hawwari, Hud b. Muhkam (d. 9th cen.). 1990. *Tafsir al-Qur'an al-'aziz*. Beirut: Dar al-Gharb al-Islami.

Hellhom, David, ed. 1989. *Apocalypticism in the Mediterranean World*. Tubingen: Paul Siebeck.

al-Hijazi, Muhammad Mahmud. 1967. *Tafsir al-wadih*. Cairo: Matbu'at al-Istiqlal al-Kubra.

Hilal, Rida. 2000. *Al-Masih al-Yahudi wa-nihayat al-'alam*. Cairo: Maktabat al-Shuruq.

Himsawi, 'Abd al-Baqi. 1992. "Tasa'ulat hawla dalalat al-nizam al-duwwali al-jadid." *Mustaqbal al-'Alam al-Islami* 2, no. 6: 49–56.

al-Hindi, al-Muttaqi (d. 1568). 1987. *Kanz al-'ummal*. Beirut: Mu'assasat al-Risala.

Hoodbhoy, Parviz. 1991. *Islam and Science*. London: Zed Books.

Huntington, Samuel. 1993. "The Clash of Civilizations?" *Foreign Affairs* 72:22–49. Revised and expanded, 1996. *The Clash of Civilizations*. New York: Simon and Schuster.

al-Husayni, al-Husayn b. Muhammad. N.d. *Tafsir-i ʿisna ʿashari*. Tabriz: Chap-i Kulayni.

Ibn Abi Shayba, ʿAbdallah b. Muhammad (d. 850). 1966–71. *Kitab al-musannaf*. 15 vols. Hyderabad: n.p.

Ibn al-ʿAdim, ʿUmar b. Ahmad (d. 1261). N.d. *Bughyat al-talib fi taʾrikh Halab*. Beirut: Dar al-Fikr.

Ibn ʿAsakir, ʿAli b. al-Hasan (d. 1176). 1995–99. *Taʾrikh madinat Dimashq*. Beirut: Dar al-Fikr.

Ibn Baz, ʿAbd al-ʿAziz. 1991. *Fatawa wa-tanbihat wa-nasaʾih*. Beirut: Dar al-Jil.

Ibn Habib, ʿAbd al-Malik (d. 853). 1989. *Kitab al-Taʾrij*, edited by Jose Aguade. Madrid: Consejo de Investigationes Cientificas.

Ibn Hammad, Nuʿaym (d. 844). 1993. *Kitab al-fitan*. Beirut: Dar al-Fikr.

Ibn Hanbal, Ahmad (d. 855). N.d. *Musnad*. Beirut: Dar al-Fikr.

Ibn Kathir, Abu al-Fidaʾ (d. 1374). 1983. *Tafsir*. Beirut: Dar al-Qalam.

Ibn Maja, Muhammad b. Yazid (d. 888). N.d. *Sunan*. Beirut: Dar al-Fikr.

Ibn al-Munadi, Ahmad b. Jaʿfar (d. 947). 1998. *Kitab al-malahim*. Qumm: Dar al-Sira.

Ibn al-Rawandi. 2000. *Islamic Mysticism: A Secular Perspective*. New York: Prometheus Books.

Ibrahim, Khalid Ismaʿil. 2002. *Al-Nadhir al-akhir: Ma yuwajihu al-ʿalam al-an fi al-Qurʾan al-karim*. Cairo: Matbaʿat Mahha.

al-Ibrahim, Yusuf. 1996. "Daʿwa li-iʿadat al-istiʿmar!" *Al-ʿArabi* 39, no. 454: 4.

Idlibi, Muhammad Munir. 2002. *Intabihu . . . al-Dajjal yajtah al-ʿalam*. Damascus: Al-Awaʾil.

al-ʿIrbawi, Nabil. 2000. *Bermuda: Al-Juzʾ al-mutafajjir min al-ard*. Cairo: Dar Salah al-Din.

Ismaʿil, Sayf al-Din ʿAbd al-Fattah. 1992. "Hawla al-tahayyuz fi mafhum al-nizam al-ʿalami al-jadid." *Mustaqbal al-ʿAlam al-Islami* 2, no. 8: 7–80.

al-Jabi, Bassam ʿAbd al-Wahhab. 1996. *ʿAlamat qiyam al-saʿa al-ʿashara al-kubra*. Beirut: Dar Ibn Hazm.

Jabr, Muhammad Salama. 1993. *Ashrat al-saʿa wa-asraruha*. Cairo: Dar al-Salam, 1993.

Jamal al-Din, Amin. 1996. *ʿUmr ummat al-Islam: Qurb zuhur al-mahdi ʿalayhi al-salam*. Cairo: Maktaba al-Tawfiqiyya.

———. 1997. *Al-Qawl al-mubin fi ashrat al-sa'a al-sughra li-Yawm al-Din*. Cairo: Maktaba al-Tawfiqiyya.

———. 1998?. *Radd al-siham 'an kitab 'umr ummat al-Islam*. Cairo: Maktaba al-Tawfiqiyya.

———. 2001. *Harmajjadun: Akhir bayan . . . ya ummat al-Islam*. Cairo: Maktaba al-Tawfiqiyya.

al-Jammal, Muhammad 'Abd al-Mu'in. N.d. *Al-Tafsir al-farid li-l-Qur'an al-majid*. Beirut: Dar al-Kitab al-Jadid.

Jirar, Bassam. 1994. *I'jaz al-raqm 19: Muqaddimat tantazir al-nata'ij*. Beirut: Mu'asassa al-Islamiyya.

———. 1995. *Zawal Isra'il 'amm 2022*. Beirut: Maktabat al-Biqa' al-Haditha.

———. 1998. *Irhasat al-i'jaz al-'addadi fi al-Qur'an al-karim*. Ramallah: Nun li-Ab-hath wa-l-Dirasat al-Qur'aniyya.

Jomier, J. 1959–61. "L'Evangile selon Barnabe." *Melanges d'Institute Dominicain d'études Orientales* 6:137–226.

al-Judhami, 'Abd al-Rahman. 1992. *Min ahkam al-tariqa*. Jerusalem: n.p.

al-Julaynid, Muhammad al-Sayyid. 1999. *Al-Istishraq wa-l-tabshir*. Cairo: Dar al-Quba' li-l-Tiba'a wa-l-Nashr.

Juynboll, G. H. A. 1983. *Muslim Tradition: Studies in Chronology, Provenance and Authority*. Cambridge: Cambridge University Press.

al-Kashani, al-Fayd (d. 1680). 1982. *Tafsir al-safi*. Beirut: Mu'assasa al-A'la li-l-Matbu'at.

al-Kashmiri, Muhammad Anwarshah (d. 1933). 1964. *Al-Tasrih bi-ma tawatara fi nuzul al-Masih*. Aleppo: Maktabat al-Matbu'at al-Islamiyya.

Kenney, Jeffery. 1994. "Enemies Far and Near: The Image of the Jews in Islamist Discourse in Egypt." *Religion* 24:253–70.

Kh., M. 1997. "Usturat al-baqara al-hamra'." *Al-Ibda'* 15, no. 12: 81–84.

Ketchichan, J. 1990. "Islamic Revivalism in Saudi Arabia." *Muslim World* 80:1–16.

Khader, Bichara. 1982. "The Social Impact of the Transfer of Technology to the Arab World." *Arab Studies Quarterly* 4:226–41.

al-Khalidi, Mahmud. 1985. *Al-Bay'a fi al-fikr al-siyasi al-Islami*. 'Amman: Maktabat al-Risala al-Haditha.

al-Khalidi, Talal. 1997. "Al-Khilafa wa-l-qiyam 'ala al-khilafa bayna al-fiqh wa-l-waqi'." *Al-Fikr al-'Arabi* 18, no. 3: 5–32.

al-Khatib, 'Abd al-Karim. N.d. *Tafsir al-Qur'an li-l-Qur'an*. Cairo: Dar al-Kitab al-'Arabi.

al-Khilfi, 'Abd al-'Azim. 1996. *Rihla fi rihab al-yawm al-akhir.* N.p.: Dar Ibn Rajab.

Kister, M. J. 1962. "A Booth like the Booth of Moses . . ." *Bulletin of the School of Oriental and African Studies* 25: 150–55.

al-Lahiji, Muhammad b. Isma'il al-Sharif (d. 1600s). 1961–62. *Tafsir-i sharif al-Lahiji.* Tehran: Mu'assasat-i Matbu'at-i 'Ilmi.

Lahmar, Kamal 'Ammar. 1995. "Al-Buritaniyya awwal ta'ifa masihiyya takhtariquha al-Sihyawniyya." *Majallat Kulliyyat al-Da'wa al-Islamiyya* 12:412–34.

Lamada, 'Atif. 1996. *Madha tu'raf 'an al-masih al-Dajjal?* Cairo: Dar al-Dhahabiyya.

Landes, Richard. 1996. "On Owls, Roosters and Apocalyptic Time: A Historical Method for Reading a Refractory Documentation." *Union Seminary Quarterly Review* 49:165–85.

Lewis, Bernard. 1986. *Semites and Anti-Semites.* New York: Norton.

Mabruk, Layla. 1986. *'Alamat al-sa'a al-sughra wa-l-kubra.* Cairo: Mukhtar al-Islami.

Madelung, Wilferd. 1981. "'Abdallah b. al-Zubayr and the Mahdi." *Journal of Near Eastern Studies* 40:291–306.

———. 1986a. "Apocalyptic Prophecies in Hims during the Umayyad Age." *Journal of Semitic Studies* 41:141–85.

———. 1986b. "The Sufyani." *Studia Islamica* 63:5–48.

Mahmud, 'Abd al-Samih. 1995. *Al-Qur'an wa-maktabat al-shaytan fi zalam al-mukhabi' li-l-Sihyawniyya al-'alamiyya.* Amman: Dar 'Ammar.

Mahmud, Mustafa. 1993. *Al-Mu'amara al-kubra.* Cairo: Akhbar al-Yawm.

———. 1997. *Isra'il: Al-bidaya wa-l-nihaya.* Cairo: Akhbar al-Yawm.

al-Majlisi, Muhammad al-Baqir (d. 1699). 1983. *Bihar al-anwar.* Beirut: Mu'assasat al-Wafa'.

Makhluf, Muhammad Hasanayn. N.d. *Al-Qur'an al-karim wa-ma'hu safwat al-bayan li-ma'ani al-Qur'an.* Cairo: n.p.

Mansur, Ahmad. 1998. *Al-Masuniyya: al-dhira' al-dariba li-l-Sihyawniyya.* Beirut: Mu'assasat al-Riyan.

al-Maraghi, Ahmad Mustafa. 1946. *Tafsir al-Maraghi.* Cairo: Mustafa al-Babi.

al-Marta'i, 'Abd al-'Azim. 1992. *Iftira'at al-mustshriqin 'ala al-Islam.* Cairo: Maktabat Wahba.

al-Mashhadi al-Qummi, Mirza Muhammad (d. ca. 1713). 1990. *Tafsir kanz al-daqa'iq.* Qumm: Mu'assasat al-Nashir al-Islami.

al-Matbaqani, Mazin b. Salah. 1995. *Al-Istishraq wa-l-ittijahat al-fikriyya fi al-ta'rikh al-Islami.* Riyadh: Matbu'at Maktabat al-Malik Fahd al-Wataniyya.

al-Mawsili, Abu Ya'la (d. 920). 1986. *Musnad Abi Ya'la.* Damascus: Dar al-Ma'mun.

al-Maybudi, Rashid al-Din (d. ca. 1126). 1339 *(shamsi)*/1940. *Kashf al-asrar.* Tehran: n.p.

al-Maydani, 'Abd al-Rahman Hasan Jabannaka. 1974. *Maka'id Yahudiyya 'abra al-ta'rikh.* Damascus: Dar al-Qalam.

Mishal, Shaul, and Aharoni, Reuben. 1994. *Speaking Stones.* Syracuse, N.Y.: Syracuse University Press.

Mowla, Khondakar Gholam. 1998. *The Election of Caliph/Khalifah and World Peace.* Self-published.

al-Mu'aliqi, Mundhir. 1996. *Al-Istishraq fi al-mizan.* Beirut: Maktab al-Islami.

Al Mubarak, Mahir b. Salih. 1991. *Risala fi al-fitan wa-l-malahim.* Medina: n.p.

Mufti, Muhammad Amad, and al-Wakil, Sami Salih. 1992. *Huquq al-insan fi al-fikr al-siyasi al-gharbi wa-l-shar' al-Islami.* Beirut: Dar al-Nahda al-Islamiyya.

Mughniyya, Muhammad Jawad. 1981. *Al-Tafsir al-kashif.* Beirut: Dar al-'Ilm li-l-Malayyin.

al-Muhadhdhabi, Milud. 1993. "Ishkaliyyat al-dimuqratiyya al-mu'asira." *Mustaqbal al-'Alam al-Islami* 3, no. 9: 151–56.

Muhammad, 'Ali. 1994. *Lama'at al-bayan fi ahdath akhir al-zaman: ashrat al-sa'a al-sughra wa-l-kubra.* Amman: Dar al-Isra'.

Muhammad, Muhammad Hamid. 2000. *'Alamat al-sa'a al-sughra wa-l-kubra.* Alexandria: Dar al-Iman.

Mul'ab, Nahi. 1998. "Nihayat al-ta'rikh 'inda Fukayama: Nazra naqdiyya." *Ta'rikh al-'Arab wa-l-'Alam* 175:64–77.

Muqatil b. Sulayman (d. 767). 1983. *Tafsir al-Muqatil.* Cairo: Ha'iya al-Misriyya al-'Amma.

Murad, Mustafa. 1997. *Mata taqum al-sa'a?* Cairo: Maktabat al-Qudsi.

———. 2000. *Ista'iddu li-qital al-Yahud.* Cairo: Dar al-Fajr li-l-Turath.

Musa, Sabri Ahmad. 1998. *Nubuwat nihayat al-'alam.* Cairo: Dar al-Bashir.

Musharraf, Hamman. n.d. "Balaghana . . . annahu kana wara' al-bahr al-'azim ilaha 'azima yuqal laha Amrika." jehad.net (accessed 1/28/2003).

Mustafa, 'Abd al-'Aziz. 1990. *Qabla an yuhdam al-Aqsa.* Cairo: Dar al-Tawzi' wa-l-Nashr al-Islamiyya.

Mustafa, Muhammad. 1998. *Damar Amrika qadim, qadim.* Beirut: Mu'assasat al-Rihab.

Mustafa, Muhammad Ibrahim. 2002. *Nihayat Isra'il fi al-Qur'an al-karim bayna al-nubuwwa wa-l-arqam.* Beirut: Mu'assasat al-Rihab.

al-Musayri, 'Abd al-Wahhab. 1973. *Nihayat al-ta'rikh.* Cairo: Matabi' al-Ahram al-Tijariyya.

———. 1998. *Al-Yad al-khafiya*. Ramallah: Dar al-Shuruq.

Nafi'a, Hasan. 1993. "Tajribat al-takamul al-wahda al-'Urubiyya: Hal hiya qabila li-l-tatbiq fi al-waqi' al-'Arabi?" *Mustaqbal al-'Alam al-Islami* 3, no. 10–11: 197–212.

al-Namla, 'Ali b. Ibrahim al-Hamd. 1998. *Al-Istishraq wa-l-dirasat al-Islamiyya*. Riyadh: Maktabat al-Tawba.

Nawfal, 'Abd al-Razzaq. 1973. *Al-Qur'an wa-l-Injil wa-nihayat Isra'il*. Cairo: Dar al-Ma'arif.

Nieuwenhuijze, C. A. O. van. 1995a. "Islam and the West: Worlds Apart? A Case of Interactive Sociocultural Dynamics." *Arabica* 42:380–403.

———. 1995b. "Islamism: A Defiant Utopianism." *Die Welt des Islams* 35:1–36.

al-Nujayri, Mahmud. 1998. *Ukhdubat al-usuliyya al-Islamiyya*. Cairo: Dar al-Bashir.

Owadally, Mohamad Yasin. 1997. *Emergence of Dajjal: The Jewish King*. Kuala Lumpur: A. S. Noordeen.

Phillips, Abu Ameenah Bilal. 1988. "A Complete Refutation of Dr. Rashad Khalifa's Theory of 19." *Islamic Culture* 62, nos. 2–3: 22–49.

Pipes, Daniel. 1996. *The Hidden Hand: Middle Eastern Fears of Conspiracy*. New York: St. Martin's Press.

Provan, Iain. 1997. "The End of (Israel's) history? K. W. Whitelam's *The Invention of Ancient Israel*, a Review Article." *Journal of Semitic Studies* 42:283–300.

Qasim, Qasim 'Abduh. 1997. "Idtihad al-salibi li-l-Yahud Urubba: Bayna al-haqiqa wa-l-ustura." *Al-Ibda'* 15, no. 12: 49–68.

al-Qasimi, Muhammad Jamal al-Din (d. 1914). N.d. *Mahasin al-ta'wil*. Cairo: 'Isa al-Babi.

al-Qummi, 'Ali (d. ca. 917). 1991. *Tafsir*. Beirut: Dar al-Surur.

al-Qurtubi, Muhammad b. Ahmad (d. 1272). 1986. *Al-Jami' li-ahkam al-Qur'an*. Beirut: Dar al-Kitab al-'Arabi.

———. N.d. *Al-Tadhkira li-ahwal al-mawta wa-umur al-akhira*. Cairo: Dar al-Qudsi.

al-Qushayri, 'Abd al-Karim (d. 1073). N.d. *Lata'if al-isharat*. Cairo: Dar al-Kitab al-'Arabi.

al-Qushayri, Muslim b. al-Hajjaj (d. 875). N.d. *Sahih*. Beirut: Dar Jil.

Qutb, Muhammad. 1991. *Ru'ya Islamiyya li-ahwal al-'alam al-mu'asir*. Riyadh: Dar al-Watan li-l-Nashr.

Qutb, Sayyid. 1996. *Fi Zilal al-Qur'an*. Beirut: Dar al-Shuruq.

Rababi'a, Ghazi Isma'il. 1993. *Al-Quds fi al-sira' al-'Arabi al-Isra'ili*. Amman: Dar al-Furqan.

al-Rahbawi, 'Abd al-Qadir. 1987. *Al-Yawm al-akhir.* Cairo: Dar al-Salam.

Reid, Douglas. 1987. "Cairo University and the Orientalists." *International Journal of Middle Eastern Studies* 19:51–76.

Rubin, Uri. 1997. "Apocalypse and Authority in Islamic Tradition: The Emergence of the Twelve Leaders." *Al-Qantara* 18:11–41.

al-Ru'ud, Muhammad 'Abd al-Razzaq 'Id. 1985. *Jami' al-akhbar wa-l-aqwal fi al-masih al-Dajjal.* Cairo.

Sa'd, Taha 'Abd al-Ra'uf. 1995. *Al-Masih al-Dajjal wa-'alamat al-sa'a al-sughra wa-l-kubra.* Cairo: Maktabat al-'Ilm al-Islamiyya.

Sadiki, Larbi. 1995. *"Al-la nidam:* An Arab View of the New World (Dis) Order." *Arab Studies Quarterly* 17:1–22.

Sa'id, Husayn Muhammad. 1993. *Qariban al-masih yahbut min al-sama'.* 'Amman: Dar al-Barayiq.

Sa'id, Salah al-Din Mahmud. 1997. *Fada'il al-umma al-Islamiyya.* Cairo: Maktabat al-Iman.

Salih, Hafiz. 1988. *Al-Dimuqratiyya wa-hukm al-Islami fiha.* Beirut: Dar al-Nahda al-Islamiyya.

Salim, 'Abd al-Ma'bud Mustafa. 1994. *Al-Mustashriqun wa-atharuhum al-sa'i 'ala al—bi'a al-Islamiyya.* Cairo: Matba'at al-Amana.

Salim, Fahd. 1998a. *Asrar al-sa'a wa-hujum al-gharb.* Cairo: Madbuli al-Saghir.

———. 1998b. *Kashf al-sirr al-ta'rikhi Yahud al-yawm hum Yajuj wa-Majuj wa-iq-taraba al-wa'd al-haqq.* Cairo: Shirket Dar al-Isha'a' li-l-Tiba'a wa-l-Nashr.

———. 1998c. *Al-Sharr al-qadim.* Cairo: Madbuli al-Saghir.

———. 1999. *Ihdharu: Al-zahf al-Irani al-muqaddas.* Cairo: Mu'assasat al-Rida' li-Tiba'a.

al-Sayyid, Ridwan. 1991. "Dar al-Islam wa-nizam al-duwwali wa-l-ummah al-'Ara-biyya." *Mustaqbal al-'Alam al-'Arabi* 1, no. 1: 37–72.

Serjeant, Robert. 1954. "Hud and Other Pre-Islamic Prophets of Hadramawt." *Le Muséon* 67:121–79.

Shabir, Muhammad 'Uthman. 1992. *Makhatir al-wujud al-Yahudi 'ala al-umma al-Islamiyya.* Beirut: Dar al-Nafa'is.

al-Shahawi, Majdi Muhammad. N.d. *'Alamat Yawm al-qiyama al-sughra wa-l-kubra.* Cairo: Maktaba al-Tawfiqiyya.

———. 1992. *Al-Masih al-Dajjal wa-Yajuj wa-Majuj.* Cairo: Maktabat al-Iman.

Shahin, Mustafa. 1992. *Al-Nasraniyya ta'rikhan wa-a'qidatan.* Cairo: Dar al-I'tisam.

Shakir, Muhammad Fu'ad. 1993. *Nihayat al-'alam wa-l-masih al-Dajjal.* Cairo: Maktabat al-Hijaz.

Shalabi, ʿAbd al-Jalil. 1992. "Mughamarat Masuni." *Majallat al-Azhar* 64:1355–57.

al-Shami, Jamal b. Muhammad. 1996. *ʿAlamat al-saʿa al-ʿashara al-kubra*. Beirut: Dar Ibn Hazm.

Shaqiq, Munir. 1990. "Al-Islam fi maʿrakat al-hadara." *Al-Muslim al-muʿasir* 56:103–12.

———. 1992. *Al-Nizam al-duwali al-jadid wa-khiyar al-muwajaha*. Nablus: Al-Nashir.

al-Shaʿrawi, Muhammad Mutawalli. 1990. *Al-Yawm al-akhir*. Cairo: n.p.

al-Sharbasi, Ahmad. 1977. "Al-Masuniyya: Muʾamara ukhra ʿala Islam." *Al-Hilal* 85, no. 6: 28–39.

al-Sharbati, Ghalib. 1994. *Aʿudhu bi-llah*. Nablus: Maktaba al-Jamaʿiyya.

Sharfi, M. Zakiuddin. 1985. *Dajjal Is Coming*. Burlington, Vt.: Darul Kitab el Islam.

al-Sharif, Muhammad. 1996. "Bayna al-Islam wa-l-gharb." *Afaq al-Islam* 4, no. 14: 26–37.

al-Sharqawi, Muhammad. 1989. *Al-Istishraq wa-l-ghara ʿala al-fikr al-Islami*. Cairo: Dar al-Hidaya.

———. 1990. *Al-Kanz al-marsud fi fadaʾih al-Talmud*. Cairo: Maktabat al-Waʿi al-Islami.

———. 1993. *Al-Istishraq: Dirasat tahliliyya taqwimiyya*. Cairo: Matbaʿat al-Madina.

al-Shaybani, Umar al-Tawmi. 1976. "Nazrat al-Islam ila al-hurriyya." *University of Libya, Faculty of the Arts* 5:9–48.

al-Shaykh, ʿIzz al-Din. 1993. *Ashrat al-saʿa al-sughra wa-l-kubra*. Beirut: Dar al-Kutub al-ʿIlmiyya.

al-Shihabi, Ibrahim. 1997. *Istratajiyat al-Qurʾan fi muwajahat al-yahudiyya al-ʿalamiyya*. Damascus: Arab Writers Union.

al-Shinawi, ʿAbd al-ʿAziz. 1996. *Al-Nisaʾ akthar ahl al-nar*. Cairo: Maktabat al-Iman.

al-Shirazi, Nasir Makarim. 1342 *(shamsi)*/1941. *Tafsir-i Namumeh*. Tehran: Dar al-Kutub al-Islamiyya.

al-Shuri, Majdi b. Mansur b. Sayyid. 2002. *Al-Thamar al-dani fi dhikr al-Mahdi wa-l-Qahtani: Al-Qahtani khalifat al-zaman al-akhir wa-maʿahu al-Durr al-maknun fi bayan haqiqat Harmajaddun*. N.p.

al-Silfi, Sulaym b. ʿId al-Hilali. 2001. *Al-Fawaʾid al-hisan min hadith Thawban (tadaʿi al-umam)*. Casablanca: Dar Ibn ʿAffan.

Slomp, Jan. 1978. "The Gospel in Dispute." *Islamochristiana* 4:67–111.

———. 1997. "The Gospel of Barnabas in Recent Research." *Islamochristiana* 23:81–109.

Smith, Wilfred Cantwell. 1957. *Islam in Modern History.* Toronto: McGill Univ. Press.

Stern, S. M. 1968. "'Abd al-Jabbar's Account of How Christ's Religion Was Falsified by the Adoption of Roman Customs." *Journal of Theological Studies* 19:128–85.

al-Sulami, Yahya (d. 1261). 1989. *Al-'Iqd al-durar fi akhbar al-muntazar.* Zarqa': Maktabat al-Iman.

Sulayman, Subhi. 2000a. *'Ala man taqum al-sa'a?* Cairo: Dar Salah al-Din.

———. 2000b. *Lughz al-masih al-Dajjal wa-muthallath Bermuda.* Cairo: Al-Hurriyya.

Sunnaqrat, Da'ud 'Abd al-'Afu. 1983. *Judhur al-fikr al-Yahudi.* Amman: Dar al-Furqan.

Surur, Rifa'i. 2000. *'Alamat al-sa'a: Dirasat tahliliyya.* Alexandria: Dar al-Furqan.

Suwayd, Muhammad. 1989. *Dawlat al-batil fi Filastin.* Mecca: Rabitat al-'Alam al-Islami.

al-Suyuti, Jalal al-Din (d. 1505). N.d.(a) *Al-Durr al-manthur fi al-tafsir bi-l-ma'thur.* Cairo: Anwar al-Muhammadiyya.

———. N.d.(b) *Al-Hawi li-l-fatawi.* Beirut: Dar al-Fikr.

al-Tabari, Muhammad b. Jarir (d. 923). 1954. *Jami' al-bayan fi ta'wil ay al-Qur'an.* Cairo: Mustafa al-Babi.

al-Tabarani, Sulayman b. Ahmad (d. 971). 1996. *Musnad al-Shamiyyin.* Beirut: Mu'assasat al-Risala.

al-Taba'taba'i, Muhammad Husayn. 1972. *Al-Mizan fi tafsir al-Qur'an.* Beirut: Mu'assasat al-Risala.

al-Tabrisi, al-Fadl b. al-Hasan (d. 1153). N.d. *Majma' al-bayan fi tafsir al-Qur'an.* Qumm: Manshurat Maktabat Ayatullah al-'Uzma al-Mara'shi al-Najafi.

al-Tahawi, Muhammad Sayyid. 1984. *Al-Tafsir al-wasit li-l-Qur'an.* Cairo: n.p.

al-Tahtawi, Ahmad Mustafa. 1997. *Al-Masih al-Dajjal wa-ahdath al-muthira li-l-nihayat al-'alam.* Cairo: Dar al-Fadila.

al-Ta'if, Yusuf. 1995. *Ghara'ib wa-'aja'ib al-masih al-Dajjal.* Cairo: Dar al-Ta'if.

Talas, Mustafa. 1986. *Fatir Sihyawn.* Damascus: n.p.

al-Ta'mi, Muhyi al-Din. N.d. *Tahdhir al-rijal min al-masih al-Dajjal.* Cairo: Markaz al-'Arabi al-Hadith.

al-Tamimi, As'ad. 1998. *Zawal Isra'il hatmiyya Qur'aniyya.* Cairo: Dar al-Mukhtar al-Islami.

al-Tantawi, Muhammad Sayyid. 1987. *Banu Isra'il fi al-Qur'an wa-l-Sunna.* Cairo: al-Zahra'.

———. 1971. *Al-Tafsir al-wasit li-l-Qur'an al-karim.* Cairo: Jami'at al-Azhar.

Tawfiq, Ashraf. 1998. *Waqayyadtu didd majhul.* Cairo: Maktabat Rajab.

al-Tawil, Yusuf al-'Asi. 1995. *Al-Salibiyyun al-juddud: Al-Hamla al-thamina*. Cairo: n.p.

Tawila, 'Abd al-Wahhab 'Abd al-Salam. 1999. *Al-Masih al-muntazar wa-nihayat al-'alam*. Cairo: Dar al-Salam.

al-Tayr, Muhammad. 1986. "Rihla 'Arabiyya li-iktishaf Yajuj wa-Majuj." *Majallat al-Azhar* 58:1672–77.

al-Tibi, 'Ukasha 'Abd al-Mannan. 1990. *'Ibadat al-awthan*. Cairo: Maktabat al-Iman.

———. 1991. *Akhir maqal fi al-masih al-Dajjal*. Cairo: Dar al-I'tisam.

al-Tihami, 'Ala al-Din. 1997. *Al-Fitna al-thalitha al-kubra*. Cairo: Dar al-Tayassur.

Tottoli, Roberto. 2002. *"Hadith* and Traditions in Some Recent Books upon the Daǧǧal (Antichrist)." *Oriente Moderno* 21, no. 1: 55–75.

al-Tusi, Muhammad b. al-Hasan (d. 1067). 1957–65. *Tafsir al-tibyan*. Najaf: Maktabat al-Amin.

al-Tustari, Sahl b. 'Abdallah (d. 897). N.d. *Tafsir al-Qur'an al-'azim*. Cairo: Dar al-Kutub al-'Arabiyya.

al-Tuwayjiri, Hamud b. 'Abdallah. 1994. *Ithaf al-jama'a bi-ma ja'a fi al-fitan wa-l-malahim wa-ashrat al-sa'a*. Riyadh: Dar al-Sumay'i.

al-'Uqayli, Sulayman (d. 1200s?). 1994. *Al-Futuhat al-ilahiyya*. Beirut: Dar al-Fikr.

al-'Urfi, Khalid Hamid. 1994. *Al-Atbaq al-ta'ira wa-sirr al-ikhtifa'at al-ghamida*. Cairo: Dar al-Bashir.

Van Koningsveld, Paul. 1996. "The Islamic Image of Paul and the Gospel of Barnabas." *Jerusalem Studies in Arabic and Islam* 20:200–229.

Veliankode, Sidheeque M. A. 1995. *Doomsday: Portents and Prophecies*. Riyadh: Dar Ibn Khozaimah.

Virailio, Paul. 1998. *"Nihayat al-ta'rikh?"* Translated by Camilia al-Subhi. *Al-Ibda'* 16, no. 7: 29–38.

Walker, Dennis. 1994. "Louis Farrakhan and America's Nation of Islam." *Journal of the Pakistan Historical Society* 42: 252–79.

———. 1998. "The Revived Nation of Islam." *Islamic Studies* 37:445–78.

Wallerstein, Immanuel. 1999. "Islam, the West and the World." *Journal of Islamic Studies* 10:109–25.

al-Waqfi, Ibrahim Ahmad. 1990. *Allah fi al-adyan al-thalatha*. Cairo: Mu'assasa al-Misriyya li-l-Kitab.

Wensinck, A. J., ed. 1936–62. *Concordance et indices de la tradition musulmane*. Leiden: E. J. Brill.

Ya'qub, al-Siddiq. 1988. "'Aqidat al-Yahudiyya bayna al-shirk wa-l-tawhid." *Majallat Kulliyyat al-Da'wa al-Islamiyya* 5:40–54.

Zakariyya, Fu'ad. 1983. "The Future of Arab Futurology." *Jerusalem Quarterly* 29:56–62.

Zallum, 'Abd al-Qayyum. 1962. *Kayfa hudimat a-khilafa?* Nablus: n.p.

al-Zankuri, Hamadi. 1994. "Al-Haki fi qissat Tamim al-Dari: Fanniyatuha wa-dalalatuha." *Hawliyyat al-Jami'a al-Tunisiyya* 35:7–60.

Zaqzuq, Muhammad Hamdi. 1983. *Al-Istishraq wa-l-khalfiyya al-fikriyya li-sira' al-hadari.* Qatar: n.p.

Zarzur, 'Adnan Muhammad, Yahya Muhammad Rabi', and Hamid 'Abd al-'Aziz al-Ansari. 1996. *Al-Thaqafa al-Islamiyya: Fi hawla jihat al-tahddiyyat.* Qatar: Maktabat Dar al-Fath.

al-Zaydi, Majid. 1996. "Al-Hurriya al-akadimiyya fi al-jami'at al-'Arabiyya." *Dirasat 'Arabiyya* 32, nos. 11–12: 103–10.

al-Zayn, Hasan. 1992. "Al-'Arab wa-l-nizam al-'alami al-jadid: Ila ayna?" *Al-'Irfan* 76, nos. 9–10: 10–13.

———. 1994. "Mabda' al-musawa'ah bayna al-Islam wa-l-dimuqratiyya." *Al-'Irfan* 78, nos. 5–6: 4–11.

Zaytun, 'Abd al-Wahhab. 1996. *Al-Yahudiyya bayna al-kharafa wa-l-mumarisa.* Damascus: Al-Manara.

al-Zu'bi, Musa. 1997. *Kayfa zayyafa al-Yahud al-kutub al-muqaddasa.* Damascus: Al-Manara.

INDEX